FILM CRAZY

Also by Patrick McGilligan

Cagney: *The Actor as Auteur*

Robert Altman: *Jumping Off the Cliff*

George Cukor: *A Double Life*

Jack's Life: *A Biography of Jack Nicholson*

Fritz Lang: *The Nature of the Beast*

Clint: *The Life and Legend*

Backstory: *Interviews with Screenwriters
of Hollywood's Golden Age*

Backstory 2: *Interviews with Screenwriters
of the 1940s and 1950s*

Backstory 3: *Interviews with Screenwriters of the 1960s*

Tender Comrades: *A Backstory of the Hollywood Blacklist*
(with Paul Buhle)

Forthcoming

Darkness and Light: *The Life of Alfred Hitchcock*

FILM CRAZY

INTERVIEWS WITH HOLLYWOOD LEGENDS

PATRICK McGILLIGAN

ST. MARTIN'S GRIFFIN
NEW YORK

www.stmartins.com

Book design by Michael Mendelsohn

Library of Congress Cataloging-in-Publication Data

McGilligan, Patrick.
    Film Crazy: interviews with Hollywood legends /
  Patrick McGilligan.
      p. cm.
     ISBN 0-312-26131-4 (hc)
     ISBN 0-312-28038-6 (pbk)
     1. Motion pictures producers and directors—
     Interviews.   2. Motion picture actors and actresses—
     Interviews.   I. Title.

PN1998.2 .M434   2000
791.43'092'27494—dc21   00—025482

First St. Martin's Griffin Edition: August 2001

10 9 8 7 6 5 4 3 2 1

For Russell Campbell

CONTENTS

On the campaign bus with the Gipper

"I told you he wasn't a dame . . ."

"What I have in mind is a happy audience . . ."

"I liked the strong characters . . ."

"You're talking to a screwball . . ."

On the set of Family Plot

Introduction

A long, long time ago, on a campus far, far away from Hollywood, I fell in with a group of people who were passionate about film. (We never said "movies.")

Although film craziness was epidemic around the country, indeed around the globe, I tend to think that the mutant strain found at the University of Wisconsin in Madison in the late 1960s and early 1970s had something to do with the unique combination of the long, subarctic winters—from which escape was desirable—coupled with the inviting central location of the film archives in the State Historical Society building.

The film archives were (are) a treasure trove. For years, archivists of the Wisconsin Center for Film and Theater Research had been quietly collecting the personal and professional documents of show business people. These included luminaries as well as lesser lights. A special effort had been made to collect the memorabilia of stage and screen figures with a history of involvement in left-wing or liberal causes. Among others in this category, the collection included some papers of the Hollywood Ten.

More important, from our point of view, some unsung archivist had managed to obtain the United Artists collection, which included the promotional materials, script files, and 16mm prints of every Warner Brothers, RKO, and Republic motion picture dating from the early 1930s through the early 1950s. This, remember, was back in an era before Ted Turner's all-movie cable channels, Blockbuster Video, and "laser discs"—words we never dreamed.

Mornings at the archives, the film-crazies would gather to watch whatever some graybeard (i.e., graduate student) had put on the schedule—say, three or four William Wellman films, the earliest, most obscure, most topical titles from his Warner Brothers period. We relished the fact that many of the films we were watching hadn't been shown in America, even in truncated form on television, for thirty or forty years. We tingled with the collective hope that any day we might discover a "lost" masterpiece.

The room set aside on the top floor of the State Historical Society building was a long, narrow concrete bunker with utilitarian chairs scattered around. There was always, I remember, a prescribed number of snafus with the projection equipment. Once started, the only interruptions were for reel changes, and we often squeezed in several films back to back, before lunch. Some of us slurped coffee or chewed gum. Some made loud comments about the film in progress, others watched silently, scribbling notes, gazing intently at the rectangle of light dancing on a far wall.

Around noon, we usually stumbled out onto Library Mall, dazed by the blinding sunlight and just in time for the antiwar (or whatever issue) rally of the day and the march that was scheduled and the protest or riot that might eventuate.

This is oversimplification, of course. Not every day did we watch three or four William Wellman films from the 1930s; sometimes it was Anthony Mann's shipboard musicals from the 1940s (not as exciting, I assure you). Nor was every film buff at the UW a political radical capable of dodging tear gas canisters. It just seemed that way.

Madison was a locus of film culture and of left-wing activity. The film-political passions were linked in some people, although in at least a couple of instances that I recall, friends with comradely beliefs came to blows, or almost, not over Marx or Mao, but over what films ought to be championed, or who were the greatest directors.

Most of us organized our own film societies to show our favorite films to other students; at the time, there were more than two dozen organizations that competed for space and bookings. Many of us cut our teeth writing program notes for the Wisconsin Film Society (the oldest, most respectable film society on campus) or reviews for the college daily. Some of us—mostly the graybeards—were on the official committee that violently debated what should be programmed into the Memorial Union Play Circle theater, with its plush seats. Most of us contributed to *The Velvet Light Trap*, a mimeographed, hand-stapled periodical (quite "periodical") that we hawked at film showings. More than we realized, it was also circulated around the world.

The articles in *The Velvet Light Trap* had a distinct sociological flavor. Our preference was for headline or historical subjects. Our heroes tended to arise out of the strengths of the UW archives. Raoul Walsh, William Wellman, George Stevens, Robert Stevenson, René Clair, and Ida Lupino were names I first heard in college, from people who were studying their work at the State Historical Society. Warner Brothers and RKO were the best, most important studios from our point of view. Warners was the proletarian one with a social conscience; RKO was eclectic, occasionally left-leaning. We knew a lot less about the others and didn't much care.

Growing up in Madison, I had seen surprisingly few movies, although I never felt deprived. We lived on a lake and spent most of our free time outdoors. My father wasn't about to spend money on a family expedition to the movies, and my mother, who once attended the Pasadena Playhouse, had a Catholic suspicion of Hollywood's negative influence on children. She passed on her love for show business—dance, theater, *The Ed Sullivan Show*—while carefully restricting even our television time.

About the only movies I recall being taken to were *Ben Hur* (perfectly acceptable to the Catholic Church) and, the next year, *The Alamo* (a history lesson from John Wayne).

By the time I was in high school I found myself drawn to the nighttime triple-feature horror fests that were being staged regularly at the downtown theaters. My group of friends liked nothing better than to hang around outside the Orpheum, pull the fire escape down, jimmy open a balcony door, and then slip inside. Walking in backward as people were exiting between shows also worked a surprising number of times. I don't remember much of what we saw, because, really, we'd see anything that was playing at the Orpheum, which was the easiest theater to sneak into. Once or twice we were detained by police. That was half the excitement.

I arrived as a freshman at college (only a couple of miles from my house) in the fall of '69, shortly after Nixon had taken over the nation's presidency and escalated the bombing of Vietnam. I went very swiftly from political science to theater to film major, and began to see more films in any given week than I had seen in any previous year. Half the time, it seemed, classes were being picketed or boycotted, and it was off to the safe haven of the film archives.

The archives closed in the evening, but the film societies and film department offered, on any given night, a smorgasbord of possibilities, with everything from Satyajit Ray to Ingmar Bergman to Alfred Hitchcock competing for space on the poster boards. Our biggest crises of conscience came when something that we really wanted to see was scheduled, during a campus-wide strike, for a lecture hall that had been declared off limits. I remember agonizing over whether to cross a picket line to watch a rare, bootleg print of Chaplin's *Monsieur Verdoux*. We debated amongst ourselves when *The Birth of a Nation* was announced for a special presentation; the African-American students center had denounced the event. Our final decision was—we liked to quote the supposed maxim of West Indian Marxist author and historian C. L. R. James (although, if he wrote it, I, for one, certainly never read it)—"Our duty is to see the film in the afternoon, picket it in the evening."

One semester, when a boycott of classes looked as though it would last weeks, I persuaded a teaching assistant to let me spend his class period watching films in the archives and researching a term paper comparing the acting styles of James Cagney and Humphrey Bogart. I had only the vaguest idea of the job ahead, and never even had seen a Cagney film. As I began to watch their programmers from the early 1930s, I found myself riveted by Cagney's persona. Bogart was floundering and erratic at that early stage of his career, he was less authoritative, and so Cagney alone became my subject.

I was very diligent, watched every available film (the archives had the bulk of Cagney's titles, since he spent so much of his career under contract to Warner Brothers), did the necessary library stuff. When I finished my paper and turned it in, the teaching assistant gave it an A and said, "Why don't you turn it into an article for *The Velvet Light Trap?*" I asked him, "Is there any money in that?" He said he thought there might be a little. I wrote the paper up more elaborately as an article and handed it to Russell Campbell, the founder and first editor of *The Velvet Light Trap*. A New Zealander at the UW for graduate film study, Campbell was a gentle soul who really *did* have a gray beard. He made suggestions, asked for revisions. Eventually he accepted the article for publication with the offhand remark, "It's quite extensive and good—have you thought of turning it into a book?" I asked him, "Do you think there's any money in that?"

I knew from my research that there were not any other Cagney books. With my article in hand I visited the UW bookstore and really for the first time found myself in the film books section. I picked out a few books that looked especially attractive and opened them up to Acknowledgments, writing down the names of publishers and editors who had been thanked. I invested in photocopying and mailing to five companies. An editor in London wrote back after several weeks, saying yes, if I could lengthen and polish the manuscript, he would contract it as a book. I was a sophomore with a book contract!

If I was the youngest (budding) author in the group, I wasn't the only one. Russell Campbell's *Photographic Theory for the Motion Picture Cameraman* and *Practical Motion Picture Photography* had just been published. Lately Campbell had been pondering the oeuvre of William Wellman on the theory (supported by the social consciousness of his early-1930s work) that Wellman was a closet leftist; it turns out Wellman wasn't, Campbell had to switch his research, and later he directed documentaries and wrote other books, including *Cinema Strikes Back: Radical Filmmaking in the United States 1930–1942*.

Gerald Peary—who had taught me children's theater while I was still in high school—was writing his thesis on the rise of the American gangster film. He and I formed a film society we called (undoubtedly the least evocative name of all the campus film societies) Tar and Feathers. "I'm Tar, he's Feathers," we liked to introduce ourselves. Running a film society was one of the best jobs I ever had; we didn't always see the films we had booked, however, because we were out in the hallway counting the piles of money and laughing at our own jokes. You could learn a lot from Gerry, who went on to edit—is still editing—important anthologies of film essays and criticism, including (with his constant cohort in those days, Karyn Kay) the first collection of its kind, *Women and the Cinema: A Critical Anthology*.

Joseph McBride and Michael Wilmington had collaborated on a book about John Ford, which, everyone knew the scuttlebutt, was finished and accepted but not yet available in stores. Not many in the film-crazy circle were "townies," perhaps the majority were from out of state, but a fair percentage, including McBride and Wilmington, were from Wisconsin. McBride stood apart from the rest of us because he wore a suit and worked for the city's morning newspaper. He was reputed to have watched *Citizen Kane* fifty times! His early efforts at selling pieces to film magazines and writing film books showed everyone else it could be done. I only knew McBride in passing at the UW; we ended up hanging around together much more later on, when I used to visit Hollywood for the *Boston Globe*. I've lost track of the times we jumped into a car and took an impromptu trip to visit Howard Hawks or Allan Dwan or Rouben Mamoulian or George Stevens. McBride continues to write books and nowadays is considered a top biographer, often with a film director as his subject; Wilmington, who impressed everyone as the best film critic on campus back then, is the first-string reviewer of the *Chicago Tribune*.

Howard Gelman (*The Films of John Garfield*), Danny Peary ("Gerry's brother" and the author of *Cult Movies 1, 2, and 3*, as well as many other iconoclastic books about film and baseball), Nancy Schwartz (who made her impressive contribution to film history with *The Hollywood Writers' Wars*, finished by her mother after her untimely death), Douglas Gomery (prolific author of *The Hollywood Studio System* and other histories of film industry practices), and others were up there on the fourth floor, watching films in the archives. It was a formidable group of people, with some of the nonwriters who never wrote books just as fascinating to listen to and learn from.

One of the odd paradoxes of those years is that we were all watching and studying films, but few of us were actually trying to make one. We saw ourselves more as scholars or historians, even then. Whenever significant film personalities—Jean-Luc Godard, Warren Beatty, Nicholas Ray—visited the UW to give a guest lecture or host a screening, we rushed them with our tape recorders and wrote down everything they had to say for *The Velvet Light Trap* or some other humble film magazine.

My own first tape-recorded interview was with the Senegalese filmmaker Ousmane Sembène, whose name meant little to me until Gerry Peary and I read it on a poster, announcing his appearance on campus. We went into a frenzy of activity, crammed by reading one of his novels. We only had the opportunity to see one of his films, *Emitai*, although that sort of drawback never inhibited us. I well remember staring at my shoes for a long time once when a famous Hollywood director, after having politely surrendered hours of his time answering my questions, finally asked one back: "Tell me honestly, you haven't seen very many of my films, have you?"

The need to learn and preserve film history, which started for many of us in the UW film archives, was closely linked to the desire, the urge, to meet and interview the actual people and hear the history from their lips. Our zeal for such encounters survived college. In fact, I graduated by mail, having already accepted a job at the *Boston Globe*. The majority of these interviews I did while working for the *Globe* from 1973 to 1976. When I traveled to Hollywood on assignment, I went without an expense account, crashed on friends' floors, and wrote twice as many articles as when I was in the office. I was allowed to make up my own list of assignments. Robert Taylor, my admirable editor, always looked at the list said, "Go ahead!" Bless him. Debra Weiner, my eternal friend, who was living in Boston during part of that time, was always up for any journalistic adventure.

For a long time, directors, especially, were the magical names; it wasn't until many years later that I woke up to the importance of screenwriters (the last interviews in this book, chronologically, are with two writers). I recall one particularly interesting day at the *Globe* when I sat at my desk debating with a fellow reporter how we should divide the assignments just offered to us by Bob Taylor. One of us would get to interview Thornton Wilder, the other would meet René Clair. An impossible choice. I chose Clair.

The film legends were mostly in their eighties, and we often felt like angels of death, heading off to meet them. Gerry Peary and I tracked down Warner Brothers contract director William Keighley at his New York City apartment. But Keighley had some strange mental disorder that made him transpose the gender of the people he was talking about. He kept referring to Jack Warner as "the big woman." Although his wife, actress Genevieve Tobin, sat nearby, gamely trying to interpret, Gerry and I, ever the gigglers, could barely make it through the session. When I met Lewis Milestone he was wheelchair-bound and attended by a nurse; there were only a few moments of intriguing lucidity amidst hours of virtually unintelligible conversation. Some of these interviews I never transcribed or wrote up. To this day, I feel an overwhelming sadness and guilt that I arrived too late on the job and missed too many people.

Stanley Kauffman, David Denby, Richard Corliss, and others have noted the lamentable passing of film culture awareness nowadays. The 1960s and the 1970s were certainly the heyday in America. The passion to understand Hollywood's past seems passé with today's generation, which dates its consciousness of cinema traditions to *Mean Streets*. It is my hope that these dozen interviews—most of them previously published, but never before collected in one volume—might help to keep the flickering flame alive.

—PATRICK McGILLIGAN

"Can you ride a horse?"

1. Interview with Raoul Walsh

Los Angeles, August 1974

by Patrick McGilligan and Debra Weiner

RAOUL WALSH

(1887–1980)

1910 *The Banker's Daughter.* Actor.
A Mother's Love. Actor.
Paul Revere's Ride. Actor.

1912 *The Life of General Villa.* Actor, script, codirector (with Christy Cabanne).
Outlaw's Revenge. Director.

1913 *The Dishonored Medal.* Actor, director.
The Great Leap. Director.
Until Death Do Us Part. Director.
The Double Knot. Actor, script, director, producer.
The Mystery of the Hindu Image. Script, director, producer.
The Gunman. Script (uncredited), director, producer.

1914 *The Final Verdict.* Actor, script, director, producer.
The Bowery. Director.

1915 *The Birth of a Nation.* Actor.
The Death Dice. Script (uncredited), director, producer.
His Return. Director, producer.

The Greaser. Actor, script, director, producer.
The Fencing Master. Script, director, producer.
A Man For All That. Actor, script, director, producer.
Eleven Thirty P.M. Script, director, producer.
The Buried Hand. Script, director, producer.
The Celestial Code. Script, director, producer.
A Bad Man and Others. Script, director, producer.
Home from the Sea. Director.
The Regeneration. Coscript, director, producer.
The Lone Cowboy. Coscript, director.
Carmen. Script, director, producer.

1916 *Pillars of Society.* Director (with D. W. Griffith).
The Serpent. Coscript, director, producer.
Blue Blood and Red. Story, script, director, producer.

1917　*The Honor System.* Script, director, producer.

The Conqueror. Coscript, director.

Betrayed. Costory, script, director, producer.

This Is the Life. Costory, coscript, director.

Pride of New York. Story, script, director.

The Silent Lie. Director.

The Innocent Sinner. Script, director.

1918　*The Woman and the Law.* Script, director.

The Prussian Cur. Story, script, director.

On the Jump. Story, script, director.

Every Mother's Son. Story, script, director.

I'll Say So. Director.

1919　*Evangeline.* Script, director, producer.

The Strongest. Script, director.

Should a Husband Forgive? Script, director.

1920　*From Now On.* Script, director.

The Deep Purple. Director.

1921　*The Oath.* Director, producer.

Serenade. Director, producer.

1922　*Kindred of the Dust.* Director, producer.

1923　*Lost and Found on a South Sea Island.* Director, producer.

1924　*The Thief of Bagdad.* Director.

1925　*East of Suez.* Director, producer.

The Spaniard. Director, coproducer.

The Wanderer. Director, coproducer.

1926　*The Lucky Lady.* Director, producer.

The Lady of the Harem. Director.

What Price Glory? Director.

1927　*The Monkey Talks.* Director, producer.

The Loves of Carmen. Script, director.

1928　*Sadie Thompson/Rain.* Actor, adaptation, director.

The Red Dance. Director, producer.

Me Gangster. Director.

1929　*In Old Arizona.* Codirector (with Irving Cummings).

The Cock-eyed World. Director.

Hot for Paris. Script, director.

1930　*The Big Trail.* Director.

1931　*The Man Who Came Back.* Director.

Women of All Nations. Director.

The Yellow Ticket. Director, producer.

1932　*Wild Girl.* Director.

For Me and My Gal/Pier 13. Director.

1933　*Sailor's Luck.* Director.

The Bowery. Director.

Going Hollywood. Director.

1935　*Under Pressure.* Director.

Baby Face Harrington. Director.

Every Night at Eight. Director.

1936　*Klondike Annie.* Director.

Big Brown Eyes. Adaptation, director.

Spendthrift. Adaptation, director.

1937　*O.H.M.S./You're in the Army Now* (U.K.). Director.

Jump for Glory/When Thief Meets Thief (U.K.). Director.

Artists and Models. Director.

Hitting a New High. Director.

1938　*College Swing.* Director.

1939	*St. Louis Blues.* Director.	1950	*Montana.* Codirector (uncredited, with Ray Enright).
	The Roaring Twenties. Director.		*The Enforcer.* Codirector (uncredited, with Bretaigne Windust).
1940	*Dark Command.* Director, producer.		
	They Drive by Night. Director.	1951	*Along the Great Divide.* Director.
1941	*High Sierra.* Director.		*Captain Horatio Hornblower.* Director.
	The Strawberry Blonde. Director.		
	Manpower. Director.		*Distant Drums.* Director.
	They Died with Their Boots On. Director.	1952	*Glory Alley.* Director.
			The World Is in His Arms. Director.
1942	*Desperate Journey.* Director.		*Blackbeard the Pirate.* Director.
	Gentleman Jim. Director.		*The Lawless Breed.* Director.
1943	*Background to Danger.* Director.	1953	*Sea Devils.* Director.
	Northern Pursuit. Director.		*A Lion Is in the Streets.* Director.
1944	*Uncertain Glory.* Director.		*Gun Fury.* Director.
1945	*Objective Burma!* Director.	1954	*Saskatchewan.* Director.
	The Horn Blows at Midnight. Director.	1955	*Battle Cry.* Director.
			The Tall Men. Director.
	San Antonio. Codirector (uncredited, with David Butler).	1956	*The Revolt of Mamie Stover.* Director.
	Salty O'Rourke. Director.		*The King and Four Queens.* Director.
1946	*The Man I Love.* Director.	1957	*Band of Angels.* Director.
1947	*Stallion Road.* Codirector (uncredited, with James V. Kern).	1958	*The Naked and the Dead.* Director.
		1959	*The Sheriff of Fractured Jaw* (U.K.). Director.
	Pursued. Director.		
	Cheyenne/The Wyoming Kid. Director.		*A Private's Affair.* Director.
1948	*Silver River.* Director.	1960	*Esther and the King* (It./U.S.). Coscript, director, producer.
	Fighter Squadron. Director.		
	One Sunday Afternoon. Director.	1961	*Marines Let's Go!* Story, director, producer.
1949	*Colorado Territory.* Director.		
	White Heat. Director.	1964	*A Distant Trumpet.* Director.

Living in retirement on his ranch, high above Los Angeles in the Santa Susanna Mountains, film director Raoul Walsh still, at eighty-eight, met visitors in Western dress, handsome and somehow dashing in shiny cowboy boots and a white ten-gallon hat. No longer, though, did he roll his own Bull Durham tobacco "with one hand," a lifelong habit Walsh recently had surrendered. These days he was smoking Silva Thins.

One eye had long been pirate-patched in black, the result of a freak accident during the filming in 1929 of In Old Arizona, his first "talkies" Western; one year later, directing another western, The Big Trail, Walsh discovered a muscle-bound ex-USC athlete by the unlikely name of Marion Morrison, a.k.a. John Wayne. Walsh's other eye had long suffered from glaucoma, and his sight was failing. But his voice was clear and his energy good; he was able to tell long, colorful stories about the days gone by, flavoring them with an occasional Oriental or Cockney accent, a reminder that before turning screen director, "Papa"—or "Irish," as he was known affectionately to the many people in Hollywood who worked on productions with him—had a fling at acting.

He led a full and exciting life that mingles history and Hollywood, a life laid out in his funny, anecdotal autobiography, A Man in His Time. Before the turn of the century, as a lad in New York City, Walsh wooed Virginia O'Hanlon, the same Virginia who wrote a famous letter to a newspaper asking if, indeed, there really was a Santa Claus. Later, he headed west and in the dying days of the frontier became a cowboy. He was privileged to ride with Pancho Villa on assignment from D. W. Griffith. He could recall a memorable dinner one night with Charlie Chaplin, Jack London, and Wyatt Earp. In his time, he would go fishing with George Bernard Shaw and horse racing with Winston Churchill. He even met Adolf Hitler (he later came to regret having not assassinated him), under rather peculiar circumstances; that was when the Nazis tried unsuccessfully to persuade the film director to pilfer a renowned portrait of the Revolutionary War general von Steuben from the private collection of his friend William Randolph Hearst.

It was after a talent scout signed the young Eastern-bred cowpoke for the role of Paul Revere in a long-lost-two-reeler that Walsh entered motion pictures. He played John Wilkes Booth, the assassin, in D. W. Griffith's epic The Birth of a Nation, before parlaying his modest thespian abilities into a directing career that had its first peak during the silent age. He mounted a spectacular version of The Thief of Bagdad starring Douglas Fairbanks in 1924, and his production of What Price Glory? two years later is considered a classic. People who attend the annual silent film festival in Italy, attest that among his lesser-known silent film titles there are other great works. In 1964, John Ford, asked by Cinema magazine to name his ten favorite *motion pictures, listed Walsh's* The Honor System, *from 1917, in second place.**

Walsh survived the eye accident and the arrival of talking pictures, and, especially at Warner Brothers, where he found a niche as the man-handler of James Cagney, Humphrey Bogart, and Errol Flynn, he thrived, lasting almost fifty years in the profession, having a hand—as actor, writer, director, or producer—in some 140 films. Many have outlasted the Oscar winners in their appeal. Walsh himself never won an Academy Award—he shared in only one nomination, with codirector Irving Cummings, for In Old Arizona—*yet his reputation, especially in France, where he was always recognized as among the best of the journeymen contract directors, continues to grow.*

How did you break into motion pictures?

People ask me how I got in pictures, and the thing that really got me into pictures was because I could ride. I got a job with a traveling *Clansman* company, riding the horse on a treadmill, being a Ku Klux Klan leader, and carrying a fiery cross. Now, when I first got that part, the leading man—a hell of a fine fella—told me to tell the assistant stage manager to give me some of the small parts to read, in case anybody got sick or drunk, you know. Well, we went all the way from San Antonio to St. Louis and nobody ever got drunk, and I never made an appearance.

Then I went to New York, and an actor called George Center took me to this agency. When the receptionist asked me my whole history, Center put down that I had played every part in *The Clansman.* She said, "Can you ride a horse?" She had heard I was from Texas. I said, "Yes." So she gave me a slip to go over to Union Hill, New Jersey, to the Pathé brothers [Charles and Émile Pathé], who were just starting to make pictures. Now, when I arrived in New York, I had some money, and the first thing I did was to go and buy a nice suit of clothes. I still had my good boots. I had my new suit on and stuff when I met these two Pathé brothers, and an interpreter

---

*The Honor System is cited by Joseph McBride in The Book of Movie Lists as one of the Ten Important Lost Movies. Ford's first favorite was The Birth of a Nation.

who spoke fairly good English. He asked me what I could do. "Can you ride the horse? . . ." "Yes," I said, "I can ride the horse," and so forth and so on, and then they signed me up for three pictures. I think I got the job because I had a good suit.

The first picture was called *The Banker's Daughter*. It was a crummy-looking thing. I was in love with the banker's daughter, and one of the other clerks that was in love with her stole some money, and I was blamed. Eventually, the police come, the girl breaks down, the bankers say, "Take him off!" and so forth and so on, and, finally, the janitor says he saw this other fella steal the money, so they set me free. That was the story.

In the next picture, I escaped from prison. A funny thing happened there. In those days, you know, in Sing Sing prison, the convicts all had striped uniforms. We were taking a scene out in New Jersey, it was a big field and it was getting down toward the end of the picture. The director—he was French and spoke broken English—says, "You go way off by those big trees, and then, when I call for you, you come running cross field as fast as you can, and then when you hear a gun go off, you fall . . . see?" I said, "All right." So I went over way behind the fields, behind the trees, and he shouted, "C'mon, start running!" So I started running across the field and four guards were chasing me and then they shot and I fell down. And, lo and behold, there was a church just a short way away and a priest came running over from the church. He had seen me. He didn't know it was a picture. And he came running up to give me the last rites. We were all surprised. I was surprised when he turned me over. The Frenchman finally talked the priest into giving me the last rites and he gave him five dollars.

Then finally comes my big day: the third picture. The director tells me, "Now, we'll see if you can ride the horse. We have good story about your famous American jockey Paul Revere." Well, I rode over half of Jersey, jumping over stone walls, hollering, "The British are coming!" The director spotted this big cemetery. He said, "Now, you jump over the cemetery wall, and jump over all the headstones." Well, I did and I was arrested. The company was arrested too and fined fifty dollars and we had to repair whatever damage was done to the cemetery. Now, fortunately, there was a young director watching, from Biograph. He saw me do all this, and he told [D. W.] Griffith about it. Griffith sent for me and signed me up. He said, "Do you want to go to California?" And I said, "When do we leave?"

Did you act in many Biograph pictures?

Well, I acted in a lot of one-and two-reelers. They were very ordinary stories with phony titles. "The Liquor That Touches Your Lips Will Never Touch Mine." Those kinds of titles . . . all that junk. At first, they used to cast me as a lover, until I finally said, "To hell with that. Let me play the heavy. Let me play the guy who robs the bank."

Why didn't you like to play lovers?

Well, most of the girls were kind of cold-blooded in those days. And then there was only the three-second kiss . . . they didn't want to get their hair mussed. I'd take them by the hair and kiss 'em anyway. You know, I played John Wilkes Booth in *Birth of a Nation*. I almost played him again once, too, when I met Hitler. I went to the opera one night years later when I was in Germany, and Hitler was sitting in the box, right up there, just as Lincoln was sitting in the box when I played John Wilkes Booth. If I had a gun or something, I could have walked around and pumped him full of lead. What the hell is one life compared to twenty million?

Then I directed a lot of one-and two-reelers, and played in them too. It was tough making pictures in those days. You had to be rough in those days to get along. I remember Griffith would ask me to go out and find a certain type for him, you know, a nice motherly woman. We had a couple of character actors, but they were always being used for other pictures. They'd shoot four or five pictures at a time, you know, on this big stage. So I'd drop by some shops that sold women's clothes or something, and look around and see a nice-faced elderly woman and talk her into coming down to the studio. Some of them stayed and made out pretty good. A couple of the women became pretty good character actors. Once, Griffith asked me to get him a minister. So I scouted around and saw this big, tall man walking down the street, and I said, "Would you like to work

in moving pictures?" He said, "Sir, I am a minister of the gospel."
So I picked the right guy, but he didn't take the job.

Had you watched a lot of movies when you were young?

All they had where I lived was nickelodeon places. And even when
we were making pictures, we never saw them. In fact, the negative
used to be sent to New York to be printed and edited there. We
didn't print any rushes [in California]. They didn't have facilities for
making a positive print.

How could you tell if you were making a good motion picture?

You'd hear from New York. [laughs] Not only that, but when you
saw this picture with the new titles in it, you were flabbergasted.
"Geez, I didn't play the scene that way."

Do you mean they edited the films in New York?

Yeah . . . they fooled around with it and stuff.

When did you begin to see rushes?

Griffith brought a fellow out who was connected with the laboratory
in New York, and they built a laboratory over where CBS or NBC
is now, in North Hollywood. Then we began to see the rushes.

Can you sum up what you learned from D. W. Griffith?

It was altogether different in those days, because there was no dialogue or anything. I learned a great deal about pantomime from him,
people telling the story just by their looks, their eyes, and their
hands. I learned about movement from him, of course, because most

of his pictures were what we always called a "run-to-the-rescue." That means that the girl is on the railroad tracks, the train is coming, her lover is coming on the horse and he gets her off just as the train goes by. All the pictures in the early days had that.

The greatest thing that he taught me? All the time that I was with him, as his assistant and as an actor, I never saw the man carry a piece of paper. Everything came from here. [points to forehead] Never looking up a scene . . . "What is this, what is that?" Never. I'm the same way. The minute I read the script the night before, I may glance at it once in the morning and that's it.

One of your big successes during the silent era was The Thief of Bagdad. *How did you get involved with that picture?*

I believe that picture was Doug Fairbanks's idea, yes, but it was always a mystery why he sent for me to do it after all the rough-and-tumble, blood-and-guts things that I'd been making. He came on the set one day when I was directing William Farnum. He and Farnum were old stage pals together. He told me he had just seen [producer] Sol Wurtzel, who had run a picture for him that I made with Tom Mix called *The Lone Cowboy*, which I had a lot of stunts in. Evidently, that picture appealed to him, and he sent for me to direct *The Thief of Bagdad*.

Who hired the crew, you or Fairbanks?

There was a set designer by the name of William Cameron Menzies. I brought him out from New York. I had met him in New York through a friend of mine, when I was going to make a picture and he gave me some sketches. "All right," I said, "Come on, we'll go to Hollywood and make it." And let's see . . . a chap by the name of Mitchell Leisen, who became a pretty good director. He designed all the costumes for *The Thief of Bagdad*. Doug Fairbanks hired him.

How was it working with Fairbanks?

He rode on his athletic prowess, you know, and he loved to exercise. He particularly liked me because I used to exercise with him. We'd run a mile each day. He wanted to keep his weight down. And then we'd go into the gym and box and fool around and get in good condition.

We understand you were also friendly with Chaplin, who admired The Thief of Bagdad.

Yes, Charlie and I were friends. He was greatly interested in *The Thief of Bagdad*. He came over to Doug's house every afternoon after he finished work. Doug had a steam bath and a pool. We all used to do some exercising and then jump in the pool. One day, Doug decided to play a gag on Charlie. That morning, Doug had the studio put in about ten big slabs of ice in the pool. Now, every day, Charlie would come out of the steam room, stand by the edge of the pool, and quote Shakespeare before he'd jump in. Well, they finally got the water in this pool so damn near frozen that you could skate on it. Then they took the ice out. Doug and I watched Charlie come out and give his oration and jump in. Christ, he nearly hit the ceiling!

F. W. Murnau was another friend of yours?

I knew him very well. They all seemed to tie in with me, for one reason or another. He used to come to my house all the time, and we would talk about different pictures, and he would ask about different people and stuff.

[Ernst] Lubitsch and I also formed a pretty good association, when he first came over. Mary Pickford brought him over. He used to come up to my house all the time. He would say, "Raoul, what's this actor by the name of so-and-so? Is he a bum or is he good?" [laughs] And I'd tip him off, you know, on people to get.

A funny thing happened. When he first came over, Lubitsch

brought his wife with him, a young German girl he had just married [Helene "Leni" Sonnet]. He also brought his writer with him, a fella by the name of Hans Kraly. Kraly was writing a script for him. So after he had been here about six months, Lubitsch came up to my house. He had tears in his eyes and I said, "What's the matter, Ernst?" He said, "My vife is having an affair with Hans Kraly. What would you do?" I said, "I'd shoot him." "Oh," he said, "I can't do that. The script isn't finished." [laughs]

Of your many films, does any single one best characterize your attitude towards life?

Oh, hard telling. I made so damn many of them. I made about one hundred and forty of them, you know. Of course, one of the first big pictures that I made, which was one of the great moneymakers of all time, was the old *What Price Glory?* I kind of liked that scene where the fella lost his leg, and then they talk about "what price glory. . . ." The War Department told me that they received more enlistments from *What Price Glory?* than from any picture or any publication that's ever been out to draw enlistments.

Despite the fact that it is an antiwar film?

Yeah, but you see those two fellas were having a hell of a time. Did you ever see it? The kids sitting in the audience figure, "Geez, if this is the Army life, I'm for it." In fact, when I was making *Battle Cry*, I was down at the training ground for the Marines down off Puerto Rico. The general of the Marines—I can't think of his name—flew down there, and I was up on a hill directing a scene. He said, "Is this going to be as good as *What Price Glory?*" I said, "I'm hoping." He said, "Well, you s.o.b., it better be. You got me into this army."

Objective Burma *is so much more gung-ho about the military. The two movies seem so different, so opposed in philosophy.*

Yes. Well, you see, that was the topic of the times. Incidentally, some friends of mine came back from Israel six months ago, and they were using *Objective Burma* as a training film.

Is that good or bad?

Well, did they win or lose? [laughs]

You made several pictures with Victor McLaglen and Edmund Lowe.

Yes, they were in *What Price Glory?* Then I made *The Cock-eyed World* with them. Then the studio insisted on doing a third one, and I said, "Look, geez, you can only go to bat so many times. You're going to kill these two guys and kill me." They talked me into it by saying, "Geez, well, we've already got it sold to theaters . . ." It was called *Women of All Nations.* It should have been called "The League of Nations" because it was a flop.

How did you become involved with **The Monkey Talks?** *That sounds like a strange project.*

It *was* a crazy thing. [Producer] Winfield Sheehan was in Paris or something, and it was a stage play. He liked it and bought it. He brought the fellow over who played the monkey and it didn't go off at all. It didn't have any story, just the monkey. [laughs] Monkey business. Oh, there were a lot of crazy ones made in those days, you know. Not only that but, you see, they'd come to you in the silent days . . . when we had a lot of girls under contract, also men, you know . . . and they'd remind you if you didn't start a picture with them on Monday, their salary would start [anyway]. [laughs] They would give you that line of junk.

What about a film called Me Gangster? *We haven't seen it, but from its synopsis, it sounds like one of the early films to treat the whole story of a gangster, from his environment to his demise.*

That turned out to be a real dog. I'll tell you why. They bought the book, *Me Gangster.* The book ended with bank robbers who took automobiles and different vehicles and surrounded this bank; they planned their getaway so nobody could apprehend them. Then they went in and blew the safe and stuff, and came out and got away. Well, the censors cut it all out. The whole bank robbery. They just didn't want anybody to see how to hold up a bank or open a safe. The picture started off good but the whole point was the holdup, which was entirely cut out. We put some phony scenes in there instead but they didn't mean anything. They had money in the picture, so they put it out, but they'd put anything out in those days.

That must be a disappointing experience for a director.

Yeah, it is. After you buy the book and read it and analyze it and say, "Gee, I'll get a great lot of suspense here."

Was In Old Arizona *your first talkie?*

Yes. I was the first one to do an outdoor talking picture. I was the first one to go for talking pictures. The other directors called me a bloody traitor. We had a big directors' meeting. They said, "We have mastered a technique of making pictures, and here you are going with the opposition to tear it down." I was doing it because it was a novelty, talking pictures. I figured, "Talking? What the hell! Let's get something new." I said, "You'll all be following me." I left the directors' organization, and that was it.

Yeah, *In Old Arizona* is the one where I lost my eye. Warners had the patent for sound indoors, but nobody had perfected anything that could get sound outdoors. I was in a theater in Beverly Hills one night and halfway into the program, all of a sudden, I heard some talking on the screen, and there was a Fox Movietone News wagon. You remember those trucks they had? I immediately went up to Sheehan and I said, "I'm going to make an outdoor Western for you." He said, "What with?" I said, "With one of your Movietone News wagons." He said, "Geez, why didn't I think of that?" So he called New York and wanted to know where the nearest wagon was. It was in San Francisco. They sent it down. Three days later, I took a crew and we went up to Utah. I was playing the Cisco Kid [in *In Old Arizona*]. It was supposed to be a two-reeler. Well, when they saw the rushes and stuff, they said, "Make it a five-reeler." I said, "Send me up a stagecoach, send me more people, I'll drag it out," and, in the meantime, I lost my eye.

Did you regret the passing of the silent era?

Yeah, I did miss the silent pictures for a while, because they were fun, they were easy to do, there was no dialogue to study and people said anything they wanted. The only thing was you had to be careful, some people could read lips. You know what happened in the case of *What Price Glory?* We hadn't figured on the lip-readers. . . .

Didn't What Price Glory? also have something to do with your involvement, in the early 1930s, with Gaumont Productions in England?

I'll tell you what happened. After *What Price Glory?* came out, the British government heard about the high enlistment here. They were only getting two hundred men a month into the army in England. So the British army sent a chap over here to talk to me, and he said, "Mr. Walsh, we're having a terrible time trying to lure recruits. We even advocated that they wear blues and carry a swagger stick. But it didn't pay off and we'd like you to come and make some sort of a picture like *What Price Glory?* We have a script over there," and so forth and so on. . . .

So I got on the boat and went over with him, and the script was terrible. It was awful. I said, "If anybody sees this on the screen, not only will they shun the British army, they'll blow the theater down." So he said, "Well, what do you suggest, Mr. Walsh?" I said, "I suggest you send for some American writer." So I sent for an American writer [Lesser Samuels], and we sat down and wrote a pretty good script, and this head fella of this studio—he was a terrible jerk—threw everything out. "Oh," he says, "Impossible. You cahn't do that. A private can nehver speak to a captain. . . ."

I had a scene where these two comics got into what they called a punt—do you know what a punt is? Well, a punt is one of those flat boats they have on the Thames. You rent those punts, you know, and a fella takes his girl and she has a parasol and he pilots the punt up the river. Well, they wouldn't allow the soldiers to be in a punt on the river! Why? I don't know. So it was a terrible disaster, called *You're in the Army Now*, although I had a hell of a fine man in it called Johnnie Mills. That picture fell by the wayside. They wouldn't let me put anything in it that would lure people into the army!

You bounced around a little in the early 1930s. Darryl Zanuck hired you to direct **The Bowery,** *right?*

That was his first picture after he and Joe Schenck bought the Fox company. They got rid of Sheehan and all of the Fox personnel. Zanuck was running the studio and he sent for me to do *The Bowery*. I got along good with Zanuck, but sometimes he would go a little bit overboard in changing things. What I used to do is, I would take a scene in a certain way so they couldn't do anything with it. I would take a scene—only with close-ups of the people—and that was the scene.

What about William Randolph Hearst? Did he interfere with you when you were directing Going Hollywood *with Marion Davies?*

This was a comedy and he'd come down to the set and sit there sometimes and laugh like hell. It made money because Bing Crosby was just coming into prominence. He was the first good box-office name Marion had with her. She was a good actress—one of the best comediennes on the stage—knew comedy well. Fine girl. Big-hearted girl. Goddarn it, her heart was as big as this whole universe.

Another film we haven't seen is Under Pressure. *According to the reviews we have read, the entire story takes place in a tunnel.*

Yes, we never got out of the tunnel. Terrible, terrible picture.

What about Every Night at Eight?

That was probably a twelve-day one. They went by so fast.

Do you remember a film called Spendthrift? *It was produced by Walter Wanger and dealt with the Depression.*

It was one of those things, I think, made in eleven days. Wanger had some kind of a tie-up with Paramount, and they were running short of pictures. Wanger said he could make a couple of pictures in fourteen days, and he asked me to do this one.

What about Klondike Annie? *Did Mae West give you a free hand?*

She insisted on bringing in a very fine-looking Chinese boy that she was supposed to fall in love with in the film. Well, there was about a reel of that sort of carrying on, and it's still on the censor's floor. They wouldn't allow that stuff in those days.

What about a mystery called **Big Brown Eyes?**

Was Joan Bennett in it?

Yes, and Cary Grant.

A funny thing happened. I'll tell you. I don't think he was married to Joan Bennett then, or engaged to her, but we started casting the picture and Joan insisted on having Fred MacMurray. I held out for Cary Grant. Now Cary Grant was in the doghouse. Nobody wanted him, but I finally got him in the picture. I cast him as a kind of slick, fast-talking house detective, and it sort of brought him back.

How did you become involved in **St. Louis Blues?**

Another one of those hurry-up things. It was supposed to be for [George] Raft, and he turned it down and I forget who we got in it. I don't know whether it was Lloyd Nolan or somebody else, and Dorothy Lamour, and that good comic at Famous Players then. But it didn't have much of a story, and it didn't play at all. The music was no good, too.

Why do you continue with a picture when you have a gut feeling it is going to be lousy?

Well, geez, you can't walk off it once you accept it, you know what I mean? You have to talk it over, and then they always con you and say, "Oh, you'll build this up, you'll build that up . . . you'll do this, you'll do that."

You made Dark Command at Republic, before you went over to Warners full-time.

It was one of the biggest moneymakers Republic ever had. I put everybody in it. Walter Pidgeon—he gave one hell of a performance—Marjorie Main, Roy Rogers, Gabby Hayes. I put everybody in it but my mother-in-law.

Did you ever make any movies that were successful by any criteria other than the box office, that were good even though they didn't make money?

Yes, there were some. I remember one which I can't remember the name of. Westbrook Pegler—you remember him—he wrote an editorial about this picture. That was way back in 1914, I guess. After I read the editorial, I just forgot about it, though. It never grossed a quarter.

It seems like you found a real home at Warner Brothers. Did Jack Warner interfere much with your directing decisions?

No, never. I got along with Jack for pret' near thirty years.

How did Warners assign stories to their different directors?

When they'd buy a story, they'd generally know it was my type of story. Adventure or gangster or suspense or whatever. Jack would call me in and say, "Here." I turned down a couple of them and made him cry, but he finally found out later on that I was right.

*Let's talk about Cagney and Bogart. You are one of the few people who directed them both, and at least once, in the same film—*The Roaring Twenties. *How did you stage the final sequence of that film?*

We always walked through a scene like that, of that length—from the house all the way down the street to the church. We walked through that with the cameraman, for the lights to follow Jimmy. It was Jimmy's idea to fall into that ashcan and knock it over, and then I told him, "Stagger up the steps." What I figured for him to do was die in the gutter. So he got halfway up the church steps, he staggered, fell, and rolled down and died in the gutter.

It's a beautiful scene.

Yes. One time I went over and gave the boys a talk at UCLA and one fella said, "Why did it take so long for Jimmy Cagney to die in *The Roaring Twenties?*" And I said, "Well, it's damn hard to kill an actor."

How did you do the montage sequences for that film?

A fella by the name of Don Siegel did them. See, they had a big library there of all scenes from way back. I told him what I wanted, you know, about the crash of the stock market, about this and about that. They were all available, and he just put them together. He was a clever man.

What were the differences between working with Cagney and Bogart?

I never had much trouble with any of them. If they got rough, I got rough, but Jimmy never got rough. He was always a gentleman. Greg Peck was always a gentleman, [Gary] Cooper and [Clark] Gable, all those fellas. I'll tell you what Bogie's trouble was. He was sore at motion pictures because he had to get up at seven in the morning and come down and work on a hot set all day, whereas he used to be on the stage where his hours were from eight to eleven at night. Then he had all the next day to continue having a good time drinking. So he fundamentally hated pictures on account of the long hours, and the retakes, and the added scenes and stuff. But I used to say, "Bogie, what about that salary check at the end of the week?" He'd say, "That's the only damn thrill I get out of this business."

How did Bogart get cast in High Sierra?

A peculiar thing. The script was bought for Raft. Raft read it and turned it down. Jack Warner called me in and said, "What's the matter with this crazy bastard? This is a good story for him. Have a talk with him." So I went over to see George. I knew him very well. He said he liked the script, but he did not want to die in the end. He said he was superstitious. I said, "George, you've killed a couple of people in the picture and the censors are going to demand that you pay the penalty." He said, "The hell with the censors, I'm not going to play it." So I went back to Warner and told him that he turned it down and Warner said, "Who the hell can I get?" I said, "You've got a young fella who has been playing second or third plots here named Bogart." He says, "He's a pretty tough guy—do you think you can handle him?" I said, "I'm a tough guy, too." He said, "Well, you're going to have trouble with him. He's going all over town telling people I'm a fairy." Which boiled Warner up.

Is it true the "Mad Dog" Earle character had to die in the end because of the censors?

That's it.

Would you have liked to see him escape?

Yes. Him and the girl and the little dog. I would have liked to see them ride away into the desert somewhere with the sun setting, but the damn censors were pretty strict in those days.

Did Ida Lupino learn anything about directing from you?

She'd ask me sometimes different things and then she went off on her own to become a director. She used to watch me, how I used the camera and stuff, and the first thing she would always say to me was, "How in the hell do you keep your temper?" I'd say, "I don't let anybody bother me." But she did, and it damn near put her in the bughouse. She'd get so excited and irritable. I told her to calm down, forget it, put some weight on.

In High Sierra, as in many of your films, there seems to be a strong motif of the desire for freedom. Did this theme attract you, partly because of the restrictions you had faced in your own career, with certain studios?

You mean that I had experienced that? You bet I had.

What was your favorite picture of the sound period?

Offhand, I might say *The Strawberry Blonde*. I kind of liked the swing of it, the old-time music, the characters and the dress. It brought me back to my childhood. I grew up in that area [of New York City], you know.

Did you deliberately sweeten the memory of your past?

Yes. A jolly time, good times, all nice people, singing and dancing.

That's the way it really was, or the way you wanted to remember it?

That was the way I wanted to remember it.

Was the entire film shot on the Warners lot?

On all those stages and lots in those times, they had what they called the New York street. Then they had the Parisian street that looked like something you would see in Tijuana. It no more looked like a Parisian street than . . . they would hang a few French signs outside and call it a French street. But they always had a big New York street.

You have said that you always shoot the toughest scene first. What was the toughest scene, then, in **The Strawberry Blonde?**

There were really no tough scenes in it, you know. It sort of went along like a summer day, from the opening scene where they picked the two girls up in the park.

How was Cagney to direct in such an atypical, sentimental role?

As I was saying, he was one man you never had to fight with. He understood everything. Of course, he came from that era, too, you know. He knew those days, the Gay Nineties.

Let's talk about some of the other Warners films. They Drive By Night is an odd hybrid. It can't seem to make up its mind between social consciousness and old-fashioned melodrama. It starts solidly with the truck drivers . . .

And then it goes into the drama. [laughs] Well, they ran out of the trucking story. It was rewritten a couple or three times. But it was a financial success, a hell of a good film.

Ida Lupino has a famous scene where she goes raving mad in the witness box.

That got her a seven-year contract at Warners. It was getting near lunchtime, and she said, "I'm hungry." I said, "You're not going to eat until you play this scene. Get up there now and go stark, staring mad, figuring you're going to get no food."

What about Manpower? *We understand there was a lot of tension on the set, between George Raft and Edward G. Robinson.*

I had to keep them apart. George was in one of his bad moods on that picture. He's a very moody fellow, and I don't know whether he figured Robinson's part was being built up or something . . . Robinson was a hell of an actor, you know. And I think I had Peter Lorre in the picture. Lorre was seated on a desk, and Raft was supposed to come in and talk to him about some plans or something, and then go out. All Lorre was supposed to do was to sit on the edge of that desk and listen. Well, Peter was always a fella who believed in doing a little bit of business, to attract attention. So when George walked up to him and started to talk to him, Lorre started to knock some dandruff off his coat and Raft knocked him off the desk. [laughs] I was behind the camera and I said, "What the hell happened to Lorre?"

**When you made a film like They Died with Their Boots On,
where were your sympathies—with Custer or the Indians?**

The Indians, and I'll tell you why. Of all the pictures that have been
made about the West, it was the only picture that's ever been made
where the Indians won a battle.

Did you always try to treat Indians fairly in your films?

Yes. In fact, I'm a blood brother of the Sioux and a blood brother of
the Navajos.

**But later on, you made a film called Distant Drums. The
Indians in that film are not treated very sympathetically.**

Yes. They are a peculiar tribe of Indians, the Seminoles. They're
bastards to handle. They threatened to kill me four or five times.
Before we went down there to make the film, some documentary
company had gone in there to use a canoe for one day's work. I don't
know whether they held the unit manager up for $250 for the canoe,
but when I wanted thirty canoes in my script, this chief wanted $250
apiece for them. Well, we couldn't afford that, so I had a big argument with him. He threatened to run me off the reservation and
stuff.

About twenty or thirty miles away, on the upper end of the
swamp, there were a bunch of renegade Indians hanging around—
all tribes, Sioux, Blackfeet, Arapahos, Mohawks. Evidently they were
on the lam from someplace and had hidden out in this swamp. I
brought three truckloads of them down, and I told this chief, "Now,
if you want to start any trouble, my men here will pick it up." We
didn't have any more trouble with him. And they also brought boats
down which we paid five dollars a day for.

When you direct a film like They Died with Their Boots On do you study the actual history?

I do a bit of reading about it, and if it doesn't turn out to be dramatic—if it's against the hero or something—I try to patch it up.

Wasn't Custer the villain, in real life?

But it's never been proven that he wanted to go in there and get all the glory. I think there are about eight or ten books out about him. Some of the books blame the commanding officer who was supposed to join him—[General Alfred] Terry.

But Custer was definitely heroic in your version.

Well, you had to do that on account of Flynn. Incidentally, that's the first picture that the audiences ever accepted Flynn being killed. Let me tell you something. There were only two people in those days that you could run through an entire film and kill 'em off—Cagney or Bogart. You couldn't kill a Cooper or Gable or Peck or any of those fellas. The audience wouldn't stand for it. In fact, the exhibitor wouldn't play it. They would accept Cagney when he died, and Bogart when he paid the penalty. I don't know why . . . they probably knew from the start that these fellas were going to end this way, you know.

What was the toughest scene to direct in They Died with Their Boots On?

I guess the killing of Custer was one of the toughest scenes. In those days, a director could demand who he wanted, you know, as extras and bit players. Well, I had put at least one hundred cowboys from all over the country into pictures because, in the early days, when we first came to California—this is seventy years ago—nobody out here could ride a horse. They were just farmers who had orange groves. Mr. Griffith called me in one day and he said, "You come from Texas, you know all about these fellas, where can we find some riders?" I happened to think about the stockyard way down in East Los Angeles—they had big stockyards there in the early days—where cowhands would come in with the cattle. Well, I got ahold of some cowhands. They were getting thirty dollars a month, and I told them we'd give them five dollars a day to work in pictures. They didn't know what pictures were. I got them in a big truck, took them out to the studio, and put them to work.

Now, when it came time to get the riders for Custer's cavalry, and also the Indian riders, which we doubled, the [Screen] Actors Guild or the Screen Directors Guild said that they were going to select the riders. Well, we had about three hundred riders, and the first day eighty of them went to the hospital. A lot of them got kicked by horses—they had never seen horses or anything. That went on for two days. We had to have two doctors on the set. Finally, when so many people were getting hurt, they told me, "Use your own men." So I got all my old cowboys, and I got the good scenes with the Indians, and the failing off the horses, and the cavalry. It was tough going, but I was glad to get it under my belt.

Yes, I worked on that scene pretty hard for quite some time. I was way up on this big platform with my camera. You see, Custer had been warned that the Indians were all around. The scout told him there was at least three thousand Sioux out there, but he never believed that. When Custer saw this bunch of Indians up on a hill—I think there were about seventy or eighty of them—he gave the orders to charge. Well, of course, this was a lure. These Indians were luring him into another valley. He gave chase to these Indians and all of a sudden he was surrounded by Indians. He took to this little hill, gave the order to dismount, and then they all got on the ground and started shooting, and the Indians came charging right in. After we got the establishing shot, then I got on the ground and right to the close-ups.

Did white people double as Indians?

Yes. Well, we had wigs on them, but they had blue eyes, so we had to keep them way in the background. Many times I sent up to the Sioux reservation, I'd bring twenty or thirty or forty Indians down, then I'd send over to Arizona and bring Navajos in—keeping them in the foreground.

How did you plan all of the shots for a scene like that?

I took my cameraman out and I said, "I'd like to shoot this scene right here. How is it going to be for you?" "Perfect." "All right, we'll shoot it here." I always consulted him for his light. If he wanted me to move forty feet away or somewhere, and it didn't affect the background too much, I'd move.

Did you often look through the lens yourself?

Very seldom, very seldom. I'd just say, "What lens are you using?" He'd say, "I'm using a two-inch." I'd say, "Put a thirty-five on."

Did you have favorite shots that you returned to over and over? It seems that you sometimes favored low angles.

Yes, and side angles and real low shots. A variety of shots instead of the same thing, as though they were in a photographer's gallery. It's all according to whose view it's from. You get up high sometimes, say, if you had a big dance scene in one of those big ancient mansions where they're doing the minuet and all that stuff. Then you get up and take the whole room—generally start on the chandelier and pan down, you know, and then pan over to the drunken musicians.

What if you were photographing, say, a love scene between Olivia de Havilland and Errol Flynn?

I considered those two the most beautiful people I ever photographed. She was a beauty and he was a handsome devil, before he took to rumming it up. So, of course, I would stay close on them so the audience could see their real beauty.

Every now and then, I'd have some trouble, particularly with a girl, when we'd first start. She'd say, "Mr. Walsh, would you mind photographing me from the left side of my face? It's my best side." Geez, if you've got four people in the scene and you had to do that, you'd be in trouble. But I'd generally do it to accommodate her, and work things around.

Did you have certain scriptwriters that you used repeatedly?

Yes, a chap by the name of John Twist. He was very fast, and also susceptible to changes. He'd call me in and say, "I have this scene finished here, I'll read it to you." Then I'd say, "Why don't you change this or do that, and let this guy do that?" "Oh," he'd say, "that's great, let's do it." That's the way we'd work.

Did you always work on the scripts of your movies?

Oh, yes, and sometimes I'd hit upon a story myself and get together with Twist and say, "Let's develop this thing and see what you can get out of it."

You'd work on scripts, uncredited?

Oh, yes, yes, yes. You always have to doctor them up. I worked on all of them, practically.

Were you yourself influenced by any authors, particularly?

To tell you the truth, I didn't read much. Now, of course, you know, in the very early days—this was nearly seventy years ago, when I started in Hollywood—we used to take books from [Joseph] Conrad and Jack London and Somerset Maugham—all those people. Never pay them.

When Doug Fairbanks hired me to direct *The Thief of Bagdad*, I went to the library and dug up some Arabian Nights tales and stuff because, you know, I had been making Westerns with Indians and this was a hell of a jump, from the plains of Santa Fe to the streets of Baghdad. So sometimes I brushed up with some research and I memorized some of the names, some of the characters and different things.

What kinds of stories did you like best?

Adventure and melodramas.

Why adventure?

Well, maybe I led that kind of life and I knew more about it.

Why melodrama?

I think you have got to do something like that to keep the people in the theater interested. Mystery, violence, chase.

Did you ever direct—or want to direct—purely romantic stories?

Love stories? No, I'll tell you a story about that. Bob Buckner, who was a very well-known producer at Warners, came to me one day and said, "Raoul, I've got a hell of a lovely, tender love story. I think it would be a good idea if you did it for a change of pace, get away from all of these adventure things. Do you mind if I ask Jack Warner if you can do it?" I said, "No, go ahead, I'd like to do it for a change." So he went to Warner and told Warner about this tender love story and how sweet and everything it was going to be. Warner said to him, "Raoul Walsh's idea of a tender love scene is to burn down a whorehouse!"

So he wouldn't let you do it?

No. [laughs]

Did you rely much on your own experiences when directing? Did you, in terms of the stories, include incidents and people modeled after what you had encountered?

Oh, yes, lots of times. Sheriffs I met in the early days and characters and bank robberies. I remember sitting and listening to people talk, and eventually, sometimes, it would find its way into a picture.

I knew Wyatt Earp, tall, thin fella, who lived in Glendale. He used to come over to the studio and sit there. I remember one time I was taking the scene of a bank robbery, and, after it was all over, I said, "Wyatt, how did it look?" He said, "I have my suspicions you were a bank robber."

Speaking about that, they tell a funny story about Mike Curtiz. He didn't know anything about Westerns or horses. He was standing up near the camera one day, getting ready to direct a scene, and he yelled off to the other people. He said, "All right, bring up the empty horses!" [laughs] I guess there was nobody in the saddle.

Maybe some critics think of you as a "man's director" because you directed so many war stories, adventures, and Westerns.

Yeah, I guess the man usually played the predominant part. You see, in the early days, you could very seldom get a girl with any kind of name in a Western, because it was all about men. The story was about the leading man. He would go off to kill the Indians and leave her on the porch waving goodbye to him. A couple of reels later, after he'd won a couple of battles, he'd come back and she'd still be knitting a shawl in the balcony.

But the women in your films—I'm thinking of High Sierra *and* White Heat, *but even* The Strawberry Blonde—*are often very strong characters. Equal to the men.*

You see, I was brought up with a rough crowd in Texas and Montana when I was young, and I guess it kind of stuck with me to like strong women.

Who were some of your favorite actresses, those you especially liked and respected?

Olivia de Havilland in *They Died with Their Boots On.* Then, of course, I made a picture with Marlene Dietrich, who was just wonderful to handle. Virginia Mayo, Jane Russell, and, way back, I can't think of some of the others.

Errol Flynn gives his best performances in two of your films— They Died with Their Boots On *and* Gentleman Jim. *Was he a good actor?*

He was a good actor if he liked the part. Otherwise, he'd walk through it. Not only that, but you see when I approached him with *Gentleman Jim,* I said, "Look, this fella, Gentleman Jim, was a great hero with the American public." And I added, "If you don't give a good performance of him, somebody is liable to meet you on the street and knock you for a loop." So there was a gymnasium on the lot. I went down there and worked with him, and I got two other fellas to work with him while I was directing. He took off about eight pounds and got in real good shape. He liked that part, loved it.

Did you stage the boxing scenes yourself?

Yes. I was pretty good at handling my dukes in those days. In the high school I went to for a short time, the professor who taught there took a great liking to me because he knew I liked athletics and knew I could box. He was "Jafsie" [John F.] Condon, the man who helped find the Lindbergh kidnapper. He taught me how to box.

In the final scenes of the film, when Gentleman Jim defeats John L. Sullivan, who is played by Ward Bond, which of the characters did you identify with?

When it came down to giving up the belt, I really felt for poor old Ward.

How did you become involved with Jack Benny in that crazy comedy The Horn Blows at Midnight?

He asked for me. [laughs] It's a terrible picture. I think he was in a band in heaven and, at the end—didn't he have the triangle?—the band played this wonderful number and he hit the triangle.

Pursued is a very bizarre Western. People call it a "psychological Western." Why did you direct that?

Oh, I would have tried anything. I would have put on "Red Riding Hood" if they would have asked me. The fella who wrote it [Niven Busch] said, "I have a hell of a Western I'd like you to do." I read it and said, "Geez, this *is* a new Western. I'll do it." Of course, I had a good cast: Robert Mitchum and Dame Judith Anderson.

Silver River *had a good cast: Errol Flynn and Ann Sheridan. Why was it such a failure?*

The reason is that the title of that picture should have been "Johnnie Walker" and "Gordon Gin." They were both on the bottle. That was down toward the last. They were both fighting with Warners. They wanted to get away from Warners. The picture was just terrible.

You directed a musical remake of The Strawberry Blonde— called One Sunday Afternoon. *But it wasn't as successful as the Cagney version. Why?*

Well, the people in it probably, and the story was too good to make a musical out of it. It's just like when they took *A Star Is Born* and made it with Judy Garland and put singing numbers into it. It was too good a story to have to shove music into it.

But you directed a few musicals in your time. . . .

Tried to. Oh, I don't know, I wasn't interested in them. I thought I'd take a chance and see what it was like to hear some music on the set, instead of beefing.

Colorado Territory *was another remake—sort of. Isn't it* High Sierra *as a Western?*

Every now and then, Jack Warner would call you in and say, "Irish, we need a picture. So-and-so has turned down a script, so-and-so isn't available. So-and-so, such-and-such." This time Warner said, "I need a picture," and I said, "I don't have any ready." So he said, "Why don't you remake one of your old ones?" So I said, "All right, I'll take *High Sierra* and we'll put it out West."

I had only one argument with it. He put Joel McCrea into the part. I wanted Bob Mitchum, because you couldn't picture Joel McCrea in jail with a rap of murder against him. But they talked me out of it, and that was that.

Let's talk about White Heat—one of our favorite Raoul Walsh films, one of our favorite Cagney films. What attracted you to the story?

The main character . . . and the fact that he got away with what he wanted—except being killed.

Did you sympathize with the main character?

Yes. I kind of liked that thing of this poor nut that was all shot-up about his mother.

Is there always something sympathetic about gangsters, because of the way they have been raised?

Could be . . . but some are born bad. I had a hell of a time selling the script to Jack Warner. Gangster pics were taboo. Taboo. The exhibitors, nobody wanted them. I read the script—it was written by [Ivan] Goff and [Ben] Roberts—and I went to Warner. I told him, "With Cagney in this part, I can make a hell of a picture." He said, "Well, you know, gangster pictures are not very good at the box office." I said, "This is going to be good or else I wouldn't make it." And he said, "All right, Irish, go ahead and make it."

Did Cagney make any particular contributions to the script?

Oh, he always did. We always sat down before a scene and read the script. We'd go over it and go over it and go over it and go over it. He'd never demand too many damn things like a lot of actors, you know. Another actor would say, "I think I ought to have a love scene with this girl." But Jimmy was never like that at all. He went along with the script. We built it up, changed some words, changed some language. Got a good cast, fortunately, and put the picture together.

Did you cast the film yourself?

Oh, yes.

Did you cast Edmond O'Brien?

Yes, yes. The Irish have to stick together.

Virginia Mayo seems rather young to be cast as Cagney's girlfriend.

With good makeup, Virginia could knock off four or five years. But Cagney always looked young, you could never guess his age. When he was out here the other day, the only change was a little big there. [indicating stomach] Because he loves to eat, Jimmy loves to eat. All he has to do is look at a steak and he gains five pounds.

He always used to come to me about three weeks before we started, and he'd say, "Irish, could you arrange to give me three weeks while I go to the gym?" I'd say, "Certainly, Jim." So he'd get on his sweatshirt and his exercise clothes and he'd go to the gym and he'd knock off twelve or fifteen pounds, and show up looking like a young schoolboy.

Can you remember any of the script suggestions that Cagney made? Was he instrumental in developing the "mother complex" in the script?

The both of us talked that over. In fact, I started it. I said, "How do you feel about sitting on the old gal's lap and playing that scene?" He said, "Jesus, that's great."

Did that include the scenes where his mother rubbed the back of his neck?

Yes, the motherly touch.

How did you shoot that prison sequence, where Cagney goes mad in the mess hall?

When he hears about his mother's death? Well, we sat down and talked it over and I said, "Jim, just go stark, staring mad, because this is your mother and you loved her, and so forth and so on." Then he walked through it, rehearsed it, just showed me what he was going to do so we could carry the lights. Then I said, "Do you feel like taking it?" and he said, "Hell, yes, let's go." Then he went and got it the first time.

You decided to photograph the scene in one long shot?

Yes, with that pan around . . . and that pan down along all those convicts who were whispering about his mother . . . coming back to him . . . and then I stayed right with him all the time.

Drawing back into an extreme long shot.

Well, I thought his yelling and screaming and acting would get it over better than a full shot. It didn't need any big heads, you know.

Who inserted that tender scene in the forest, with Cagney, before the final shootout?

I did. I thought it was time to slow down. Things were moving pretty fast. And get a little soliloquy or something, and then keep going. Instead of go, go, go! I thought I'd see if I couldn't get a bit of sympathy for this fella

How did you shoot Cagney's death scene?

Oh, the original scene was in the script . . . at the end he ran up those stairs to the top of that tank and was killed. I happened to be looking at a newsreel one night and I saw this big explosion of this tank. So I got the company to buy the negatives and we double-printed it. Jimmy was up there on top of the tank, but he was never up there when the explosion went off, otherwise he would never have been out here to see me, as he was recently. We caught up touches about the old days, you know.

Do you think the film was too violent in places?

Yes, but a lot of people have copied it. It's a terrific hit in Japan. It plays there every Saturday night on television because all Japanese pictures end in tragedy. And, of course, blowing this man up in a ball of fire is one of the greatest things they ever saw in Japan. I make many trips to Japan, and when I go into a restaurant or something, they always call me, "Mr. Whitah Heatah." Mr. Whitah Heatah.

You directed Rock Hudson's first movie, Fighter Squadron.

Somebody sent him in to me—I don't know who it was. He was a big, tall, good-looking fella, but he was soft. I was making a picture for Warner Brothers at the time, and, at my expense, I took him on location up to Flagstaff, Arizona, and put a couple of cowboys with him. I said, "Show this bum how to get on a horse and how to get off and how to ride. And rough him up." I asked, "Fellas, what time do you get up in the morning?" They said, "We get up at five." I said, "Get him up at five." And by the time we were finished making the picture, he was a pretty rugged, tough-looking guy. Then I sold his contract to Universal, he did no more exercising or anything, and he became kind of soft-looking again.

Did you direct The Enforcer *under a pseudonym?*

No, I'll tell you what happened. Milton Sperling was producer of the picture, and he engaged a young director—do you know his name?— Bretaigne Windust. I think they got through a reel and a half, and Windust got into a terrible fight with Sperling. They parted company. Sperling went to Warner and said he was up against it, and would Warner let me take over? Warner agreed, but I had an agreement with Sperling that I wanted this man's name on the picture. He was a young fella and what the hell, I didn't want to take all the credit and stuff. I directed way more than half of it, and I retook some scenes and things. But I still insisted I didn't want any credit. . . .

Oh, I've done that ten or fifteen times. I can't tell you the names of some of them. The director would get drunk or wouldn't show up. Warner would send for me and have me finish it, but I always insisted that the other director's name went on it, no matter what I did. I did one with Bette Davis which I won't mention, because we had a lot of trouble.

Captain Horatio Hornblower *is one of your underrated*
movies. It has one of Gregory Peck's best performances.

A funny thing happened during *Captain Horatio Hornblower*. I had
this big frigate down in a place called Villa France in the Mediter-
ranean, south of France. And I had a scene with Peck standing up,
giving the helmsman orders to bring it up to this big wharf. Now,
right close by this wharf are a series of cheap apartments. Most of
them have a balcony. They are very cheap places; in fact, they are
all inhabited by prostitutes. So when we got ready to take this
scene—Peck was giving orders to the helmsman to come in closer
to the dock—all of a sudden, up on one of these balconies, a naked
woman appeared. Stark naked. Right in the center of the camera.
So I had to stop the scene. [laughs]

I told my French assistant to call out to them, that if she wanted
to watch the scene, would she put something on? Well, you know
the French talk so long . . . they talked and talked, and finally she
disappeared. Then we turned the boat around and came back, and
as we started to approach the dock again, out she came, stark naked,
with a big picture hat on. That was her change of clothing. [laughs]

What happened to A Lion Is in the Streets, *the movie you*
made with Cagney for his independent company? It's hard to
follow the continuity of the story.

I'll tell you what happened. Bill Cagney was the producer, and he
talked Jimmy into buying the book. They bought the book, *A Lion*
Is in the Streets, and they hired a writer—I can't think of his name
[Luther Davis]. He started to write the script for it, and he wrote a
pretty good script using most of the good scenes from the book,
dramatizing them. One week before we were to start the picture, two
lawyers from Louisiana showed up, representing the [Huey] Long
family; they said if anything was photographed from that book, they
would bring a lawsuit. And it knocked us right on our can. I suggested to the producer, "Bill, call it off." He said, "Oh, we have pret'
near seventy or eighty thousand dollars in it already." I said, "Well,
you may never get it back, because what they're cutting out is the

guts of the story." We went ahead with it but they had the lawyers watch everything, so we couldn't take anything from the book. Nothing from the book—we had been threatened. Of course it broke Jimmy's heart when we told him, "Jim, you can't photograph the book. You bought a book and now you can't make it. We have to write a new story." So they got this other writer and another writer and a couple more writers, and we tried to put the thing together, but it didn't pay off.

You started using CinemaScope in the 1950s. Was it easy for you to adapt to?

Not at the beginning it wasn't, because it was very difficult to get close up on anybody, you know. Whereas with the old-kind 35mm camera, you could get right up to a fella's eyes and head and know what he was thinking about. Here you had this huge vacant space on either side of him.

Was the book also the problem with The Revolt of Mamie Stover?

Yes. The biggest mistake we made—I didn't make it, the studio made it—was they bought that damn book, *The Revolt of Mamie Stover*. Well, that book is all about prostitution in Hawaii. They knew they couldn't show prostitution and yet they bought it. They wrote a script and we put it on. And it was nothing.

The King and Four Queens?

No good, no good. Some strange things happened on that picture that I wouldn't want to talk about.

Band of Angels?

I kind of like that. Clark [Gable] was all right, and I thought the girl [Yvonne De Carlo] looked like a mulatto and played the part fairly well. They cut a lot of scenes out of that, too—between Yvonne [De Carlo] and Sidney Poitier—that they didn't like. Not too many.

Would you have been more frank with the sex scenes in your films if it hadn't been for censorship?

The pictures I'd have made would have set the theater on fire. [laughs] The censors always cut out dialogue and substituted stuff, weakened the whole story, weakened the characters. The original dialogue would be good and strong, and they'd water it down.

What's the fella that wrote the Marilyn Monroe book? Norman Mailer? Well, he wrote *The Naked and the Dead*. The censors cut out all the naked and just left the dead. [laughs] I had a marvelous sequence with Lili St. Cyr at the beginning of the picture, with all these Marines. It was her act, a marvelous act in the bathtub, very artistic, but not too raw. But they just didn't want her on the screen. So they cut the whole thing out.

Were you disappointed by A Distant Trumpet, *your last film?*

Yes. Those people didn't belong in it. No . . . no . . . didn't belong.

What is the common element in a Raoul Walsh film, whether it is a comedy, adventure, or western?

I think it's the tempo. Breaking it up and hustling it along. Keeping the pace a-going, keeping it a-going, keeping it a-going. Don't dwell too long on one spot. Don't let the interest die. Don't let the audience get ahead of you. Let them see the scene, then give them a new view of something. Keep them a bit hypnotized.

Is there a key to your own personality in the movies?

I always liked a picture that had some roughness and toughness to it. I don't know why. I figured it woke the audience up. I liked to make the lead character more strong, rather than him just walking through it as a good-looking leading man.

Were you influenced by other American directors?

No. To tell the truth, I very seldom saw pictures when I was making a picture.

Did you ever discuss directing with other directors? When you saw John Ford, for example, what did you talk about?

The directors were a peculiar lot. There was not great camaraderie among them. Each one had his own objective in making a picture, and they didn't talk about things. Well, we were all friendly when we met, you know, but then we sort of disappeared and didn't see each other for years. Jack Ford? We were at a directors' meeting one night and he said, "Irish, tell me about your eye. What did they do?" I said, "They cut it out. They said it was a mush eye and it would hurt the vision of the other eye if they left it in. So I told them to cut it out, and they did." I said, "I'll tell you what I'll do, Jack. You lie down on the table here, and I'll get a fork and take yours out for you." He didn't speak to me for three months.

What have you done since your retirement?

Well, I had several offers. How old was I then? Pret' near eighty. I had several offers to go to France to make pictures, but my lovely wife talked me out of it. She said, "It's too much trouble to go over there, if anything should happen to you . . ." and so forth. Then the Japanese came over and wanted me to do a big spectacle up in Mongolia. A Japanese fella came and he said, "Well, Mr. Walsh, very good story for you, very good. Two thousand camel and two thousand horse and many, many thousand soldiers." I said, "How's the story?" "No story." But he came back again and said they had a story, but a guy my age fooling around up near Upper Mongolia, with the Chinese on one side and the Russians on the other, you know, I would have landed in the clink. Bound to.

You also wrote a Western novel that's been published?

In France and Italy and Spain—and it's going to be published here. *Come Hell or High Water.* It's a big Western story about three fellas after the Civil War that go west. It's a hell of a good, rough story. Real rough Western. It would make a hell of a Western. Besides, it's got three girls in it that are real powerful.

Have the movies of today changed from the early years?

Oh, the glamour is gone. In the early days at Grauman's Chinese Theatre, when they had an opening, all these stars arrived in their chauffeur-driven limousines, dressed in creations from Paris, Rome, and London. They all looked elegant, the men in their tails and stuff. Now, the leading lady arrives in a leather jacket, a pair of hot pants, and her escort is wearing a muffler and a jockstrap. [laughs]

The stars? They've got no glamour to them. There are no glamorous people. Look at Flynn. He'd get into a jam every other day. There'd always be something to write about. Now, these columnists have nothing to write about.

What do you think you would have done if you hadn't become a movie director? If you couldn't ride a horse?

Well, at one time, you know, I was going to go into a circus. I had become a very good rope twirler, and a fella was going to take me into the circus with him. But that wouldn't have paid . . . because I would have earned about fifteen pesos a month. It's hard telling, hard telling. I never would have been in one place long, I know that. I probably would have followed the route taken by Marco Polo and ended up in a Chinese jail or a Chinese laundry, doing work or something.

"Is it okay, is it okay . . . ?"

2. Interview with Clarence Brown

Beverly Wilshire Hotel, September 1974

by Patrick McGilligan and Debra Weiner

CLARENCE BROWN

(1890–1987)

1920	*The Great Redeemer.* Director (under Maurice Tourneur's supervision).
	The Last of the Mohicans. Codirector (with Maurice Tourneur).
1921	*The Foolish Matrons.* Codirector (with Maurice Tourneur).
1922	*Light in the Dark.* Coscript, director.
1923	*Don't Marry for Money.* Director.
	The Acquittal. Director.
1924	*The Signal Tower.* Director.
	Butterfly. Director.
1925	*Smouldering Fires.* Director.
	The Eagle. Director.
	The Goose Woman. Director.
1926	*Kiki.* Director.
1927	*Flesh and the Devil.* Director.
1928	*The Trail of '98.* Director.
	A Woman of Affairs. Director.
1929	*The Wonder of Women.* Director.
	Navy Blues. Director.
1930	*Anna Christie.* Director.
	Romance. Director.
1931	*Inspiration.* Director.

	A Free Soul. Director.
	Possessed. Director.
1932	*Emma.* Director.
	Letty Lynton. Director.
	The Son-Daughter. Director.
1933	*Looking Forward.* Director.
	Night Flight. Director.
1934	*Sadie McKee.* Director.
	Chained. Director.
1935	*Anna Karenina.* Director.
	Ah, Wilderness! Director.
1936	*Wife Versus Secretary.* Director.
	The Gorgeous Hussy. Director.
1937	*Conquest/Marie Walewska.* Director.
1938	*Of Human Hearts.* Director.
1939	*Idiot's Delight.* Director.
	The Rains Came. Director.
1940	*Edison the Man.* Director.
1941	*Come Live with Me.* Director, producer.
	They Met in Bombay. Director.
1943	*The Human Comedy.* Director, producer.
1944	*The White Cliffs of Dover.* Director.
1945	*National Velvet.* Director, producer.
1947	*The Yearling.* Director.

		1952	*It's a Big Country.* Codirector (with
	Song of Love. Director, producer.		five others).
1949	*The Secret Garden.* Producer.		*When in Rome.* Director.
1950	*Intruder in the Dust.* Director, producer.		*Plymouth Adventure.* Director.
	To Please a Lady. Director, producer.	1953	*Never Let Me Go.* Producer.
1951	*Angels in the Outfield.* Director, producer.		

A native of Clinton, Massachusetts, who moved to the South when he was eleven, Clarence Brown attended the University of Tennessee and earned a double degree in mechanical and electrical engineering. Starting out as an auto engineer and salesman, Brown heard about a job in motion pictures and was hired as a twenty-dollar-a-week assistant to Maurice Tourneur at Peerless Studios in Fort Lee, New Jersey. Tourneur, one of the silent era's great pictorialists, became his directing mentor.

Brown became best known, perhaps, as Greta Garbo's favorite director. No one directed the enigmatic, sometimes ambivalent star more often. Brown directed Garbo in two of her greatest silent pictures—Flesh and the Devil and A Woman of Affairs—in her first talkie—Anna Christie—and in five other successes—Romance, Inspiration, Anna Karenina, and Conquest. No other American worked with Garbo more than twice.

Yet Brown's three decades of credits show range and diversity. His silent period included a beautifully atmospheric Last of the Mohicans (codirected with Tourneur) and the smoldering The Eagle, starring Rudolph Valentino and Vilma Banky. The 1930s and 1940s were, besides the Garbo vehicles, a time of smoothly crafted "women's pictures," historical epics, and, especially, MGM-style Americana: Ah,Wilderness!, Of Human Hearts, Idiot's Delight, Edison the Man, The Human Comedy.

National Velvet, released for Christmas in 1944, may be Brown's late-period masterpiece. Another appealing adaptation of children's literature, The Yearling, remains an unusual and winning film. Intruder in the Dust was a brave rendering of Faulkner from a fellow Southerner and a statement on race relations that probably only Brown, because of his close friendship with Louis B. Mayer, could have made at MGM.

During his long reign as one of the studio's top directors, Brown wielded virtual carte blanche on the MGM lot. Throughout the industry he was regarded as a master of visual effects, a wizard at certain subjects. One of his curious distinctions is that rarely, unlike many top directors, did he take any script credit or do any writing on his films.

His early retirement, in 1953, had a hint of disillusionment over changing times. A superpatriot who was active as a "one hundred percent American" in the Motion Picture Alliance for the Preservation of American Ideals during the blacklisting era, Brown said, in this interview, that he "retired at exactly the right time" because Hollywood had become so entwined with foreign coproduction. He never looked back, and he thrived as a businessman. He claimed to have never even visited the MGM studio again, except once, when he agreed to give a friend's daughter a tour.

When we met Brown, he was eighty-five, white-haired, his cataract-afflicted eyes framed by thick black glasses. But he was also vigorously healthy, the result, he said, of eating yogurt and Grape Nuts regularly and maintaining a globe-trotting lifestyle. We dined for lunch at the magnificent Beverly Wilshire Hotel, which was one of his early investments. Hardly, he told us with a wink, one of his greatest investments. "I made a lot of money in real estate," Brown admitted, "more than I ever made in films."

After ordering, Brown proudly produced a copy of the Clarence Brown Film Festival program from the University of Tennessee at Nashville retrospective in his honor in 1973. A Clarence Brown Theatre, endowed by him, exists at his alma mater. But he expressed little interest in contemporary Hollywood or show business in general and said he would rather spend time talking about the first love of his youth: cars. He still loved to tinker with cars, Brown said. He owned several Mercedes-Benzes, and he liked nothing better than to crank one of them up to top speed. "That's my weakness," the former director told us. "I still open it up to a hundred and forty miles an hour in the desert."

I had my first job with Maurice Tourneur for twenty dollars a week as an assistant director in 1915. He was my master and my lord. I worshiped him. I first started with Tourneur as an assistant director, and I was still an assistant director when World War I came along. I went into aviation for one and a half years. When I came back, I joined Tourneur again. That's when I made my first picture.

Tourneur was making *The Last of the Mohicans* at that time. He produced and I was his assistant. But he fell off a parallel when the picture was no more than two weeks old, and I had to do practically the whole picture with him in the hospital. "Is this okay, is this okay?" I'd ask him from his bedside. My schooling in pictures was from Tourneur, who was a great artist. I learned about composition and lighting from him. I wasn't influenced by my other contemporaries, although I copied from myself a couple of times. But a man's got a right to steal from himself, doesn't he?

How did I go to work for MGM? It's a long story. I wouldn't know where to start, it's so long and complicated. I had made several successful pictures, including *The Goose Woman* and *Smouldering Fires* and *The Eagle* with [Rudolph] Valentino. I was still working for Tourneur, and I bought the rights to this story. Soon after, someone at the studio told me that MGM was going to make that story. "Impossible!" I said. "I have the rights for the story from the author." Well, MGM called me down to their attorney's office. The attorney said that the paper I had to the story was wrong, and that the story was in public domain. "We understand that you put up some money for this," he said, and I had. I had paid $1,500 which was $15 million at that time. "We want to pay you for it," he said. He handed me a check for $1,500. I tore it up into little pieces and dropped it on the floor. "I'm sorry," I said. "It's not for sale." The attorney called [Irving] Thalberg and told him I wouldn't sell it. "See if he's got a price for it," Thalberg said. Right off the top of my head, I said, "$15,000." He told Thalberg, "His price is $15,000." "Give it to the son of a bitch," said Thalberg, "but he'll never work a day in his life for MGM." Within a year, I had a contract with MGM, and worked there for thirty years—never anywhere else.

Except once—I was loaned out to 20th Century Fox because they wanted to make a picture with Myrna Loy called *The Rains Came*. She said she wouldn't make a picture without her director. I was her director. Now I had a hundred percent ironclad contract with MGM, and I told Thalberg I didn't care to leave. "I'm very happy here," I said. He told me to go on over and tell 20th Century that I didn't want to make the picture. They made a date for me to go over. I walked into [Darryl] Zanuck's office and waited for about five minutes, until he finally called me in. He was swinging his golf club, which is what he always did while he passed the time of day. "Well," I told him, "I understand you are a son of a bitch to work for." With that, he really started swinging his golf club. After a while, he cooled off. "Mr. Brown," he said, "if you make this picture, you'll reserve that statement until after the picture." And I had the happiest time ever making that picture. I had the run of the studio. I even had Shirley Temple's six-room bungalow. It was a successful picture, too.

Fox was very good to me. At MGM, I had to fight for my freedom. It was a studio of departments. Each department worked for itself, to make money for itself—and not for the studio. Camera, art, costumes, everything was a department. Each department head tried to cut everything they could in order to get their books to shine. But I fought them all the way. If I didn't get what I wanted, I'd make them tear it down and build it up again. Eventually, they'd give me everything I'd need to make a 35mm film, from every angle of production. But I had to fight for it.

Louis B. Mayer? He and I were always friends. Wonderful friends. Never an argument. From the day I met him until the day he died— and he practically died in my arms. I wasn't like [Erich] von Stroheim. Mayer never raised his voice to me in forty years, and he never locked me out of his office. After he retired—his last six or seven years—we were practically never separated.

I got along with Thalberg, too. I'd be working with a writer on a script, and we would come to a scene that we didn't know how to go around. We'd call Irving and go up to his office and fifteen minutes later we'd come out of his office with a scene that was probably the best one in the picture. A genius, an absolute genius. I say that unequivocally. It's a pity he died so young.

I worked differently from a lot of people, you know. My cameraman, Bill Daniels, would follow me around in rehearsal, both of us thinking of setups. I always expected the cast to know its lines when they came in for scenes. We'd shoot the whole sequence and later cut it up into scenes. We'd do the long shots first, and then cut it up into close-ups. In *A Free Soul*, there was a scene with Lionel Barrymore, who was playing an attorney in San Francisco. His big scene was when he got up before the court and pleaded for his defendant's life. When he finishes, he drops dead to the floor. Well, he just played the hell out of it. Everyone in the studio was applauding him afterwards. He came to me and said, "Clarence, I haven't got it anymore. I've given it everything I've got. I don't know about the close-ups." "Don't worry," I said, "I've everything I want. I had six cameras on the scene, and we shot every angle we wanted." And he won the Academy Award.

I had my hand in everything, though I don't write at all. I admit it, I couldn't write a line. But I can tell good writing when I see it, and when I wanted to change a scene in a script, I always sent for the writer. Frances Marion did a script for me—a brilliant writer— and I did one picture each with Anita Loos and Dorothy Kingsley. I refused some stories, of course. Oh God, yes. The story is the most important element. Without a story, you can try and work your heart out, but if you haven't got a story, you haven't got anything. Usually, I went to the studio with a story I wanted to do. But I did take a couple sometimes to keep the big stars, who were getting $5,000 a week anyway, from being idle. But usually I went to them with a story I wanted to do. I found stories everywhere. I'd pick a script out of the gutter, if I liked it. I found the story for the first picture I ever made, *The Great Redeemer*, in a newspaper. A priest wrote the script for *Angels in the Outfield* and I loved it.

My first picture with Garbo, *Flesh and the Devil*, was a silent. I made seven pictures with her. Nobody else could make over two. I had a way with Garbo that didn't embarrass her. Garbo is a very sensitive person and, in those days, directors used to yell from behind the camera. I never—never—gave her directions in front of anyone else. I would tell her privately what she should do. I knew she would be a star from the beginning. She had something none of them had, something that photographed from behind the eyes. I took very few takes with Garbo. She was always up on her lines. Sometimes she wasn't happy with her scenes; sometimes, after four or five takes, she still wouldn't be happy; but when you saw her on the screen, oh, something was there.

She had only made one picture or so in Europe before coming to MGM, with Mauritz Stiller, who discovered her. Stiller was as-signed to direct her but he spent so much money on her that Metro eventually took him off the film. He then went to Paramount. But he was madly in love with her. He was the only real love of her life. He was the man who made her an actress. But after they came to the United States, he went to Paramount and she went to MGM, and that's when she fell in love with John Gilbert. Stiller went back to Sweden and died of a broken heart. That's why she never married. Don't ask me about the details. I know, I was there. Certain things happened.

I directed her in her first picture, *Flesh and the Devil*, with Gilbert. We had cast Gilbert and then decided to make it the first big picture for Garbo, even though Gilbert had never met her. I was worried about whether he'd like her or not. But when they met on the set—I introduced them—it was love, immediately. That's why the love scenes came off so well. They went for each other like hook, line, and sinker. Real love. It came right from both of their hearts. They showed *me* how to do a love scene. And I'm no prude. I've been married four times, the last for twenty-seven years—the only love of my life.

Her first talking picture was no problem. We picked a story [*Anna Christie*] in which the star was a Swedish whore, so she had the dialect already made. "Garbo Talks" read the posters. That was all that was needed. She was MGM's most popular star, though—you may not realize this—she was more popular in Europe. During World War II, when the European market went right out the window, things got rough. MGM, you know, had made the European theaters take all the other pictures before they could get Garbo. Now, MGM thought the American market for Garbo was going to go, too, and thought that it could not even afford to make her pictures. Even though she only had one more picture to do on her present contract, Mayer called her into his office and handed her a check for $200,000—for a picture she wasn't going to make. "I can't take that," she said. "I haven't made the picture." She returned the check and never made a picture after World War II. Quite a gesture. That was Garbo. By me, she could do no wrong.

Some people call me a woman's director. I guess, because in my day the thinking was that to make a picture, all you needed was to take a little shopgirl and wind up with her married to the governor of the state. The true-to-life shopgirl goes to see the picture and thinks, "Maybe I can do that too." But I guess the real key to my success was love stories. You can't miss with a triangle love story. When you put on a billboard *Wife Versus Secretary*, with [Jean] Harlow the harlot, [Myrna] Loy the wife, and [Clark] Gable the man, you don't need a story. You've got all you need right there. Yeah, Gable was the greatest male ever on the screen. Valentino may have been the greatest women's actor. But men liked Gable and women liked Gable. He had them all.

But, you know, one of my best pictures had no women in it at all, *Intruder in the Dust*. When I was sixteen, I spent the summer in Atlanta, Georgia. There I went through a whole race riot. I saw sixteen black men murdered by mobs. It made quite an impression. So when I read this story, I didn't walk, I *ran* up to the front office at MGM. "I've got to make this picture," I said. "You're nuts," said Mayer, because the hero was a black man. "If you owe me anything, you owe me a chance to make this picture," I said. "Okay, go ahead," he said. I had trouble, too. I made the picture on location with the people in Oxford, Mississippi. They didn't want me to make it originally. So I went before the city fathers and told them that if I didn't make it down here, I would make it in Hollywood anyway—the way I wanted to. So, finally, they agreed. The first showing was in Oxford, and all those people loved it. It was the greatest night ever in Oxford. There were four pictures that came out at that time about racial difficulties. I started first, but Metro's wheels grind very slowly. Mine was the last, but by far the best, that came out. I even had a riot in the picture. It was pretty damn good. Well, I got an award from the British Academy, but nothing from the United States. Too hot to handle.

I tried historical films, too—with so much history that when I made *The Gorgeous Hussy*, about Andrew Jackson, I set my native state, Tennessee, on fire. I had done pretty thorough research, and I had found out that Mrs. Andy Jackson smoked a pipe. So we had Mrs. Andy Jackson sitting on a rocker, in front of the fire, smoking a pipe. When we ran it in Nashville, I thought the people there were going to hang me by the heels. They were furious about Mrs. Jackson smoking that pipe. We wrote back and told them, "Sorry, but we can't change history."

My favorite picture ever, though, is *The Yearling*. Victor Fleming, one of the greatest directors, originally started the picture. But he had just come off the greatest picture ever made, *Gone with the Wind*, and he just wasn't at home with three people. He went on location to Florida and tried, but it was lousy. They shelved it for a year, and then I took it up. Fleming's problem was the kid. He was lousy. They had publicized in all the papers down South that they were looking for a boy to play in *The Yearling*. All the mothers brought their kids, from two to twenty. When I shot the picture, I went to seven different cities myself, looking for the right kid. I told everyone, even the teachers, that I was a building inspector. I was in Nashville, the day after Valentine's Day, and I saw this boy in a fifth-grade classroom at Nashville's Eakin Elementary School, taking down the valentines from the wall, and I knew it was him: Claude Jarman, Jr. He was only ten years old. Almost an alley kid. He had never seen a film, even a camera. When I first talked to him, I told him I was from the University of Tennessee and that I was hunting for football players—and I wanted to start early. He fell for it. His parents didn't want any part of it at first, but finally they agreed. He won an Academy Award on this picture. And he later played the boy in *Intruder in the Dust*, when he was six feet four inches.

I had a way with kids, I guess. I get along with them very well. I directed Liz Taylor's best picture, *National Velvet*, and she says that too. She was just a punk kid of eleven in the studio school, with violet eyes and a beautiful complexion. But we got along fine.

I also made one of President Eisenhower's favorite films, *Angels in the Outfield*. I found that out when, during one interview, Eisenhower was asked what his favorite films were. He said *Bridge of San Luis Rey*, some other big ones, and then he mentioned another ditty, *Angels in the Outfield*. Well, I read this, and when I heard he was playing golf at a nearby course here in California soon after, I introduced myself as the director of *Angels*. We became very good friends. He was crazy about that movie. He had personally worn out three copies of the film. Once he told me, "I could see it one hundred times but my friends are getting sick of it." Another time, he called me up because he wanted to show *Angels* to some friends but he didn't have a print available. "Can you get me a copy?" he asked. But I didn't own one, MGM didn't do that. So I got on the phone— this was on a Saturday morning—and called up some rental companies in Los Angeles, and finally I managed to locate a print. I sent it over to the Santa Monica airport and his personal helicopter picked it up. And he showed it that night. Well, the weekend passed, Monday morning arrived, and he didn't return the print. I was a little worried, because it didn't belong to me. I called up and discovered that it was packed aboard his plane, bound for Washington—he intended to take it along. I didn't know what to do but finally I got hold of him and explained the matter. Well, what do you know? He sent it back to the airport on his helicopter.

I retired at exactly the right time. The picture business, as we knew it then, had gone completely to hell. They go all over the world now. They don't make them in Hollywood now. It got to the point that I felt I had had it. When I signed my last seven-year contract with Louis B. Mayer, I told him, "This is it. I'm going to go out that door and down the street and never come back." And that's exactly what I did.

3. Interview with René Clair

Martha's Vineyard, August 1973

by Patrick McGilligan and Debra Weiner

RENÉ CLAIR

(1898–1981)

IN FRANCE:

1920   *Le Lys de la Vie.* Actor.
        Les Deux Gamines. Actor.

1921   *Le Sens de la Mort.* Actor.
        L'Orpheline. Actor.
        Parisette. Actor.

1924   *Paris Qui Dort/The Crazy Ray.* Script, director.
        Entr'acte. Script, director.

1925   *Le Fantôme du Moulin Rouge.* Script, director.

1926   *Le Voyage imaginaire.* Script, director.

1927   *La Proie du Vent.* Script, director.
        Un Chapeau de Paille d'Italie/The Italian Straw Hat/The Horse Ate the Hat. Script, director.

1928   *La Tour* (documentary short). Director.
        Le Deux Timides. Script, director.

1930   *Sous les Toits de Paris/Under the Roofs of Paris.* Script, director.
        Prix de Beauté. Script contribution.

1931   *Le Million.* Script, director.

À Nous la Liberté. Script, director.

1933   *Quatorze Juillet/July 14th.* Script, director.

1934   *Le Dernier Milliardaire.* Script, director.

IN THE U.K.:

1935   *The Ghost Goes West.* Director.

1938   *Break the News.* Director, producer.

IN FRANCE:

1939   *Un Village dans Paris* (documentary short). Coproducer.
        Air Pur (unfinished). Director.

IN THE U.S.:

1941   *The Flame of New Orleans.* Director.

1942   *I Married a Witch.* Director, producer.

1943   *Forever and a Day* (one episode). Codirector, coproducer.

1944   *It Happened Tomorrow.* Coscript, coadaptation, director.

1945   *And Then There Were None.* Director, producer.

IN FRANCE:

1947 *Le Silence est d'Or/Man About Town*. Script, director.

1950 *La Beauté du Diable/Beauty and the Devil* (Fr./It.). Script, director.

1952 *Les Belles des Nuit/Beauties of the Night* (Fr./It.). Script, director.

1955 *Les Grandes Manoeuvres/The Grand Maneuver* (Fr./It.). Script, director.

1957 *Porte de Lilas/Gates of Paris* (Fr./It.). Script, director.

1959 *La Grande Époque* (French version of *The Golden Age of Comedy*). Narrator.

1960 *La Française et L'Amour/Love and the Frenchwoman* ("Marriage" episode). Script, director.

1961 *Tout l'Or du Monde* (Fr./It.). Script, director.

1962 *Les Quatre Vérités/Three Fables of Love* ("Two Pigeons" episode, Fr./It./Sp.). Script, director.

1965 *Les Fêtes galantes* (Fr./Rum.). Script, director.

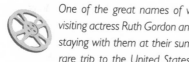

One of the great names of world cinema, René Clair happened to be visiting actress Ruth Gordon and her husband, writer-director Garson Kanin, staying with them at their summer home on Martha's Vineyard. It was a rare trip to the United States for the French filmmaker, and he wasn't seeking any publicity, but we learned of his visit and asked if we might interview him. He agreed to spend an afternoon answering our questions.

Clair, born René-Lucien Chomette in 1898, grew up above his father's store in Les Halles, the market district of Paris. As a youth he staged puppet plays and wrote poetry. Voluntary service in World War I, ambulance-driving at the front, led to an injury, a period of invalidism, and retreat to a Dominican monastery. It wasn't until 1921 that Clair first became involved in motion pictures, initially as an actor in Feuillades serials.

His earliest films as a writer and director remain highly regarded. Paris Qui Dort, which Clair wrote in one night in 1924, established, in Ephraim Katz's words, "the core elements of Clair's cinema—the stylish charm, the exhilarating wit, the celebration of movement, and the intuitive sense of comic timing." Entr'acte, produced for a surrealist ballet with music by Erik Satie, was as original as it was stylish, and The Italian Straw Hat is still seen as his silent masterpiece. Two of his first sound features, Le Million and À Nous la Liberté, were hugely popular as well as artistically acclaimed.

In the mid-1930s, Clair worked briefly in England. Of the two films he made there, The Ghost Goes West, starring Robert Donat, is more characteristic, a comedy about a Scottish spirit from a director who in his career often tilted towards fantasy subjects. Clair directed documentaries in France before World War II, and then he escaped to America. He didn't exactly flourish in Hollywood, but minor gems like I Married a Witch and It Happened Tomorrow upheld his reputation for fatalistic wit and love of humanity.

Returning to France after the war, Clair continued to develop with more personal, philosophical, and tragicomic works such as Le Silence est d'Or in 1947 and Les Grandes Manoeuvres in 1956. He was honored with induction into the Académie Française in 1962 and completed his last film, Les Fêtes Galantes, in 1965.

Above all, the seventy-five-year-old Clair told us, he considered himself a writer. After he stopped directing he published several volumes of film essays, books of his screenplays, and three novels. (He was the French translator of Garson Kanin's play Born Yesterday.) When we interviewed him, he was still sharp and keeping busy with writing projects. Those few films he neither conceived nor wrote—his perfectly respectable version of Agatha Christie's And Then There Were None is one—he blankly disclaimed.

You are known primarily as a writer and director of comedies. Why are you inclined towards comedy instead of drama or tragedy?

My dear . . . why are you blond or brunette? Naturally.

At the beginning of your career, in 1923, you directed your first film, entitled Paris Qui Dort or The Crazy Ray. Like so many of your later films, The Crazy Ray blends science fiction and farcical humor. We have not seen the film, because it is so rare, but a friend of ours recently saw a print here in America.

Excuse me, but I must say that your friend did not see The Crazy Ray. I know the print which is owned by Henri Langlois and the French Cinémathèque, the Museum of Modern Art, even in Moscow and everywhere. The print is a bad one . . . the original negative of the film was lost somewhere, nearly thirty years ago. I recut the film myself two or three years ago after I found parts of the original negative. It is now more or less as it was—a little shorter, but more faithful to what I intended it to be at the time I made it. Unfortunately, this print does not exist yet in America. And this version which belongs to the Cinémathèque . . . well, I don't understand it myself.

Our question, nevertheless . . . we are told that there is a recurrent image in the film that seems to be significant— a fellow who is frozen in the path of his suicide leap off a Parisian bridge. He reappears several times in the film, as do many of the other Parisians who are "frozen" by the Crazy Ray which has paralyzed the city. Presumably, he will complete his suicide jump when the ray vanishes at the end of the film. Is this intended as rather an ironic comment, a deliberate juxtaposition of humor and pathos?

No . . . The Crazy Ray is a farcical comedy, even slapstick. The city of Paris is suddenly put asleep and all the people stay in the positions they have. This fellow was waiting to jump into the Seine River and he was stuck there. But all the people in the film are stopped in different gestures and on different occasions. It was just one of the various gags about people being stuck in the middle of their activities.

This device—repeating a particular joke or gag—happens again and again in The Crazy Ray. In fact, it seems to be a technique which you have used during your entire career.

There are two things about gags which, for me, are very important. First, when a gag is going to be good, the public feels it and laughs before the gag. That's a very strange thing which I have never been able to explain . . . they know better than we do. And secondly, about the repetition of gags . . . when you invent a gag which is good, it is all right once . . . if you repeat it twice, it is better . . . the third time, even better, they laugh more and more. If you go and repeat it a fourth or fifth time, it stops. You never know when. It is very strange. I've stopped gags too soon. It infuriates me and I don't want to see the pictures again. "Oh Christ," I say, "if I knew they weren't going to stop, I'd have done it once or twice more." But you never know in advance . . . that's the thing about comedy, do you see? It is the opposite with tragedy. Poor mother there . . . her child is sick . . . you go for a doctor . . . the snow is falling . . . it can go on for twenty minutes like that, but in comedy you can't. Nothing is more dangerous. You never know when they are going to laugh. There are some things in a picture I made in England, called *The Ghost Goes West*, which, for a long time after seeing the film, I didn't understand why the audience was laughing.

Perhaps one reason why audiences laugh at **The Ghost Goes West** *in places that you had not expected is because of the difficulty of making a film in other than your native language. How did you cope with overcoming the national sensibility, when you worked first in England and then in America?*

I always worked in collaboration on my English and American films. I wouldn't dare write without the help of an American or a British collaborator. There is a difference and I must be very careful of that.

When you are in a different country with different types of actors and different types of mentality, you must adapt yourself to these new conditions. I don't believe you can make intelligent or exciting films unless you make a very good national film, expressing the qualities of your race. A Russian picture has to be Russian. An American picture has to be American.

That is why I am not very satisfied with the trend in French production. Their important productions need American money, which really is very bad because of American influence. It would be just as bad if French influence were too strong in America.

You must notice that I was very careful and I never made a Hollywood picture in England or America. You need English or American collaborators. I tried my best because I had seen German directors come to Paris and make a French picture and it made me laugh.

I will tell you the real story of *The Ghost Goes West*, if you are interested. Once I was in London for the premiere of one of my French pictures and had dinner with Alex Korda. I knew Alex when he was in France, and then he went to England to become a producer. "Oh, I just bought a very, very short novel published in *Punch* which might interest you," he said. "It's called *Sir Tristan Goes West*." I read it and liked it and I asked Alex, "Did you buy it? Yes? Would you sell it to me?" He said, "No, I don't want to sell it, but if one day you are free you can make a picture for me." Well, I didn't think at the time that I would be free, but suddenly things happened. I went to Alex and said, "Are you still interested in the film?" and he said, "Yes." He gave me a great writer, Robert E. Sherwood, the dramatist, and we wrote the script together, Bob and I. He was terribly helpful to me because he was a great writer and, simply, because for the first time I was writing something which was not coming from my country, or from my language.

Do most of your films have what may be described as happy endings?

A comedy has to have a happy ending. Otherwise, it is not a comedy. More or less happy, that is. That is why the ending of a comedy is almost always false, because things don't finish happily in life. It's almost a little trick, but in Shakespeare's comedy or Molière's comedy or even my comedy, they finish happily because that's the law of comedy. It's much more difficult to make a good ending to a comedy than a tragedy, because in a tragedy you just kill everybody off and it's finished. I know very few comedies with a good ending. I mean a natural ending. It's always a little false, you know.

On the other hand, many of your comedies have deliberately tragic overtones and have been nicknamed comédies tragiques for that very reason.

I have called them that myself. Why? Because they are deeper and more tragic than the traditional comedy: to give them a sense of life.

For example, there is a film I made called *Les Grandes Manoeuvres*. Have you seen it? That you should see. . . . Here are certain parts I'm satisfied with. It's a long story, rather deep, and it is supposed to be rather moving. Well, I would not call it a comedy—there are some comedic scenes in it—but the real tendency of the story is not, in fact, comedic, but tragic. It is a sad little story. Very sad, in a philosophical sense. It is, you know, the first time they were speaking of the atomic bomb and I made an allusion that the devil was, in spirit, this scientific disaster.

Do your films affect you, or affect audiences, in the same way as they did when they were first produced?

No, never. Even among the great masters . . . Chaplin, for example . . . I'm old enough to have seen *The Gold Rush* at its premiere in Paris . . . well, people were literally dying of laughter. I know, that, for myself, I couldn't look at the screen. I was sick with laughter! Since then, thirty or so years later, I have seen a very good reissue of *The Gold Rush* . . . and people were again laughing but it was not the same. Do you see? It was not the same.

And I had an experience myself with one of my own pictures. When I made that film, *Beauty and the Devil*, it was first shown at two main theaters in Paris. In one of the theaters, the picture stayed twelve weeks, which was an enormous amount of time, and for three or five years—I don't know exactly how long—it recorded the highest number of public. About ten years later, the picture was shown again in a theater in Paris which was, I would say, a distance of three hundred yards from the first one. It stayed one week. Same film. Same film, same district!

I would say that most films, like most plays, have a certain radioactivity, like sparkling water. Then you open the bottle . . . after that, it is the same water and the same bottle and it is still full but the radioactivity has disappeared. Which is not true with novels, because with novels the printed pages give the imagination more liberty. In film it is impossible. It remains the same.

We know that you have written most of the films you have directed, but did you also always edit your own films?

Of course . . . even in America. I was lucky to be able to do it in Hollywood.

When you wrote your film scripts, did you ever include technical instructions such as camera angles or editing schemes?

In the beginning, yes. In the beginning, I was very careful about technical things. Practically everything was written. Then, when the time came, and I was writing my own material, I knew what I was going to shoot, more or less. Then I had no need to put technical instructions into the script. I don't know whether everybody is the same . . . When you begin as a director, you're much more interested in camera technique, and it's a rather long time after that that you become interested in directing actors.

Which of the various tasks of the filmmaker do you consider to be the most important?

Like a few directors who write their own material, I prefer to write myself. There are three operations—conceiving the idea and writing it, editing, and direction. If I had to make a choice of two of these things, I would take writing and cutting. For me, direction is less important, because if a film is well written, the director cannot do very much . . . the difference is not very important. If a person does not have control of the editing, the editor can do anything he wants with his film. For me, control of the film is the most important thing and control should be made first by writing it yourself and then by editing it yourself.

*You were a genuine auteur before the word—are you familiar
with the auteur theory?*

I have read about that, occasionally. I really don't know what it means.
I know it is a theory, and applicable, perhaps, to a director like Chaplin, who wrote what he's shooting, or René Clair, who wrote what
he's shooting, or Ernst Lubitsch, who frequently cowrote what he was
shooting. But what is the auteur theory? What does it mean?

*Simply, that certain directors' films represent a body of work
with coherent themes or styles, sometimes regardless of
whether that certain director wrote his films or not. Howard
Hawks, for example, is widely considered to be an auteur.*

Howard Hawks was chosen by his studio because the studio had a
property which seemed convenient for the him. [laughing] No . . .
those people have not known the old Hollywood. They speak of the
dream Hollywood. If you shoot A Midsummer Night's Dream, the
author of the play is obviously Shakespeare. You can direct it in your
own way, but . . .

*You have always been a severe critic of Hollywood, even
though you spent your wartime years in America, working in
Hollywood. How did you adjust to the Hollywood method of
filmmaking?*

After the success of my first film, I was asked to come to Hollywood
many times, but I always turned the offers down because I knew that
their system of production was completely opposed to my individu-
alism. In France I could do practically anything I wanted to. But in
1940, I had my choice between Hitler and Hollywood and I preferred
Hollywood. [laughing] Just a little.

I went to Hollywood and it was difficult, of course. But I was
rather lucky because I could work more or less independently, so I
did not have big troubles. I was offered a seven-year studio contract,
which I turned down because I did not want to become a slave of

the producers. I made much less money than my American counterparts because I made pictures only when I felt that I had a chance of doing something that I wanted to do. I didn't do everything that I wanted to, no, but I was not obliged to do things that I would not like to do. That's why I only made four films in five years, while my American counterparts were making a dozen or so. Of course, you must admit that a few of them were working like me: Frank Capra, Preston Sturges, and sometimes Ernst Lubitsch. They were people who were writing or cowriting while they also were directing films that they had not written or not even cut.

No . . . I'm not antagonistic to Hollywood. I'm antagonistic to the big Hollywood system which deprived us of geniuses like von Stroheim who could have made many more pictures if Hollywood had not killed him. Or Orson Welles . . . he was a great man and he couldn't get along with Hollywood because he was too much of an individualist. But Hollywood has given us a lot of great films . . .

You have written that American films were among the most unrealistic films ever produced by any country.

In the old days, Hollywood was a paradise, a dream. And I wrote, too, that we cannot speak of realism in that era of the American picture because, after all, America was a great country of farmers where you never saw a farmer on the screen. It was an artificial world. Now, it's changed. Things are much closer to the real thing.

Didn't you sue Chaplin long ago, claiming that he had modeled his Modern Times after your À Nous la Liberté?

À Nous la Liberté and Modern Times! If you could see the two films at the same time, at one sitting, well, you would be struck by the comparison. And the truth is that, of course, Chaplin never admitted it. The company for which I made À Nous la Liberté sued United Artists, which had made Modern Times, for plagiarism. And, of course, I was asked to take part in the suit and I always refused. I said I know that Chaplin has seen À *Nous la Liberté* . . . it is enough to look at his film. I know, according to the date that he had made his film, two or three years after mine, I had no doubt about that. But I said . . . like many directors, I have found many inspirations from Chaplin's work and it is a great honor for me if he took his inspiration from my work. That's all I can say.

Do you ever regret the passing of the silent cinema?

Sound came too soon, before we could explore all the visual possibilities of film. What I felt—and it happened—was that directors or writers, with sound at their disposal, with the easy way of expressing themselves of an action, they would not go on trying to find a visual expression of an action. Talk became so important that you could close your eyes and listen and understand what was happening. That's not cinema, that's radio. Many directors, like von Stroheim, Chaplin, and me, were really hoping that we could build a sort of visual Esperanto all over the world with silent films.

Who influenced your style of comedy, literary and cinematic?

Literary?

Molière?

Oh, Molière? Yes, very much. [Eugène] Labiche? Yes, Labiche wrote *An Italian Straw Hat*, from which I made a film. And, of course, cinematically speaking, the very, very early kinds of motion picture, and the primitive French film. After that, no doubt, the American films which I saw before I was interested in motion pictures, while I was still a journalist. Mack Sennett, Chaplin . . . that great gang taught me a lot of things. Now, literarily, speaking—that is, when I write motion pictures—and this will surprise you, I have been influenced by a great English writer named G. K. Chesterton.

Throughout your career, you have been steadfast in your inclination towards fantasy. You seem utterly opposed to any sense of realism. Why do you prefer to work within a framework of fantasy?

It is true that I don't like realism very much. I could not explain it exactly . . . maybe it is because I like, as much as I can, to create a little world of my own, which I could not do with realism.

Is your aversion to a realistic cinema the principal reason why you almost always utilize soundstage or interior sets as opposed to exterior or outdoor natural scenery?

The real answer is that, in the old times, the sensitivity of the film itself was much less than it is today. You could not shoot a film in a room without a lot of light. We had to use certain studios in Hollywood because certain studios were more practical for lighting. That was the natural reason.

Now, the film is much more sensitive, allowing new directors to work with a camera, moving around without the big amount of material we needed in the old days. That is, more or less exactly, the difference of style of the new cinema.

Another reason—for me, the general reason—is that, in certain pictures, I like to create an imitation of reality in order to give the film a certain style. I remember a picture which was released here under the title *The Gates of Paris* that I shot almost entirely in the studio, interiors and exteriors. Then, for one little scene, I needed a street. Well, I could not build a street. For one thing, it was much too expensive. So I decided to go outside with my camera and crew and two actors. We shot the scene. It was easy. Later, when I was in the cutting room, I wanted to put that scene in the middle of two other scenes, but I couldn't because the difference was too obvious. I cut it. I cut it because it was a completely different style.

It is especially intriguing that, in perfect complement to your antirealistic visual expression, so many of the subjects of your films are of a wholly fictitious, often fantastic nature—ghosts, life after death, witches, and the like. Why?

It's probably a disposition of mine. It's true that my first film, *The Crazy Ray*, was something fantastic. It would even be called science fiction today. The second film I made was *Entr'acte*, something different; it was a dadaist, surrealist, small film made for a ballet, not the normal cinema. The third film I made was *Le Fantôme du Moulin Rouge*—hmmm? My fourth film, it is true, was *Le Voyage Imaginaire*, which, as you know, is a story about dreams. After that I stopped for a while. I came back to fantasy when I made *The Ghost Goes West*.

Do you believe in ghosts? Or reincarnation? What is your attitude toward death?

Like everybody else, I will have my own sort of death. You'd be a damned fool if you didn't think you'd have to die someday. Of course, nobody can escape. But I don't think I've made any allusions to reincarnation in my films. Speaking of death, I will quote Hemingway, who said something one day. Someone asked him if he believed in God and Hemingway answered, "Sometimes at night."

Your films seem to have one thematic element in common: a distrust of science and contempt for technology. Why is that?

Like many comedic authors, I am more or less a pessimist. I don't believe that humankind is going to progress. [laughing] And like all comedy authors, I am more or less a moralist.

Are there any contemporary directors that strike you as being especially talented?

Well, you know, I'm not very interested in motion pictures nowadays.

Are you currently working on any motion picture projects?

I don't think I will ever make another picture after being in the business so long. I don't need to make another picture because, after so much time, I would not like to repeat myself. And, really, I've made enough. While if a brilliant idea would come, I do not say that I would turn it down, even if the idea would come from the outside. But I'm not terribly excited about the prospects. . . . I have other things to do. I am going back to my original tendencies. I write. I am finishing a book of short novels; I have a play that will be produced in Paris next February or March. And I direct on the stage now. I just directed an opera of Gluck's *Orpheus* for the reopening of the Paris Opera House.

Do you consider yourself a classicist?

I would be very, very happy if other people would consider me a classicist. Well, well, well . . . every author has the hope of approaching some form of classicism, even as revolutionary as I tried to be myself in my youth.

4. Interview with George Stevens

The Brown Derby, September 1974

by Patrick McGilligan and Joseph McBride

GEORGE STEVENS

(1904–1975)

1924	*The White Sheep.* Cameraman.
	The Battling Oriole. Cameraman.
1925	*Black Cyclone.* Cameraman.
1926	*The Devil Horse.* Cameraman.
	The Desert's Toll. Cameraman.
	Putting Pants on Philip. Cameraman.
1927	*No Man's Law.* Cameraman.
	The Valley of Hell. Cameraman.
	The Battle of the Century. Cameraman.
1928	*Leave 'em Laughing.* Cameraman.
	Two Tars. Cameraman.
	Unaccustomed as We Are. Cameraman.
1929	*Big Business.* Cameraman.
	Doctor's Orders. Coscript, cameraman.
1930	*Ladies Last* (short). Director.
1931	*Call a Cop!* (short). Director.
	High Gear (short). Director.
	The Kickoff (short). Director.
	Mama Loves Papa (short). Director.
1932	*The Finishing Touch* (short). Director.
	Boys Will Be Boys (short). Director.

	Family Troubles (short). Director.
1933	*Should Crooners Marry* (short). Director.
	Hunting Trouble (short). Director.
	Rock-a-bye Cowboy (short). Director.
	Room Mates (short). Director.
	A Divorce Courtship (short). Director.
	What Fur (short). Director.
	Flirting in the Park (short). Director.
	Quiet Please (short). Director.
	Grin and Bear It (short). Director.
	The Cohens and the Kellys in Trouble. Director.
1934	*Bridal Bait.* Director.
	Ocean Swells. Director.
	Bachelor Bait. Director.
	Kentucky Kernels. Director.
1935	*Laddie.* Director.
	The Nitwits. Director.
	Alice Adams. Director.
	Annie Oakley. Director.
1936	*Swing Time.* Director.
1937	*Quality Street.* Director.
	A Damsel in Distress. Director.
1938	*Vivacious Lady.* Director, producer.

1939	*Gunga Din.* Director, producer.	1951	*A Place in the Sun.* Director, producer.
1940	*Vigil in the Night.* Director, producer.	1952	*Something to Live For.* Director, producer.
1941	*Penny Serenade.* Director, producer.	1953	*Shane.* Director, producer.
1942	*Woman of the Year.* Director.	1956	*Giant.* Director, coproducer.
	The More the Merrier. Director, producer.	1959	*The Diary of Anne Frank.* Director, producer.
1948	*A Miracle Can Happen/On Our Merry Way.* Uncredited direction (segment).	1965	*The Greatest Story Ever Told.* Coscript, director, producer.
	I Remember Mama. Director, executive producer.	1970	*The Only Game in Town.* Director.

 The son of vaudeville parents, George Stevens had some experience as a child actor before entering films in 1922 as an assistant cameraman. He became a full cameraman for the Hal Roach Studios in 1924, and in the next six years he photographed dozens of two-reel comedies, including such classic Laurel and Hardy shorts as Putting Pants on Philip, The Battle of the Century, Two Tars, and Big Business. His later films as director would show the imprint of his visual sensibility as well as the patient, improvisatory pacing he learned as an apprentice in silent comedy.

His filmography includes official classics of the American cinema (Gunga Din, Woman of the Year, Shane, A Place in the Sun, Giant), as well as many less famous if thoroughly entertaining productions (Annie Oakley, Vivacious Lady, Penny Serenade, The More the Merrier) that some critics think have aged just as well, if not better.

Actors behave like three-dimensional people in Stevens's films. Stars such as Katharine Hepburn, Elizabeth Taylor, Cary Grant, Jean Arthur, Ginger Rogers, Irene Dunne, Alan Ladd, and Fred Astaire gave some of their most relaxed and endearing performances under his indulgent gaze. Stevens was willing to stop the plot to let his actors feel out their relationships with one another—sometimes, it must be said, to the detriment of the films as a whole, but along the way allowing wonderful moments of behavioral observation. Even in the light comedies that he made before World War II, Stevens was an affectionate humanist who placed a high premium on human values.

During the war, Stevens volunteered as a military photographer and was with the troops that liberated Dachau. He returned from his overseas experience a changed and sobered man, turning his always painstaking working methods to a succession of increasingly high-blown, emotionally intense, exquisitely photographed, self-consciously *artistic works:* A Place in the Sun, Shane, Giant, The Diary of Anne Frank, *and* The Greatest Story Ever Told. *During this postwar period, the films stretched fewer and farther between, and Stevens became one of the directors most honored by the Hollywood establishment, winning two Best Director Oscars, the Irving G. Thalberg Award from the Motion Picture Academy, and the vaunted D. W. Griffith Award for career achievement and several other awards from the Directors Guild.*

Shane, especially, still looks like a masterpiece, a perfect blending of subject and theme, but as Stevens's budgets and shooting schedules grew, so did his problems with the studios and critics. The production of The Greatest Story Ever Told *took three years, cost almost $25 million, and resulted in the death by heart attack of cameraman William Mellor, who had experienced combat photography with Stevens. The film's critical and financial failure virtually destroyed Stevens's career, though he managed to make one last film,* The Only Game in Town, *a charming but unsuccessful throwback to his earlier comic style.*

Though when we met him Stevens seemed eager to talk about his career, the interview was difficult to arrange because he was hospitalized at the time for his annual checkup. He was still wearing his plastic hospital ID bracelet as we talked in a shadowy corner of the Beverly Hills Brown Derby, where all the waiters knew him by name. A bulky, craggy-faced man with a shock of gray-streaked hair, Stevens was nattily attired in a blue velvet jacket, gray pants, and an ascot. In person, as in his movies, he was leisurely and ruminative. He nursed a single Bloody Mary during our four-hour conversation, chasing it with a fast cup of coffee on farewell. He seemed fit and trim, and little did we suspect that six months later he would be dead, at age seventy. His casket-bearers included the surviving elders of Old Hollywood—fellow directors and longtime friends King Vidor, Rouben Mamoulian, and William Wyler.

How do you think your own films were influenced by Laurel and Hardy?

I was very much influenced by Laurel and Hardy. I remember one time, in *Alice Adams*, Katharine Hepburn, who was the great lady at RKO, had to go to the dance. She got her gown and I put her in a little Ford with her brother driving. I took a shot of them going down the street and the back wheels were wobbling, which caught the audience off-guard, and there was a very good laugh. Something like that was always going on in those pictures.

I was a youngster when I worked with Laurel and Hardy, in my formative years. The *whole thing* was formative—nobody knew that Laurel and Hardy were going to be comedy stars. They were two hacks around the lot; they had to make a picture, so they put the two of them together.

Was it the slow pace of their films that made them stand out at the time?

I think a little better definition was that in the fast-moving comedies, the only people that thought about what was happening were the audience, but in Laurel and Hardy's comedies, when something happened, the injured one thought about it, and the onlooker looked at him and thought about how horrible it was. They had the presumption to stop the hand-is-quicker-than-the-eye concept of comedy, which was Larry Semon and the Keystone Kops and all that hurried stuff. Before you could examine the situation, another object had crashed through the window, and it was time for the chase.

The beauty of the Laurel and Hardy shorts to me was their absolute deliberation, their great poise, their Alphonse and Gaston relationship with one another. The Laurel and Hardy concept moved over into other films considerably, with Cary Grant, Roz Russell, Irene Dunne doing the late take and even the double take. That had come out of the personalities of Laurel and Hardy, and the people that worked with them.

There's a little bit of Laurel and Hardy in the ending of Woman of the Year, *the long sequence of Katharine Hepburn comically destroying the breakfast she's trying to cook for Spencer Tracy.*

It's exactly that. Those were retakes because the finish didn't work out. I had to put something on at the end.

A Damsel in Distress *was an example of the script not being finished when production started, wasn't it?*

It was a very fragile little plot. There was a little story written by P. G. Wodehouse called "Lucky." The character's name was Lucky, and he was a gambler. We had a very fine writer on it, Howard Lindsay, the playwright who wrote *Life with Father*—a dreary guy to talk to but a funny writer. We gave him lots of time to do it, but after we got so far with this, I couldn't get him on the phone. He left a note, "Dear George, I'm on my way to New York, by way of the Canal. I'm sorry, I'm written out." I had to use Ernie Pagano, a gag man around the place, to work on the script, and I don't know who else [S. K. Lauren]. We got it out the best we could as we went along.

We had a sad thing on that picture, too. This is the first picture that Freddie [Astaire] did without Ginger [Rogers], and it was like Laurel without Hardy. Ginger was a great friend of mine. But she went to Big Bear to do her own picture, and Joan Fontaine was the one who was going to be with Fred Astaire. Now, I never thought too much of that, but I had gone ahead and started to work. Joan had been with me for a little bit in *Quality Street*, and she had done it very well. As far as I was concerned she was in the picture, and we were going to do the best we can, and somehow or other it was going to work out. But Freddie's a great worrier, and he starts worrying about Joan Fontaine. After I've been shooting for about four weeks, Freddie and Pandro Berman, the head of the studio, came down on the set and said, "We're very disturbed about Joan Fontaine. It seems to us that we've got to make a change." I said, "If we take this girl out of this picture, she'll kill herself." They said, "Well, now, that's an exaggeration." I said, "It probably is, but I'm not going to say, 'You can do it, but I'll be elsewhere.' I'll just say one thing: I'm going to stay here and you're not going to do it. We've got to put her through this picture." I can understand Freddie, he's a great artist, but she was a girl with problems, you know, she cried and all that. So they went back and they thought it over, came back with a plea for Ruby Keeler, somebody that could dance. I said, "I'm not going to take this girl out of the picture." Freddie said, "Go ahead, let's make this goddam picture." They were right, she was the wrong girl in the wrong spot. She never knew that they wanted her out of the picture, or she would have collapsed.

How did you deal with her limitations?

It wasn't *Top Hat*, but Freddie's got a couple of good numbers in the picture. We did that thing on the creek with the fog and [cameraman] Joe August ["A Foggy Day"], that's one of the popular numbers. She didn't have to dance at all; he did all the dancing. And it was very pictorial. We did what we could to make the picture work.

A Damsel in Distress *was the first film you did with August, who was certainly one of the greatest cameramen in the history of Hollywood. [They also worked together on* Gunga Din.*] How was he to work with?*

The interesting thing about Joe August was that he was almost totally inarticulate. He always had to sort of pantomime anything he wanted to tell you, with sound effects. Having done that sort of work myself when I was young, I had developed the same [way of communicating]; I thought it was style. I realized that Joe August was an artist. And he's as mute as Quasimodo. So the fact that he's tied around the larynx gives all the muscularity to the visuals. That's one of the reasons why the John Ford pictures he photographed are so beautiful. Remember *The Informer?* And Joe was no Irishman. But he knew what went on in that Irishman's mind. He had a boldness. He always liked to do something that was dangerous. He liked the chance that he was going to blow it. One time I was with him on the stage, and we needed more set. The production manager and the grips are thinking about how they are going to get a piece of wall in there. He says, "Forget it." And they say, "What did you say, Joe?" He says, "Forget it, I'll take care of that." Then he throws a streak of light along the wall, high, and turns a light on up there and makes it accent the set. He could be so tremendously good.

You often take a long time cutting a film. What kind of working relationship do you prefer with your editor?

My problem, from the first two-reeler I ever made, was that I had to get up in the cutting room and put the damn thing together so it could be shown. You can't ask another man to unsnaffle all the parts of things that were done, sometimes with hope, other times from necessity, and other things that you've shot and would like to work in, if possible. I really rehearse on film; you know, your film stock is the cheapest thing you have. So I get a rough cut that comes along from an editor when I'm doing a film and I suffer through it and then go to work and apprise him of what those cuts are. To make the film work, to create a kind of poetic feeling, well, there are a thousand ways to cut it. It's like playing a piano—the right notes to hit, and the emphasis, the *sotto voce* and the *profundo*. We used to get very good directors, great directors, way back in the history of film, like [D. W.] Griffith, who knew how to wake an audience up and make film work as it had never done before and, in some ways, hasn't since.

Is it true that you came onto Gunga Din *at a late stage?*

We were fighting for our lives to make a film of that. [Ben] Hecht and [Charles] MacArthur had written a script, and Howard Hawks was going to do it. But Hawks had gone on, and they asked me if I would make a picture of it, because they had two actors, Cary Grant and Vic McLaglen, who were committed for big salaries. I liked the [Rudyard Kipling] poem—I knew it wasn't related to the picture at all—so I read the script. It was impossible, because it was all inside. "The Rover Boys in India," but inside the barracks, and that was just not going to work for the Occidental audiences. If they are going to be in India at the Khyber Pass, the audience is going to want to see something of it.

I said, "I want half a million dollars to take the story outside. I want to do it on three elevations, the desert, the semi-uplands where there will be rugged rocks, and high ground. And I want a third character so the story will move." This was rather a sleight-of-hand trick, you know. So I said, "Doug Fairbanks, Jr., is free. Doug has his disadvantages. He's rather stiff. But this is going to be a very light role, and to lighten him up will be fine."

How did you get a final script?

I called Joel Sayre, who is a good short story writer. Joel and Freddie Guiol and I went to Arrowhead Springs and took two stenographers and we walked around there and read books for three or four days. The poem was about a true cult that existed, and the history could give us some authenticity. Then I went back to the studio and got Perry Ferguson, who was my art director, and we got airplanes and took to location. Fred and Joel arrived on the location the day after we started shooting, they stayed at the hotel at Lone Pine, and Joel did some very good writing.

Freddie was going to shoot the second unit for the battle scenes and I would take care of the close-ups. But Vic McLaglen used to get loaded at this saloon, and one day Freddie—he was always a very tough guy—met Vic in the street, stopped him, and said, "Where the hell do you think you're going?" Vic said, "Anywhere I damn please, laddie." And Freddie says, "To hell with that, McLaglen, you're going to bed. You have to work early in the morning." So Freddie put McLaglen to bed. But Freddie's a terrible bottle man—and he was so exhausted he himself went up to have a drink. And by daylight they're putting *him* to bed, you know? Before we got to the end of the picture, Freddie developed a heart condition and he had to go home.

So I was stuck up in that country with Joe August, one of the best cameramen in the business, but we had no second unit, and it meant doing everything ourselves, you know. The studio was after me to come on in to do the interiors, but I figured I just couldn't get it all in the studio, because on location I had alternatives. Finally we got to the point of, "What do we need to do next in this damn picture?" and so help me, we couldn't think of anything. So I called the studio and told them we were coming in. I guess there were some heads shaking, but our footage was quite good.

Where did you shoot the ending?

We did that down in L.A. It was my idea to put in the recitation of the poem. We got a beautiful night and a beautiful dawn, out in the Valley somewhere where the real estate is now.

Then we had to cut the picture. I had an awful lot of cutting to do with all this battle stuff, and Jesus, some guy at the studio put it together and it didn't make any sense. So I went over to the comedy department and got an old timer who used to be my comedy cutter to come over and cut the battle scenes together. "You know," he told me, "You can cut no piece of film shorter than six feet." I guess there's a lot of guys he's told that to who believed him; it was one of the rules handed down from Zion. Eventually we had eighteen-frame cuts all the way through that picture, and I had to lose him; he wouldn't cut a piece of film that short.

Cary Grant did some of his most offbeat work for you, in Penny Serenade and Talk of the Town, as well as in Gunga Din.

I didn't want to do gag pictures with Cary Grant; Cary was doing nothing but comedies then, so I wanted to do something slightly different. Cary was always ready for everything. In *Penny Serenade*, we had a scene where he goes in to see the judge about the child. His heart is breaking—and he's got his hands in his pockets. Cary didn't hold up on doing that at all. Not any more than he held up on putting his hat on backwards in *Gunga Din*. He thought that was pretty silly, but I suggested he do it, and he did it. Jesus, we put a bellboy's uniform on him, the dress uniform of that particular group, but I don't remember Cary having a problem with it. That's the way he was. And Cary's perfectly capable of suggesting changes in the script and coming up with ideas.

Whose idea was it to put Spencer Tracy and Katharine Hepburn together for the first time, in Woman of the Year?

There's a lot of indefiniteness about that, but I'm quite sure it was Kate Hepburn.

Why do you say that?

Because that's the way Kate gets things done. Kate is terrific on ideas. She doesn't wait around for people to think of things. Kate brought the script to me and asked me to read it. It was forty pages short of conclusion; it was never concluded until we got down there shooting. I said, "This is great, Kate, bring it to Columbia. Let's do it." She said, "You missed the point. I've already promised Louis B. Mayer because he's been very helpful to me." I said, "I can't do that, I'm making pictures with these people down the street." She said, "Oh, those things aren't so difficult to solve," So I went down to Metro to do the picture while Harry Cohn burned. I never went back to Metro after that—too damn many story conferences. Good directors didn't stay long at Metro.

What about Clarence Brown?

Clarence Brown is a *marvelous* director.

You directed Jean Arthur in Talk of the Town, The More the Merrier, *and her last film,* Shane. *How was it working with her?*

She was interesting because she seemed to be rising above her personality. Anytime she has a charge to make against someone or a defense of something, it always seemed that she felt herself dangerously exposed, kind of heroic in the most ordinary circumstances—even if she had to put her left hand out in traffic in order to turn. You had to treat her like a child when you directed her—she was terribly anxious about everything.

The More the Merrier *was your last picture before you went into the service. What was the shooting like?*

We had fun on that picture; I don't usually have fun on a picture because I've usually got a little too much writing to do. I knew it was my last picture, and I had a limited time to do it, and I wanted to enjoy it. There was no question about how it was going to develop; it was going to develop well. And the circumstances, as we went along, just folded in nicely.

For the first time in years, I took a film out for a preview and didn't take it apart. I'd put in for a commission, I got it, and the war was on in North Africa. It's hard to get a fifty-yard-line seat like that. So I took one more look at it and left it like that; I never saw the film again. I never heard anything more about it except once, in *Yank* magazine, in Algiers, I read where the film was up for the New York Film Critics' award.* That was good news but I knew it was a good film. Anyway, by then I was out of the film world, entirely.

Could you relate some of your experiences during the war?

One night, we were over in the Persian Gulf, which is the dullest place in the world, and there were a hell of a lot of troops in a sort of amphitheater; there must have been twenty thousand guys there, and they were going to see a movie [*I Wake Up Screaming*]. It was a film you would avoid seeing. I was very fond of Betty Grable, she was a friend of mine [Stevens directed her in *The Nitwits*, 1935], but she was in it, and it just wasn't my cup of tea. But I sat there with twenty thousand other guys and I saw the Passion Play. I had a *tremendous* experience watching this film. There was a good sister and a bad sister, and the foreign chap, and what do you think? It's the bad sister who's winning all the way. Betty Grable is the good

---

*The More the Merrier was voted Best Film of 1943 by the New York Film Critics' organization.

sister, because she's glossy and cute and the GI's dream. Everybody just sat there and there was a catharsis.

The film was fifty times the weight on each individual it was designed for, at home in their own theater, where this game was happening in their own lives. Here, they're cut off from all of that. Here, like in a cathedral, it brought them face to face with simple experiences that can be the most profound experiences in a person's whole lifetime. I was a little bit more of a person after seeing that. It was more important than B-47s or B-48s or the Afrika Korps and divisions moving and casualties going back, that ridiculous life which was the most exciting life in the world at the time.

I had gone to Africa because the U.S. Army didn't have any war films. The British came out with their *Desert Victory* and we had nothing. I got into a division outside of Algiers and I picked up Bill Mellor, the cameraman who was with me for so many years. Here they had a Hollywood cinematographer and they didn't know whether to send him into the MP or the KP or what. They gave us some tanks, with powder men—that's one thing the army had, great powder men—and we were shooting over the moving tanks with stuff blowing up in front of them. We were down there about two weeks, sending it back to Frank Capra to make the American film on the African war [*Tunisian Victory*].

In Algiers I got in to see Eisenhower. It was two days after Rommel surrendered, and I asked Eisenhower if he had talked to him. I would have liked to hear about it. I never forgot this, especially when he was running for president. He says, "I'm here to kill Germans, not to talk to them." That s.o.b. You've got to be eight years old, you know, to have your masters talk to you like that and not have it have an effect. All the time he was campaigning for president, many a time he was on the television, I would make that remark and lose a couple of votes for him. It wasn't enough.

Your unit filmed concentration camps at the end of the war in Europe. Can you talk about that?

We cut the barbed wire to go into Dachau, and that's beyond description. The only way you can talk about it is in photographs. I came around the corner of a building, in my uniform, and these people were absolutely in a stupor or a tension of fright. They were wearing these dismal stripes, they know it dehumanizes you. As I came around the corner, this one man went from however he was to the most upright figure. I guess he'd been a soldier. He was terribly thin. And he was so stricken: he saluted me. It oppresses the individual that he's reacting to, terribly. I mean, you must be one of the worst kind of villains of all time. I guess if they didn't salute just right or stand at attention just right, or breathed wrong, they would be on the woodpile. So help me, where they had the furnaces and all of the bodies are stacked up, they had sort of a purple ink on them that said "Pole" or "Czech." Some had tags on their toes. There was an enormous gassing oven; at first we didn't know quite what it was. And there was a tremendous pile of bodies on one side of the building all during the time I was there, although they were burying a lot of them.

How do you think your war experiences affected your later work?

It causes a most profound adjustment in your thinking. I don't suppose I was ever too hilarious again.

You did direct a comic segment in A Miracle Can Happen *[a.k.a.* On Our Merry Way *] for United Artists in 1948, didn't you?*

[Producer] Benedict Bogeaus was trying to get a lot of stars in a picture, a *tour de force,* and he offered a fantastic sum if I would do a comedy sequence. It had Jimmy Stewart and [Henry] Fonda—I'm smiling already. And I wasn't worried; these people are going to be funny. We put a Laurel and Hardy thing together. With ordinary actors I've tried this, and it's like playing music without an instrument, but these guys could do anything. We had a hell of a lot of fun and I got my feet wet, you know, making something which was hilariously funny without a note of humor in it. It was all structural. My partners got $50,000 for it and that did my ego some good.

*You mean Frank Capra, William Wyler, and Sam Briskin, your
partners in Liberty Films. Why did you become involved with
Liberty Films after the war, instead of returning to Columbia?*

Harry Cohn and I had met in Paris at the end of the war and he
said, "Now are you coming back to Columbia?" What could I say in
the Ritz Bar in a worn-out uniform—no, I'm not? I guess I said yes;
well, this created undying enmity between Harry Cohn and me, the
only guy to ever tell me I broke a contract. And he meant well, he
was just being sweet, and I should have come back with Columbia,
because I had had wonderful pleasure working there. But Frank
Capra had organized this company, and Willy [William] Wyler was
there, so I joined them.

For some crazy goddam reason—maybe I wanted to throw a slow,
soft pitch or something—I got hold of a comedy story that was very
interesting [*One Big Happy Family*] and I went to work on it for
Liberty. Ingrid Bergman had agreed to star in it. I worked on it
for some time, and I didn't mind that it wasn't maturing well because
I've had that happen before. Ingrid went to play Joan of Arc in the
theater, but I really wasn't getting anywhere with this comedy. We
had taken Sam Briskin as a production man, a partner, and he kept
an eye on things. Frank was making a big picture [*It's A Wonderful
Life*], and I had to cosign all the checks. I never paid for so much
snow in my life. I said, "Jesus Christ, I wish this Capra would stop
spending so much money, I've got a sore arm." It got to the point
where Sam Briskin said, "Ingrid is *so* interested, I wish you could go
back and talk to her."

I said sure, that's just what I need to do. I'll quit fooling around.
But by the time I talk to Ingrid, I'll have to tell her something that's
pretty good. So I didn't take the airplane, I took the train. I figured
that would give me plenty of time. I met Ingrid in the alley after the
play. She asked me, "How are we coming with our comedy?" I said,
"You know how these things are," and we had a couple of drinks at

"21." And she said, "Well, you have to tell it all to me." Ingrid pours a little cognac, she's all smiles, and I said, "Ingrid, we're not going to make a comedy." I felt like a heel. I said, "It just isn't working for me." I just didn't see a goddam funny thing about it at all.

How did you settle on I Remember Mama then?

RKO was going to make it with Irene Dunne, and somebody there suggested that she should talk to me about it. I'd seen the play with Barbara Bel Geddes in New York, coming out of the Army, and it was a nice little play. It was set in San Francisco and I was a kid there during that period. I thought it would be fun to reconstruct the period. It was at the most a play that committed itself only to mom and the family. Nothing contemporary.

As time went on, however, I kept feeling I should do a picture about the war—all the other guys had done or were doing pictures about their war experiences, [John] Ford, [John] Huston, Wyler, and so on. And here I was avoiding the subject. Until I found *Shane*—it was a Western, but it was really my war picture. The cattlemen against the ranchers, the gunfighter, the wide-eyed little boy, it was pretty clear to *me* what it was about.

I did an unusual sound effect in that picture. In most Westerns, you know, people are shooting off guns all the time, until you don't even notice it anymore. I wanted people to be really jolted out of their seats the first time Shane uses his gun. It didn't happen until maybe an hour into the film; I very carefully kept gunshots out of it up until that point, to make the first one more emphatic. So I got a little cannon, put it right off-camera, and when Alan Ladd fires his gun, I had them shoot off the cannon and it made a tremendous roar.

Why did you choose A. B. Guthrie, Jr., to write the script of Shane?

Bud was a good friend of mine, but he was very reluctant to be down in this area. In fact, they were doing *The Big Sky* [based on a Guthrie novel] across the street at RKO, and they had tried to get Bud to do the screenplay. I had read a couple of Bud's novels; he was the only damn Western writer that could get Westerners to be as voluble as GIs were in bull sessions. He wrote GI dialogue. It wasn't just a parody of other Western writers, who seem to put a limitation on how much a man should say. I'm not sure those Westerners were so much silent as their authors were ungifted.

I called Bud in Montana, told him what we were doing, and he said, "I think I'd like to do that." I said, "C'mon down and see if you can." So he came and I told him what I had in mind; I hadn't lined out the thing completely, but I wanted to get him interested in it. He said, "Well, what do you got for me to read?" I gave him this Jack Schaefer paperback. This was a Friday afternoon. He said, "Do you have any film scripts around?" I said, "Oh, gosh, there are a lot of those around this building." He said—he was teaching school— "I want to see how the form goes." I said, "Let's leave that for later as far as I'm concerned." He said, "Well, I'm curious, so let me have one or two of those, will you, so I can take them to the hotel over the weekend." So he did.

Monday morning, Guthrie walks in the door, and he's got a script of the paperback. He has something like thirty-seven pages, numbered, with the fade-ins, and the fade-outs and the cut-tos. I said, "Christ, don't take this over to the writers' building—people see you walking in with a script on your first day, you'll have a bomb over there in your room. The theory is you stooge around for about ten days before you get started." It was damn good. Bud Guthrie was putting himself into another tale, and it was excellent. But we got about two-thirds of the way through the script and Bud had to go back to Montana. School was starting up again or something. He rushed through some sort of a conclusion, and let it ride. I never really got through a whole script before we started. After we straightened out the chronology, the night before or sometimes during the day, we were still doing some scenes to finish it. But by then I knew the actors, and it's very easy to write to the actuality of a situation.

Alan Ladd as Shane was such a marvelous piece of casting but unconventional, particularly because he was so short for a Western hero.

It was an interesting thing for the picture because he didn't tower above the others—the mountains did. We kept him as high off the ground as possible so he wouldn't be dwarfed by people.

One of the greatest and best-remembered shots in Shane *comes at the beginning, when Ladd is riding toward the homestead in long shot and a grazing elk in the foreground of the frame lifts its head just at the perfect moment to frame the horse between its antlers. How did you do that?*

I sent out and got a little elk and a couple of bucks with big spreads. What I did was to have the buck alert us to the rider; the figure on horseback comes straight down—it's not across the screen or interesting, just progression, a kind of monotony. We lined it up and then worked with this buck to have him in the foreground; we had some dry stuff or weed up there that he went after a few times. We rehearsed with Alan Ladd and got Ladd back—he's going to move along at a signal—then we moved the camera over to where the buck was grazing. There's a fella out there, hidden back in Ladd's direction just out of frame, with a bucket and some rocks in it. During the take the fella shook the rocks; it sounded a little bit like rain. Once we did it and the buck looked toward the rocks. We took it again, the buck stayed right there with his good downtown hay (it's unusual for him), and on cue, a silent cue, we watched this rider come along.

And it was a coincidence, the horn was right in the middle—it was awful good. So I decided to shoot the works, since I was going to get lucky. I kept it quiet, let the animal graze, got Alan all the way back there, silent signal for him to start on, silent signal for the camera, he's coming on and pretty soon we call up the cue for the buck. Not quite. A little more cue. He looks up, and Alan is right between the antlers. Three takes. You're either going to get it or you're not going to get it. There's no use persisting; it just had to work that way.

*Do you think that in period films, such as Westerns, using
long takes and a deliberate pace, as you do, helps draw the
audience into the period subconsciously?*

I suppose that's true, and not only for the Western, but of all films
to some degree. Perhaps it's more true of the Western—I never
thought of that. I know we are often aware of the *aficionados* of
rapid cutting; we're not always aware of people who like to see
things build suspense or energy with one particular piece of film.
It's related to music or painting, the arrangement of film, and it
has an enormous effect on an audience. They never relate to it as
being devised, any more than I presume I'm seduced because Renoir devises the composition of what he shows me in a painting. I
know he sweated it out, erased it, but he got it. There's no question about it, there's the grand man.

It surprises me how well audiences, also critics, reward a film
that has that kind of thing in mind, by design, not because it just
happened. Sometimes we find really fine quality in a film by looking
at it, looking at it, and then looking *back* at it—why, this darn thing's
designed as the *Bolero* is designed! In one of those long takes, the
camera gets rooted in one place almost as if it has discovered something of extraordinary importance. It doesn't move in to examine it
closely; it draws the audience in to make an effort to see more. The
audience must explore it, discover why there is this muted telling of
some significant point. They're in a position where they can have a
reverential look at something.

*Around this point in the interview, Stevens looked at his watch and asked,
"Anybody want one for the road?" So we ordered coffees, bringing the
interview to a rapid conclusion. That meant we had to rush over most of
his other work in the 1950s and 1960s (A Place in the Sun, Giant,
The Diary of Anne Frank, The Greatest Story Ever Told) if we were
going to draw Stevens out on his current attitudes toward the film business
and on his last film, The Only Game in Town. On that film, as on A*

Damsel in Distress, *Stevens's loyalty to an actress took precedence over more sensible casting.*

How did* The Only Game in Town *come together? Casting Elizabeth Taylor with Warren Beatty was rather odd.

My wife and I wanted to go to Paris. And Liz Taylor is a buddy of mine. And Warren Beatty is a real buddy. So I read the script [by Frank Gilroy, based on his play]; it's a very nice little script, but it's none of my work. I wasn't going to take that script apart and give it more size and space, but I liked it. And I said I'd do it. Frank Sinatra and Liz Taylor were part of the deal. That script? I don't see how they made the deal. Now with Liz and Frank Sinatra, it's all going to be considerably unreal. But if you can make it pretty real, it's going to be rather interesting. Frank Sinatra fell out of it, and I called up Warren. He said, "Count me in." Now I've got a problem. It won't work. Liz Taylor won't work with Warren. And so we've got to use this other girl, what's-his-name's daughter, the Irish director's daughter—

Mia Farrow [daughter of the late John Farrow]?

Mia, yeah. She's fragile. She's sensitive. She can stumble around and be a little problem. But with Warren Beatty in this fragile little piece, it could have been real. Warren is very human and bucolic in a young domestic situation. I said, "Okay, we can still do it." Dick Zanuck, who was running Fox, flew over to Paris, and I said, "We can't do it with Liz Taylor, now that we've got Beatty. The frank thing to do is just to tell Liz that it will not be good for her and put Mia Farrow in the picture." Dick is all for it. Well, somebody told Liz. Jesus, 1:55 A.M. and somebody's banging on my door at the Georges V. In comes Liz. She says, "Well, I've had a new experience in my life, thanks to you. I've been fired from a picture." I said, "What do you mean, fired?" "You don't want me in this picture." "Certainly, Liz, I want you in the picture. But the way this is working out, you don't want to be in this picture. It's not right. Taylor and Sinatra fine—Taylor and Beatty no good. Drop Beatty, get someone that goes with Taylor. But the two are not going to make the story believable." Well, anyway, by that time Zanuck has come. And she gives him hell and all of that, and then [Richard] Burton arrives. They all arrive in my room. I said, "What the hell. Let's go ahead and do it. See what happens."

Do you have any plans for more films?

No, I haven't. I'm avoiding it. Too many other things to do. Too many other things to read. Do you ever read scripts? They're impossible. "Cut to close-up," scenery, meaningless description. Jesus, some of them are written in Arabic. I can't follow a script at all. I got tangled in a couple of projects and I always managed to get out—I was going to do *Butch Cassidy*; I got pretty mixed up in that, then I said no. And then *Funny Girl, Nicholas and Alexandra*—but somehow or other I always escaped confinement. I'm escaping it with more adroitness now.

Don't you have any desire to make a film?

Here's the story. Here's exactly the story. I'd *love* to make another film. But the way I make a film, nobody would make it. You know, it means I've got to take three years, two years anyway; I've got to work on the story. If somebody just gives me a script—I've done this, I've gone nuts—I won't shoot it. It's no picture. And then I've got to go to the bank.

Jesus, one time when I was doing *The Greatest Story Ever Told*, I needed $5 million to continue. I was shooting process, which is the dullest thing in the world, and they told me that the Bank of America people are coming. We had a lovely restaurant at the old Ince studio, but I called the property man over and I said, "I've got to have lunch here on the set. Put a bridge table over there, chairs for the four of them, get ham and cheese sandwiches and coffee." We all sat down for lunch and they knew I needed a lot of money. We started with radishes or some other very unpopular vegetable. One smug little guy, a fat older guy, takes a deep breath and says, "You know, every time I get in this atmosphere of a motion picture studio, I get terribly, terribly uneasy. All the things which happen in this business give us problems." I said, "Brother, do you remember 1930? Everything I had in the world was in the First National Bank in Culver City. Did you notice when you came by that building it's still empty? I still haven't got my money out of it. I get terribly nervous when I eat with bankers, so we are both going to have a nervous lunch." Exactly as friendly as that. This is the guy who took my $2,100, everything I'd saved from Laurel and Hardy and the other pictures, and blew it. I brought that up a couple of other times. Jesus, bankers! We got our $5 million.

Talking of The Greatest Story Ever Told *put Stevens in mind of Carl Sandburg, who worked with him and James Lee Barrett on the script, receiving the unusual billing of ". . . in creative association with Carl Sandburg." We gathered that Stevens had become quite fond of Sandburg, finding a kindred soul in the rough-hewn romantic poet. Stevens's description of their last meeting lingered in our minds as we took our leave of him on the street a few minutes later.*

I kept pretty close to Carl as he was getting old. He was always so vital. A man gets that old, people start to worry about him, but you never worried about Carl. When he was out here, we arranged that he would get up about ten and come in around noon; he loved to work late, he loved to go to parties. Anyway, I'd go see him at his home [Connemara Farm in Flat Rock, North Carolina] from time to time, and the winter he passed on, I went after not having been there for a year. We had some laughs; he was a wonderful man for laughter. When I bade him goodbye, he reached in his pocket and pulled out a piece of white rock. On it was written, "George, from Carl. A piece of the rock." The guy is poetic even with a chisel. Because that's the rock he has looked at out his window for the last forty years, a great big rock sitting out back. Anybody put a chisel in that, he would have brained him. So I was shook up. I said goodbye and started walking down the trail. I knew what he meant by that—it was farewell. The more I thought it over, I decided to take a look back. And as I self-consciously look back, he self-consciously looks over *his* shoulder to see if *I'm* looking back. He waved at me. Geez, I hated to see that man go.

That was the last time you saw him?

Yeah. "A piece of the rock." People look at that and say, "Who's Carl, a bartender?"

5. Interview with Joel McCrea

A restaurant in the Valley, September 1974

by Patrick McGilligan

JOEL McCREA

(1905–1990)

1941	*Reaching for the Sun.*		*Black Horse Canyon.*
	Sullivan's Travels.	1955	*Stranger on Horseback.*
1942	*The Great Man's Lady.*		*Wichita.*
	The Palm Beach Story.	1956	*The First Texan.*
1943	*The More the Merrier.*	1957	*The Oklahoman.*
1944	*Buffalo Bill.*		*Trooper Hook.*
	The Great Moment.		*Gunsight Ridge.*
1945	*The Unseen.*		*The Tall Stranger.*
1946	*The Virginian.*	1958	*Cattle Empire.*
1947	*Ramrod.*		*Fort Massacre.*
1948	*Four Faces West.*	1959	*The Gunfight at Dodge City.*
1949	*South of St. Louis.*	1962	*Ride the High Country.*
	Colorado Territory.	1970	*Cry Blood, Apache.*
1950	*The Outsiders.*	1974	*The Great American Cowboy*
	Stars in My Crown.		(documentary). Narrator.
	Saddle Tramp.	1975	*Mustang Country.*
	Frenchie.	1985	*George Stevens: A Filmmaker's*
1951	*Hollywood Story.*		*Journey* (documentary).
	Cattle Drive.	1990	*Preston Sturges: The Rise and Fall of*
1952	*The San Francisco Story.*		*an American Dreamer*
1953	*Shoot First.*		(documentary).
	The Lone Hand.		
1954	*Border River.*		

His grace was in seeming exactly what he was, with no pretensions: a California kid who loved to surf the ocean waves; peddled newspapers to a showman named Cecil B. De Mille; rode his bicycle down to Sunset Boulevard to watch D. W. Griffith shoot Intolerance; *learned to ride a horse and dreamed of becoming a cowboy; read* Ramrod, Four Faces West, *and* Union Station *and wished himself into the stories.*

Joel McCrea was artless as an actor—likable, agile, and heroic, one of the screen's most endearing light comedians, one of the most durable Western stars. He had a long apprenticeship for stardom and sometimes was the studio's second choice for the lead, after Gary Cooper or Cary Grant had dropped out of the running. He continually surprised directors and redeemed lesser films, as his stature grew.

His serenity set him apart: Surrounded by chaos or screwball lunacy, he always seemed an island of placid strength. William Wyler, Howard Hawks, William Wellman, Gregory La Cava, William De Mille, George Stevens, and Alfred Hitchcock used him well, but probably nobody understood Joel McCrea's easygoing charm better than Preston Sturges. The lightweight movie director in search of a serious theme in Sullivan's Travels; the jilted husband haplessly trailing after his kooky wife in The Palm Beach Story; the unfamous inventor of anesthesia in the bitingly ironic (and not particularly comic) The Great Moment—these are among his greatest moments.

When he felt himself growing too old for comic or romantic parts, McCrea turned to the love of his youth: westerns. In his time he would play Wyatt Earp, Buffalo Bill, Bat Masterson, and the Virginian; he built the stagecoach express, forged the intercontinental railroad, fought outlaws, Indians, Mexicans, what-have-you. Ride the High Country, in 1962, has McCrea opposite Randolph Scott as one of two aging lawmen tempted by the gold they have been hired to transport from a mine to a bank. McCrea is the one who refuses to go crooked and dies. Director Sam Peckinpah's elegy to the vanishing genre was the perfect coda to his good-guy career. There was not much after that until 1977, when McCrea was coaxed into the offbeat Mustang Country, about an ex-rodeo champion teaming up with an Indian boy to capture a wild stallion.

When I met with him, at a steak house he recommended in the San Fernando Valley, McCrea was doing some publicity for Mustang Country. He was seventy-one, but had lost none of his vigor, warmth, or self-deprecating humor. His frame was strapping, his voice familiar, choked with age. Dressed in a ten-gallon hat, bolo tie, and frontier regalia, he looked indeed like a man comfortable, on or off screen, on a horse. His face was tanned and lined, his hair long and silvery, glistening fiercely in the hot California sun.

McCrea had come down from his ranch in Camarillo; he had another in the Southwest. Real estate investments had left him wealthy and mobile, but the West was his homeland. His wife, the former actress Frances Dee, kept trying to talk him into an extended European vacation. But, McCrea explained, all he could think about was the desert, the mountains, and the ranching, which he preferred, so he stalled.

He stalled over lunch too, happy to reminisce at length as unnoticed hours slipped by. A splendid raconteur, McCrea was also a surprisingly dead-on mimic. He delivered marvelous impersonations of a petulant Hitchcock; a chronically insecure Jean Arthur; a magnanimous Cecil B. De Mille, "my booster," who introduced the actor to thousands of extras on the set of Union Pacific as "my former newsboy"; a saintly Will Rogers, who profoundly influenced McCrea's humanitarian outlook; always returning in the conversation to Gary Cooper—Coop—his friend and personal hero.

The only training I ever had was when I went to college and took a couple of courses in public speaking and drama at Pomona College. There was a fellow there who was head of the Drama Department, named Benjamin David Scott; he was a little Irishman, red-haired, and just a terrific guy. He said to me, "Why did you take these subjects?" And I said, "Well, they fit in well with my other classes." He said, "Well, don't you want to do something with them?" And I said, "Yeah, but . . ." Because I wanted to be a rancher. I wasn't intending to be an actor at all when I was that age. I was about twenty-one, I guess.

So he said, "Well, you know, I've noticed in class, in your readings, that you have ability. You're making a big mistake if you don't try to do something with it. First of all, you were raised in Hollywood, you have contacts with everybody, it could be your best bet. Second of all, you're big. Every big woman star wants to look up; that's her best angle. You're making a mistake. You want to be a rancher but you're going to work thirty, forty, or fifty years before you own a ranch. But if you go in and do western pictures, you'll still be playing a cowboy, and you'll own a ranch while you're still young enough to enjoy it, because you'll make so much more money than the seventy dollars a month you'd make on a ranch. You ought to do it."

Then Robert Taylor came along—who was then Arlington Brough—and went to the same college. Benjamin David Scott sent Bob to me. Marion Davies was giving a big party at the Cocoanut Grove; Norma Shearer was there and I was there with Joan Crawford—because she wasn't married and neither was I. You know, Metro put us together just for the big party. All the big Metro people were there: Jack Gilbert, Virginia Bruce, all of them. And when I went upstairs to the men's room at the Cocoanut Grove, I met this good-looking young guy. He said, "My name's Arlington Brough. This is a terrible place to do it, but I was afraid to come with all those big stars. I have a letter of introduction to you." And he gave it to me. It was from Dr. Benjamin David Scott and it said, "This is a boy . . . maybe too handsome . . . but he really has talent as an actor and, if you can do something for him, I'd appreciate it." He knew I appreciated what he'd done for me.

Well, I took him out to Metro and they tested him and the next thing I knew he was doing *Camille* with Greta Garbo. I was playing opposite Stanwyck at the time—whom he was crazy about and later married—and I said, "Look, I did something for you. Now you're bigger than I am, you can do something for me." I kidded him about it—we were great friends. When he went into the service, he retired his horse, Comanche, on my ranch. Barbara Stanwyck had married him by that time. Yes, we were great friends and, of course, I was great friends with Stanwyck, too.

The Captain of the Ship

The director is captain of the ship. Clark Gable told me that. He said, "No matter when I was supposed to be king at MGM, the director was captain of the ship." I don't care how big a star you become, much bigger than I ever did, like a Gable or a Gary Cooper, the director tells you how the scene should be played, and then he picks the takes. So you pick a script, and you pick a director, and your troubles are over. You don't even have to worry if the leading lady's gonna be any good, if you pick a George Stevens, a Frank Lloyd, a Gregory La Cava, a Preston Sturges, or a Willy Wyler. You just say, "Well, it's in good hands."

I found that out when I was a kid watching D. W. Griffith do *Intolerance* down on Sunset Boulevard. I rode my bicycle down there and watched him down on Sunset and Vermont. They had the great set there for years—it was the biggest set you ever saw—and, of course, in those days you can imagine how amazing it was. Griffith would sit back there in his chair, and he looked better than the leading man, you know; he had a kind of a flair, anyway: he was more romantic than the leading man, and he always wore that hat. Billy Bitzer was the cameraman, the same one that was on *Birth of a Nation*. Of course, I didn't know Griffith, but I rode my bicycle down there with another kid from Hollywood High School and we watched him. And you could tell. . . .

Then I watched Rex Ingram, who made *Four Horsemen of the Apocalypse* and who really discovered [Rudolph] Valentino. I got to know Valentino well; he was a charming guy. Terrific athlete, you know, and he wanted to do everything himself, really wanted to give. He wanted to give. Whether it was ego or whether he just wanted to give to the public, I don't know, but he was offering something.

The Showman: Cecil B. De Mille

I went to school with De Mille's daughter, Cecilia, and did a play with her and stuff. Then, when I got out of college, I went to Metro, where De Mille was making his first talkie, *Dynamite*, with [Charles] Bickford and Kay Johnson and Conrad Nagel. Carole Lombard and I were extras together, and we went out there and De Mille made a test of us. Then I went into his office. He had three secretaries—Gladys Rossen was the last and most important of them, but I don't remember the names of the first two—and they said, "Well, you can't see Mr. De Mille." And I said, "Well, I'd just like to talk to him. I've been to his home, I know him, I went to his daughter's birthday party." They said, "Well, he's a busy man . . ." And he was a big man; it was his first talkie, you know, a big deal.

So I sat down in the office and I said, "Well, I'll just wait until he goes out to lunch." See, because it was about 11 A.M. So I just sat out there. Well, when he came out to go to lunch, he walked by me and looked at me. I was real tan—I went to the beach a lot and rode waves. He looked at me and said, "How are you? What are you doing here?" And I said, "Well, I came to see you, but they told me I couldn't see you." He said, "You did?" And I said, "Yes." "Well," he said, "What do you want?" And I said, "Well, I'm out of college. I graduated from college, and I've been working as an extra for about a year and a half, and I know you're going to make a new picture and it's a talkie. The only experience I've had is in college plays and stuff, where I had to talk, so I just wondered . . ."

So he said, "Come on in the office." So I went into the office. And when I came out I had a stock contract with him for $100 a week, which to me was a helluva lot of money. And he was my booster. Interesting thing: I had delivered papers, and I used to throw his paper up on the porch when it was raining. He came out one time and he said, "The other kid threw it in the rain—you threw it up on the porch." And I said, "Yeah, well, you want to read it, don't you?" And he reached in his pocket, and he took out a silver dollar and he gave it to me. So when I went into his office that day, I told him, "You know, I've still got that silver dollar. . . ."

Now he carried me through that picture, as just really a glorified extra. That was in 1929. Then, in 1936, Cooper and I were very good friends; Cooper asked me to come over when De Mille ran *The Plainsman* there in Room No. 1 at Paramount; De Mille was the biggest director at Paramount. So we went in one afternoon and saw *The Plainsman* with Jean Arthur and Coop. And I said, "Gee, that's the best . . ." I didn't say it was the best that De Mille had ever made, because I didn't want to be presumptuous, but I thought it was better-directed than many of the others. He didn't have any bathtubs or eight thousand soldiers or anything. I thought he did a great job, so I said so. And he said, "How would you like to do a history of the Union Pacific Railroad with me?" And I said, "You're better off with Cooper." He said, "But I can't get him. I wanted to because I love Cooper. But I talked to his agent, and he's committed at Warner Brothers and at Goldwyn; he can't do it. So would you like to do it?" And I said, "Sure." So he sent it to me, and I read it, and that's how I happened to do *Union Pacific*.

The first day on the set of *Union Pacific*, he got up there on the boom and he said, "Now, we're gonna start the picture . . ." We had about seventy-five extras, working the railroad and stuff, and he said, "My former newsboy is now my star." What a showman! Right away, it sets me up. It sets me up with all the people who said, "Who the hell is McCrea? . . . He isn't very well known. . . ."

Well, De Mille was an interesting guy. Everybody thought he was a big, cold guy—only made bathtub scenes—but he had sensitivity. He was great with a lot of people. He could handle them, and make it look right. As people say, he was kind of hammy, but I think it was showmanship; I think it was like P. T. Barnum and the circus, you know? He was a showman, a showman on the set and a showman with the picture—they don't have too many of them nowadays. He made the kind of pictures that he thought people would like to see, and I enjoyed working with him. I never looked down on him. A lot of big directors that I worked with afterwards said, "Well, you know, what the hell, De Mille . . . he just has all the money and the big sets and the bathtubs. . . ." But he did some good pictures. He couldn't have lasted otherwise. He once told me, "The critics don't like my pictures very much, but the people do." He was right, too.

King Vidor: A Helluva Nice Man

The month before King Vidor started *The Crowd*, Jimmy Murray and his brother, Harry Murray, and I were extras together in a picture that Fred Niblo was directing with Lillian Gish [*The Enemy*]. And when we came in on the bus to Metro, King Vidor was already a big director. He had made these pictures with Jack Gilbert, like *The Big Parade*. When we got off the bus, King went up to Jimmy Murray, Harry's older brother, and he said, "I want to make a test of you, come over here." And he went and made a test and costarred Jimmy Murray in *The Crowd*, with King's then wife, Eleanor Boardman. The guy became a leading man overnight. King did it. He never asked the guy if he could act or anything.

After a few years, it got to be so much for Jimmy Murray that he began to drink quite a bit, and he drank himself out of the business and finally passed on at a very early age. He was a nice guy, but it was too big for him. See, I think many people, either they have to have confidence, or else they have to have the humility to know that we're all created with some talent, with ability of some sort. I always felt that if you did your best, if you were a street-cleaner and you did your best, you were fulfilling something in your life and you were making other people happier. Because the job was well done. You don't have to say, "I'm gonna be a great star." You just have to say, "I'm gonna be a great something." Maybe it'll be a shoe-shiner, but you ought to give the best shine they've got anywhere.

Later, I went to King's office myself. I'd got to know him then, and I was hoping he'd discover me in the way he did Jimmy Murray. King was very quiet, very calm, very assured. I mean, when he took me in a picture, he hadn't seen anything I'd done, because I had done hardly anything. I'd only played the juvenile lead in the two Will Rogers pictures and stuff. Anyway, I went in there and talked to him and he said, "Oh, yeah, I remember you. I picked Jimmy Murray to do *The Crowd* and you kept crowding in there. You wanted me to see you, too." I said, "Yeah." We became great friends. We did *Bird of Paradise*. David Selznick was the producer. Fine, you know? Later, we were gonna do another picture together, but it didn't work out because it was at Metro and I was under contract to Sam Goldwyn.

But King and I are still great friends. I call him every once in a while. He's working on scripts now. He'll never give up. That's his life, his life. He came here from Texas with a briefcase and an old Ford I think it was, with Florence Vidor, who was his first wife. He had these stories, you know, *Wild Oranges* and different things like *The Crowd*, he had these ideas in his head. He's a creative filmmaker and a helluva nice man. A real nice man.

William Wyler and Frank Borzage?

I'll tell you, I started with Wyler in a picture called *These Three*, Lillian Hellman's play, *The Children's Hour*. We started out and he didn't want me; he wanted someone else, I don't know who it was, Bob Montgomery or somebody, maybe Cary Grant. I was under contract to Goldwyn, with a pretty good salary, so Goldwyn said, "No, you're gonna use McCrea." Well, he had just done a picture with my wife and Francis Lederer called *The Gay Deception*, which was an excellent picture. And I had gone on the set to get my wife, and I met him. Anyway, he said, okay, he had to do it, because Goldwyn was the boss.

So we started this picture, and after about a week he came to my dressing room—he was a funny little guy, you know—and he said, "You know, I didn't want you." I said, "Yeah, Goldwyn told me." He said, "He did? I didn't tell him to tell you. But now that I've worked with you, you're great. I want you, you're great." And he never made a lot of takes with me. He was just fine with me, he liked me. Everybody else told me how many takes he usually made, and how hard he was on people. I know, for example, that it was a big thing when he had [Charlton] Heston and [Gregory] Peck and [Charles] Bickford in *The Big Country*, a big Western type of picture. And he just rode Bickford into the ground. It was surprising to people, because nobody talked back to Bickford.

Anyway, Wyler and I didn't have any problems, never made many takes or anything. You know, lots of times it has to do with a fellow like that who's real bright, and if you're a little phony, they immediately see it. Now I know some directors look for that, and they ride the hell out of an actor and they get a good performance out of him. [John] Ford used to do it. Ford was a sadistic son of a bitch. A great director, but a sadistic bastard if he wanted to be. And he'd get performances out of people. I never worked with Ford, so I don't know personally, but I knew him well and admired his work and went to see him just before he died. He was a great director, like Wyler, but I wouldn't have thrived on that. I wouldn't have put up with it.

I had to have a director who was like La Cava, like Sturges, like Frank Borzage, the man who made *Seventh Heaven*. Borzage made tests of me for *Liliom*, when I was unknown, to do with Janet Gaynor. Fox already had this team of Gaynor and [Charles] Farrell, they'd done *Seventh Heaven*, big team. So Fox was going to put me in to establish a new actor, but at the last minute Winnie Sheehan said, "No, we'd better not split up Farrell and Gaynor, This is a sure thing." So I didn't get it. But I took a test with Borzage, and his brother [Danny] played the accordion during it. It was a silent test. It showed how sensitive Borzage was, because he played mood music for me. I took the test for *Liliom* around, and it got me interviews on the lot. It really helped me. It got me the Will Rogers picture with Henry King [*Lightnin'*], because Henry King didn't know who the hell I was. Nobody did. Borzage was just that kind of a guy, with tremendous confidence.

Frank Lloyd: Greatness and Dignity

One of my favorite directors was Frank Lloyd, who was Scots-Irish and got three Academy Awards, for *Cavalcade*, *Mutiny on the Bounty*, and *Wells Fargo*, which I was in. I learned more about integrity and sincerity from Frank Lloyd than from anyone else, just by example. He would call in the whole crew at the beginning of each day and tell everybody, grips, electricians, and stars, "This is what we hope to accomplish today." Just like a general. He was meticulous and knew exactly what he wanted. He took the full responsibility of planning. And he was always on time; boy, you'd better believe he was on time. I was supposed to meet him one day at noon at a restaurant and I was late. He said, "Laddie, when you tell a person you're going to meet them somewhere, do your utmost to be on time. Be able to be counted upon."

I carried him to his rest. He was a great friend. Everyone was important to him. Gable told me, "When I did *Mutiny on the Bounty*, he was my saving grace." He is not as well remembered as Sturges today, perhaps, because he wasn't as colorful. But he was a fine guy, just a tremendous man. I talked to the stuntmen who worked with him and they said, "This man had greatness and dignity."

Gregory La Cava: Absolute Confidence

La Cava was a top director, and he picked me a few times, which was very unusual. I remember two pictures, one of them called *Private Worlds*, which was [Charles] Boyer's first picture over here, with Claudette Colbert, Joan Bennett, and Walter Wanger was the producer, and Wanger didn't want me. But La Cava said, "No, I want him." And Wanger said, "I can get Robert Montgomery." He was quite a name at MGM. La Cava said, "No, I don't want Robert Montgomery. I don't want [Douglas] Fairbanks, Jr. I want Joel McCrea." And Wanger said, "Well, he isn't as good an actor as either one of them." La Cava said, "He will be with me." See, that's the kind of confidence he had; that's the kind of man he was.

He was just great with actors, just great. He took people like me, when I really didn't know very much, was just starting, and he treated me with ease. He had absolute confidence in himself, in what you could do, and in what he could tell you to do. And you did it. If it took more takes and more time, fine; if it didn't, fine. The producer could wait and not bother us. We were making a picture.

La Cava wrote a great deal; it was kind of like working with Sturges, only he wasn't as prolific a writer as Sturges. But he did know; he knew when a line was right. I don't know whether it was his own ego or not, but he picked me two or three times when the producer said, "I can get so-and-so who's better." We all agreed that "he" was better, but La Cava didn't want him.

I remember, in one picture with Ginger Rogers, *Primrose Path*, they picked somebody else because the producer said, "Well, we have a commitment to this particular actor. You'll just have to use him, because I'll have to pay him if you don't." And La Cava said, "Well, pay him. I don't want him." The guy was as big, or bigger, a name than I was. So I asked La Cava, "How come you felt that way? I mean, it's great, I love it and I don't care but I would just like to know." He said, "Well, he came in, and I didn't have a script finished, because I never do." He never did. Then he said, "He asked me to tell him what the story was about, so I told him what it was about. . . ." Actually, it was more Ginger's picture, she was the bigger star, so this fellow said, "I don't see that I motivate anything." And La Cava turned to him and said, "Well, to tell the truth, you don't motivate a damn thing." You know what? The actor was furious and he went out. He thought his part should be built up equal to Ginger's or better, so La Cava got rid of him. They paid the actor not to do it. He was quite a name, too, although I can't tell you who.

Yes, *Primrose Path* was an excellent picture, too. Joe August was the cameraman and he was wonderful, just wonderful. Actually, that's the picture that Ginger really won the Oscar on; Frank Capra said that. *Kitty Foyle* wasn't that great in comparison. But they were afraid of the subject matter [of *Primrose Path*] in those days.*

Barbara Stanwyck: Underrated and Professional

Barbara Stanwyck was a true professional. And if you had to do more than one take, because of my fault or something, she was fine. She'd say, "C'mon, McCrea, goddammit, get with it. . . ." She was in burlesque, you know, and came up the hard way. I did five or six pictures with her.

The first one I did with her was called *Gambling Lady*. Pat O'Brien was the heavy; I was C. Aubrey Smith's son, from a famous, wealthy family. And she was a moll, going around with a gangster, Pat O'Brien. It was a Warners picture; Archie Mayo was the director. The first day, just before noon, they started taking stills. Well, the

---

*Ginger Rogers's mother, played by Majorie Rambeau, was a prostitute in the story.

Warner publicist thought, the hell with McCrea, I was borrowed from RKO, where I was under contract to David O. Selznick, getting only $150 a week. So they were making stills of C. Aubrey Smith and Pat O'Brien and Barbara Stanwyck, stills and stills and stills; they were big stars. They never called me, it got to be 12 P.M., so I just went off to lunch, see? When I came back, afternoon, I thought Archie Mayo would say something, if anybody, but Stanwyck said, "Where the hell were you for stills?" And I said, "Well, they didn't need me; I'm not very important. You're one of the big Warner Brothers stars and you were doing it...." And she said, "Listen, kid, if you want to make it in this business, be professional. You come to work like you would if you were digging postholes on a ranch, and you get your ass in there and you do what you're supposed to do, if you want to get ahead." You bet she was serious, and she was right.

I was a little temperamental and my pride was hurt a little bit. I thought, "Well, the hell with them." Again, the director never said a word; but she did. She said, "Just wait around. I was in burlesque. We used to have to change our clothes on the train, and our makeup, and we couldn't take a bath and we lived out of a suitcase. You've grown up in California where you go to the beach on your days off and ride waves, and you're a happy Southern Californian kid. Just get off your big fat ass and get to work and do it, learn your part, and be professional." Well, now, instead of being sore, I had brains enough, thank heaven, to know she was absolutely right, see? I did what she said, and by the end of the picture we became great friends.

So the next picture she did was the first Dr. Kildare that was ever made. It was called *Internes Can't Take Money* and it was by Max Brand, who wrote that whole Kildare thing. Paramount borrowed her from Warner Brothers and Al Santell, who had directed *Winterset*, directed the picture. And she asked for me. She said, "I want this guy—he's gonna be a good leading man." Then in *Union Pacific* we were together again. And people began to like us together, because they believed in us. We both kind of hit the same note; we were both sincere, we both weren't egotistical, we weren't afraid the other one was gonna have the best part. We were pros and we acted like pros. Then I did another one called *Banjo on My Knee*, with her, out at Fox. Then, later, I did *Trooper Hook*, which was bought by Metro for Spencer Tracy before he finished his twenty years there and left; they asked me if I'd do it, so I did *Trooper Hook*. And I asked for her; I paid her back.

She really is one of the most underrated and one of the best actresses I ever worked with. What was the thing she did that was so great? She should have gotten an Academy Award. Well, one that she did with me, called *The Great Man's Lady*, she should have had an award for that. She was great. She aged to one hundred and four, remember? And what was the thing King Vidor did with her? *Stella Dallas*. She was great in that, a helluva actress. I tell you, I learned from her.

William Wellman: Nothing but Guts

Yeah, I made three pictures with Wellman. He could be tough. He shot real bullets and stuff. He was careful, you know—he had a sharp shooter and he wouldn't let the actors shoot at you—but he'd have somebody shoot close to you and it'd hit a board and go "w-i-i-i-n-g." He had nothing but guts. He became a very good friend of mine, and actually he called me up when he heard I was gonna do *Buffalo Bill*. Now I had just done *Reaching for the Sun* with him and *The Great Man's Lady*. So he said, "I want to direct *Buffalo Bill*. I've always liked that story. I had an idea once of doing it with Cooper." Wellman had made *Beau Geste* and other pictures with Cooper. But they'd already assigned me to be Buffalo Bill. So I said to him, "Why not?" The producer gave me a list of five directors—by this time, it was the 1940s and I had an okay of who directed—and I said, "Wellman."

He was a wild little bastard but I liked him. If you were professional, he really worked fine with you; like he worked fine with Cagney in *Public Enemy* and he worked fine with Cooper and with Freddie March, because he would hold Freddie March down from escaping into the ceiling, overacting and everything. He would raise hell with actresses sometimes, if they were a little phony. He loved actresses like Stanwyck, who was his favorite, and Carole Lombard, another of his favorites; people like that. But if the actress was a little prissy or a little synthetic or phony, why, then he would ride hell out of them.

He never made more than three or four takes if he didn't have to, because it bored him. He was a vigorous, virile, gutty little guy and I liked him. But he could be tough on people, yes. He didn't like one of the actors in *Buffalo Bill* and boy, he just rode him. He was a good actor, too, Tommy Mitchell, a helluva good actor, won the Academy Award. He was in *Stagecoach* and *Gone with the Wind* and he was wonderful. I knew him and I liked him, but Wellman thought he was hamming it up too damn much. He wasn't playing the character, Ned Buntline; he was playing Tommy Mitchell. So Wellman rode him, to cut him down, to cut him down. He could be tough, like Ford could be tough.

Preston Sturges: A Brilliant Fellow

Preston Sturges and I were great friends. After *Sullivan's Travels*, he lined up six pictures with me, and I loved working with him; but, of course, I had to commit myself other places and so I couldn't do them all. I did three with him. But it was a very interesting experience, he really was a brilliant fellow. He wrote dialogue that I could remember; I mean, he'd give long speeches and different things, but it was very easy to remember it because he'd talk it out [as he wrote]. If you get somebody who types it out but doesn't say it, sometimes it doesn't flow so easily, you know; it's often kind of difficult.

Yes, Sturges is finally coming into his own today. I remember De Mille wanted me for a picture called *Reap the Wild Wind* and I said no, because I was going to do *Sullivan's Travels* with Preston Sturges. De Mille said to me "He's some writer . . . the picture will be forgotten. But a picture with me . . ." And I said, "Yes, C. B., but I'm not getting a percentage of your picture; I'm just working for a salary. And this fellow has a great script." That's what I based all my opinion on for doing a picture; it wasn't how much money they're going to pay me, it was the script.

You see, a director like Sturges helps you tremendously because he gives you confidence. You get confidence the day he comes to you and says, "Here's a script that I've written, and I want you to play the director." Well, immediately, you knew that Sturges could go to Cary [Grant] he could go to [Henry] Fonda, he could go to Jimmy Stewart, he could go to anyone else if he wanted to. I wasn't a Paul Newman draw; so if he gave it to you, you knew he wanted you. Immediately, at least with me, you felt confident in yourself, you tried different things and he helped you. He helped me tremendously. He gave an interview to *Collier's* once, I remember, saying that when he cast a picture, he didn't cast it as to somebody who was available; he said he wrote it with them in mind. That gave me confidence.

He told me that he wrote *Sullivan's Travels* from watching me around Paramount, working there with De Mille and Wellman and different people. I knew him as a writer for a long time before he even became a director. I told him, "Well, Preston, that's very flattering that you said you wrote it for me. No one writes things for me. They write them for Gary Cooper, and if they can't get him, they use me." "Well," he said, "That isn't the instance here. I could have gotten anybody; I could have gotten Gable, Cooper, anybody for *Sullivan's Travels* and I wanted you. I wrote it for you. You're the one." Well then, right away, a fellow who's not real cocksure of himself, like me, I needed that kind of compliment, because then I would cut loose and do things and live up to what was expected of me.

We rehearsed very little with Sturges because he would talk it over with us and he was so articulate, you see. Some of the directors I've worked with, some of the better directors even, like Wyler, are not articulate, so they'll rehearse and rehearse and rehearse, and then they'll take many takes. Wyler did thirty-eight takes of many things with people like Walter Huston in *Dodsworth*. It was a great picture; but Wyler made them do it over and over until, finally, his ear and his eye saw everything he wanted and that was it. But he wasn't articulate, really. George Stevens was articulate. And Preston Sturges was particularly articulate, because he wrote the thing as well as directed it, so he could tell you exactly what to do, and he never superimposed things that would be different from your character. And very seldom would he change anything.

His being so articulate and writing such good dialogue made it easy for me where, if I worked with a poor director, I wouldn't be as good. Some actors have this tremendous confidence in themselves; I don't want to name any of them but you know who they are. But I didn't have that ego or confidence. Except when I got on a horse, I had confidence. Yeah, I never worried about any competition there, but on the things where I didn't have the confidence, it was a great thing to have a director who was articulate.

Sturges also had a great sense of humor. He just thought everything was funny. He was so quick. I remember the first time we came in, and he told us about a scene, and I said, "Well, I don't know . . . how can I do that? It seems to me it's contrived." He said, "Well, you're absolutely right. But we'll do it this way, and then we'll do this, and then we'll do that." And I said, "Ah-hah!" Well, he hooked on to that "Ah-hah!" and he used that all the time with me. He would come in and say, "Well, what about tomorrow. Will you be on time?" We were on location doing *Sullivan's Travels*. I said, "I'll be there at the same time you are." And he said, "Ah-hah!" You know, he would get things like that.

Then we had quite a little trouble with Veronica Lake in *Sullivan's Travels* because she was pregnant and she hadn't told anybody. The day she came in and told us that she was pregnant, she wasn't showing at all. When we came to the scene where we had to jump on and off that freight car, living like bums, it made some problems. Preston said, "Well, that makes it kind of difficult. Now we have kind of a predicament . . ." So she said, "Well, there's nothing you can't do if you're pregnant." And I said, "See?" You know, see what you've got? Well, Preston just laughed and laughed. A lot of people didn't get it. But to him, he had such a sense of humor that I didn't have to say to him, "Now, see what she's done to us, and see now how you're gonna have to have a double." All the different things that "see" could mean, he got them. Oh, he was a really bright fellow.

He put a lot of things like that in the picture. I used to get colds during pictures; they used to kid me about it. The directors would say, "Well, we won't let him know when we're going to start the picture because he's liable to get a cold." I used to do it half because I had just finished another picture and I was kinda tired, and so forth. So I'd try to get them to postpone the beginning of the other picture, because I was sometimes doing three or four pictures a year, and it was too many. Anyway, I remember when we were on the freight car in *Sullivan's Travels*, and I caught cold and as I was saying, "I want to make this picture . . . want to make it . . . I've made these great comedies, but I don't want to . . . *Achoo!*" Well then, Sturges worked it in; he had Veronica Lake catch cold later and we're both sneezing. But the original idea of getting a cold, I gave him.

I look at the opening scene of *Sullivan's Travels* today and wonder how I did it. We were used to shooting about four pages of script a day. That scene was nine pages long, from the pan away from the screen and the opening shot of the men on top of the train to a shot of me jumping up and shouting, "I've got to make a picture like that!" I said, "Preston, I'm never going to be able to make it." He said, "You don't know what you can do." We shot it in one take and I was sent home by 10:30 A.M., through with work for the day.

An old man once told me, if you don't stand for something, you'll fall for anything; your life is what's important, not your job. I think of that when I remember when Preston Sturges went to work for Howard Hughes. I went over to see him at the studio one day. "Joel," he said—very big, because everything Preston did was very big—"I have Howard Hughes's money now. I don't have to write anything. Nobody has asked me for a script for a month." I said, "Preston, it will destroy you. You stood for something once. What's important is when you sold *The Great McGinty* for only ten dollars cash, with the proviso that you had to direct. What's so important about money? This is the idea of *Sullivan's Travels*, the last scene, that laughter is what's important. These were great ideas, Preston. They couldn't be bought with money." But he only looked at me and smiled, very big. "Don't worry, Joel," he said. "I have Howard Hughes's money."

Foreign Correspondent

Walter Wanger was the producer. He told [Alfred] Hitchcock that he wanted someone else. But his assistant, Joan Harrison, suggested me. What Hitchcock said to Wanger was, "This picture can't be done with a sophisticated limey like Cary Grant. I want Johnny Jones, an American kind of country square." Then this girl, Joan Harrison, helped me get the part. He was very good to me, Hitchcock was—he surrounded me with good actors: Herbert Marshall, Laraine Day, Robert Benchley, and Edmund Gwenn. He and I got along wonderfully.

Hitchcock had a habit of drinking a pint of champagne at lunch,

I remember. After lunch, one day, there was a long boring scene with me just standing there and talking. When the scene was over, I expected to hear "Cut!" and I looked over and there was Hitchcock snoring with his lips sticking out. He had fallen asleep. So I said "Cut!" and he woke up and asked, "Was it any good?" I said, "The best in the picture!" And he said, "Print!"

George Stevens and Jean Arthur

The More the Merrier was one of my favorite comedies, particularly because of George Stevens. Now George Stevens asked for me. Jean Arthur was under contract to Columbia, and she came out to the ranch. I had known her since she and I were extras, and she came out and brought nine pages of what this Robert Russell had written, called *The More the Merrier*. He was a young guy just out of the service. And she said, "I wish you'd do this picture. It's my last picture I have to do at Columbia, and I want to get away from Harry Cohn." So I went in and saw Harry Cohn. You know, he was a four-letter-word user and kind of a tough guy, but he and I hit it off well, too. So I went in there and said, "Well, I don't know, I've been working a lot. . . ." He said, "You lazy sonuvabitch. Do the picture!" I said, "Well, I don't know . . ." and hung back, and it made me all the more desirable to Harry Cohn. So he sent me in to see George Stevens, and Stevens and I hit it off immediately. We began talking about the early days when he was a cameraman photographing Laurel and Hardy. He was a very, very sensitive, meticulous worker. And he said, "You've got to do the picture."

So we started. The great thing I found out later is that he could have had Cary Grant—he had just done a picture with Cary Grant and Irene Dunne called *Penny Serenade*, which was excellent; and he could have had Robert Montgomery and several other people who were better known and bigger box-office and better actors. But he wanted me; so it instilled that kind of confidence that I needed.

He would build up things. We'd do a scene, rehearse a scene, and then he'd build it up, and say, "Well, when you come in, instead of doing that, why not . . ." And then I'd do some little gag. I had to take a shower in that picture while I was rooming with Charles

Coburn in his crowded little apartment in Washington. So I got in the shower and I was squirting water with my hands, and Stevens said, "Do that, do that in the scene." A lot of little things like that. Well, this adds confidence and everything. I think Stevens is one of the best directors that our industry has ever had. I really do.

I loved working with Jean Arthur too. She was always saying how old she looked. She told me once, when we were doing *The More the Merrier*, "I'm not gonna do any more pictures after this. If I do, I'm gonna do them with Coop and you." Because she loved Coop. She said, "Because if they put me with Tyrone Power, I'd look like his mother." And I said, "Gee, you look great, you photograph great." George Stevens and I used to build her up. We would say, "Jean, you look marvelous today." And I'd say, "George, just because you're the director, let me talk to Jean for a while." You know, we pretended like we were kind of a little jealous of one another. She was married to [writer] Frank Ross at the time so neither of us were gonna do anything, but we kind of pretended like we were a little overinterested, and it helped her. She needed her ego boosted; it was surprising, because everybody just loved her voice, they loved her, she looked great and she was good. She's one of the actresses I liked working with the most.

I talked to Stevens about *Shane*. He wanted me, because we'd done *The More the Merrier* and we got along so well. I'd go home with him often; he was separated. And he would bring young George, who's now big in the AFI but who was about twelve years old at the time, out to the ranch. Anyway, George and I got along great. We were big USC fans and so we'd go to the Coliseum and he'd get tickets because all the USC players were very fond of him. So when he was gonna do *Shane*, he wanted me to play the Van Heflin part, see?

Well, I didn't want to do that. I loved working with George, I would have worked with him for nothing. But, I thought, Alan Ladd was Paramount's star, and a very good friend of mine, and a small fellow, you know. I was through with Paramount; I'd been there seven years and now I was freelancing. I thought, "It's gonna look like I gotta have another star to carry the picture." Now, if it had been an even thing, like *Ride the High Country*, I would have done it. But this way, it wasn't. The part was for the married guy, and he was kind of a backward character. Matter of fact, I thought Van Heflin was better in it than I could have been, frankly, although I didn't know at the time that Van Heflin was even going to be up for it.

But George wanted me to do it. And I said, "George, I'm not ready to do that yet, I'm not ready to play second . . ." I'd play equal with Alan, because I like him, and his size doesn't bother me at all; it bothered Alan a helluva lot more than it did me. When Coop and I would ever go on a set to see him, he'd go over and sit down immediately so we wouldn't be standing together and the whole company would see the difference. But he was a great kid and a very fine actor. I thought the world of him, and I thought the world of George, but I just didn't think it was going to help me at the time. I didn't owe Paramount anything. So I just said, "No, thanks." And they got Van Heflin. I thought he was great, and I loved the picture: it was just an excellent, wonderful picture.

The Western: Growing Old Gracefully

It's peculiar, because most people don't remember that I did some comedies, like *The More the Merrier* and the Sturges pictures. Of course, I thought Cary Grant was the best comedian of them all. We had the same agent, too. He used to get scripts and if it was some sort of Western he'd say, "Send this to Joel." And if I got something where there was a light comedian, I would say, "Send this to Cary." We were good friends and got along very well. But I enjoyed doing comedies, I really did. Especially if I got with a director like Sturges, who had this tremendous talent for dialogue. Why, sometimes, I remember in *Sullivan's Travels*, the butler had better lines than the leading man.

I liked doing comedies but as I got older I was better suited to do Westerns. Because I think it becomes unattractive for an older fellow trying to look young, falling in love with attractive girls in those kinds of situations. Take [John] Wayne, in the Western field: he's kind of grown old gracefully. I enjoyed doing those comedies, but as I got older, I felt much more comfortable in the Western. I felt at home in them, you know?

See, I started as a teamster and as a cowboy on ranches. I worked summers; I lived in West Hollywood but I worked on ranches up in the Tehachapis Mountains and other places. The fact that I started that way, as a young kid, about ten years old, driving teams of horses, made me feel at home doing it.

I remember when I had a small part in an early picture; Walter Brennan and I were thrown in just for our names, because we were under contract to Goldwyn. It was called *They Shall Have Music* with Jascha Heifetz and the Junior Symphony Orchestra. We had to do the picture—it was nothing but we were under contract and on a salary. But I remember talking to Heifetz one day: they had great shots of his hand playing the violin and I said, "That's the greatest thing I've ever seen." He said, "Well, you do great things with your horse." And I said, "What do you mean?" And he said, "I know nothing about riding a horse, but I know you're doing it right." You see? He instinctively knew. He didn't have to know how to ride a horse; he didn't have to know about cowboys, not when he saw it done right. And I said, "When I see you play the violin, I don't know how to play either, but I know you're doing it right." That kind of thing gives you what we used to call "artistic integrity." And there's too little of it in Hollywood now, too little of it.

Then, after World War II, I didn't have a Preston Sturges; La Cava had gone. Those fellows sometimes burned themselves out or, for some reason, got out of it; they couldn't get along with the management. I remember La Cava used to call the head of our corps "Der Fuehrer." They really got into big battles. I always find that it's better if you make a constructive comment to people. I never felt that you could cut yourself off from anybody.

Anyway, I always felt so much more comfortable in the western. The minute I got a horse and a hat and a pair of boots on, I felt easier. I didn't feel like I was an actor anymore; I felt like I was the guy out there doing it. When I was doing Wyatt Earp in *Wichita*, I believed it. I even went back to the period, because I had read *Frontier Marshal*, the Stuart N. Lake book, and I knew all the things Earp was thinking and it gave an authenticity to it. The audience believed in it, and I believed in it. I kind of knew my limitations, and I never tried to exceed them until I'd had enough experience. In other words, I waited ten years before I would accept some parts, but by that time I had confidence enough to go ahead and do them. My wife kidded me, "After you're been in pictures ten years, the notices will come out and say, 'This boy is really improving, he's getting great.' "

Raoul Walsh

An American director whose life and work mirrored history.

Clarence Brown

Garbo's (and Louis B. Mayer's) favorite director:
Clarence Brown on the set of A Free Soul *in 1931.*

Photofest

George Stevens

George Stevens with James Dean on the set of Giant *in 1956.*

Photofest

Ronald Reagan

The role Ronald Reagan played for the rest of his career. The Gipper.

Robert Stevenson

Director Robert Stevenson, seen with child actors Matthew Garber and Karen Dotrice on the set of his greatest success, Walt Disney's version of Mary Poppins.

Walt Disney Productions

Sheridan Gibney

Sheridan Gibney with dictaphone, a studio publicity photo.

Ida Lupino

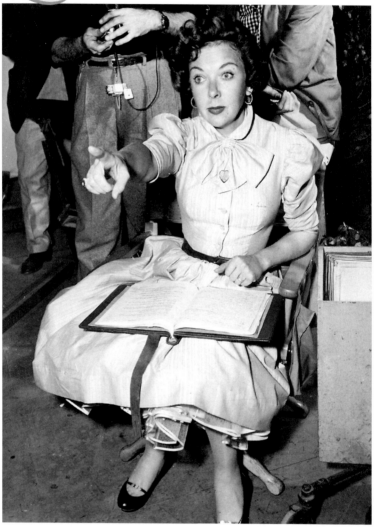

"The Female Hitchcock" in action: actress turned director Ida Lupino.

Photofest

William Wellman

On the set of Beau Geste *in 1939:*
director William Wellman (third from the left) with actors
Ray Milland, Gary Cooper, and Robert Preston.

Joel McCrea

Director Preston Sturges, owner of The Players on the Sunset Strip, seen with actress Frances Dee (Mrs. Joel McCrea), Mrs. Robert Hakim, and Joel McCrea on the restaurant's opening night in 1942.

Dory Schary

Rise to power: Dory Schary, seen in 1955, when the onetime contract writer ruled MGM.

Acting: The Authentic Approach

I wasn't instinctively an actor. My association with people like Valentino and Paul Muni taught me a lot about what to do. On Sundays, I would make up to see how I looked as Emile Zola or something: you know, like Muni. Now I admired Muni tremendously, because he gave his whole life to acting; acting was his love, his life, it was everything. I have great admiration for John Wayne in his way, not because he's the kind of actor Muni was, but he's dedicated to the motion picture business. He doesn't play golf or run a men's clothing store on the side. He's given his whole life to motion pictures. Consequently, he's gone where he wanted to go, and I admire that.

But I had a different approach. I wanted to do western things that I'd read, like *The Virginian*, which I eventually did do. Different things like *Ramrod*, and *Four Faces West*, which was a Eugene Manlove Rhodes story. I never pretended to be a great actor; I didn't try to create a character the way Muni did with Zola and Pasteur, which I gratefully admired. I didn't feel qualified to do it and I didn't try to do it. I tried to be Joel McCrea as Wyatt Earp, how I would have been if I'd have been there in that day. Because I thought the worst thing you could do—in my day, I don't know about today—was to make a pretense of being something you weren't.

Yes, I read a lot and I tried to research everything. I read everything I could. I read *Union Pacific* as a kid. I read *Stage to Lordsburg*, which turned out to be one of the great things Ford did with Wayne, *Stagecoach*. Whether it was Wyatt Earp or Buffalo Bill or when I played Sam Houston in a picture called *The First Texan*, I tried to rehearse for them and make them as authentic as I could. To me, it was not only a responsibility to show things as nearly as they were, rather than some kooky modern idea of the thing, but also to make it more easy for me to play it, because once I'd researched it, I knew everything about Buffalo Bill. I knew what he would do. Sure, he fought with the Indians and everything, but he loved the Indians. I remember, after some senator had gotten up and said, "The only good Indian's a dead Indian," then Buffalo Bill got up and made a long speech about Indians being human beings. He said, "Sure, I've fought them. I've hunted with them, and I've hunted against them;

they've stolen horses from me and I've gone and gotten them back at night. But they're people and a statement like 'The only good Indian's a dead Indian' turns my stomach."

It's very important to me to be historically authentic. Like they have you drive in on a wagon or a stagecoach and throw the reins out on both sides and then get down. You never do that. You always hold the reins. You get down and you hold the reins. And you never unhook the neck yoke first—that's up on the front of the horse. You always unfasten the traces first, and then the neck yoke, so that if they happen to run away or bolt, if you've undone the neck yoke, the tongue sticks in the ground and the stagecoach will flop over and destroy itself. A lot of these young producers don't know what happened in the old days. Well, I can remember back to when nobody'd heard of a bulldozer. There wasn't any bulldozers when I was a kid. We had teams and horses and mules. You had gang plows and what they call a Fresno scraper. If you mention a Fresno scraper to people today, they don't know what you're talking about.

Squawking About Parts

In the old days, they had big stables of people under contract; there are very few people under contract today. And they used you because they were paying you. So you had the advantage over the freelance player, unless he was great; they'd say, "Well, we've got this guy under contract, we're paying him every week, we're publicizing him and so forth, so give it to him." Well, I got parts assigned to me at times that really would have been disastrous for my future. So I'd go in and squawk about it. Well, the head of the studio might be a guy without much imagination and he'd say, "Well, hell, you're on salary and you're an actor, you're supposed to be able to do anything. Go ahead and do it; we'll give you something better next time."

Well, there might have been no next time: if I'd done some of them, it would have been a disaster. So if the girl was a big star, which most of the women for the first ten years were—Constance Bennett, Irene Dunne, Ginger Rogers, people who were bigger than I was—I would go to them and say, "You know, I don't have a clue as to what this thing is about. I've got to be honest with you. I just worked on a ranch and I was a cowboy and I don't really know anything. . . ." I would scare them a little. So they would work on my side in getting me out and getting Robert Montgomery or Cary Grant to do it.

I remember when they wanted me to do the Will Rogers story. I went to Michael Curtiz. I didn't know him very well but I went to see him. He said, "Well, we've got a commitment for the picture." It was a big picture, Warner Brothers, and I hadn't worked at Warners for quite a while at the time. And I said, "I can't play Will Rogers. I mean, sincerely, I'm not qualified to play him. I would just give an imitation, ape what he did. . . ." I didn't want to ape Will Rogers; I loved him just the way he was, and I didn't think anyone could really do him justice. So I wanted to get out of it.

Well, Jack Warner said, "You don't have script approval. We're giving you $150,000"—or something like that—"to do the picture. It's one of our biggest, best pictures. Mike Curtiz is one of our best directors." I said, "Yeah, I'm not complaining about anything in the picture, but I'm telling you that I'm not qualified to do it." Well, of course, Jack Warner paid no attention at all. He thought it was just another actor that had something better he wanted to do, or something different, so I went to Curtiz. I told Curtiz, "You know something? If you force me to do this picture, it's gonna all be on you. Because I'm telling you before we start, I'm not qualified to do it. No one's ever accused me of being a great actor. I'm a helluva man on a horse, but no great actor. So it's all on your shoulders." Curtiz— he was Hungarian, you know—said, "This is the first sonuvabitch actor who admitted he wasn't good enough; they all say the part isn't good enough, the picture isn't good enough. But for an actor to come and say he isn't good enough, I've got to believe you." He went up to Jack Warner and said, "I don't want him. I believe him. He's sincere." It got me out. It was a big plum but it wasn't for me.*

They tested Bing Crosby, they tested John Wayne, they tested Stuart Erwin, they tested everybody and ended up with Will Rogers, Jr., who you could forgive, see? Because he did it like his dad, and I

---

*Joel McCrea was announced to play Will Rogers in the autumn of 1944, with Mark Hellinger producing; the film was finally made with Will Rogers, Jr., as *The Story of Will Rogers* and released in 1952.

thought he was very good in it. It wasn't a terribly big success but Curtiz did a good job. And, actually, any one of those guys, had they done it, would have found out what I was backing away from, what they should have backed away from. Because people would say, "Well, that's not Will. . . ." It's like somebody doing Jack Benny today; who the hell is going to do it? Who can do it? You can do Sergeant York and you can do Buffalo Bill because people have seen you as much as they've seen them. But you can't do Jack Benny, and you can't do Will Rogers, I don't think. Frankly, I really don't like to see some mediocre Hollywood actor do those unique big stars. And I just felt that if I did the Will Rogers thing it would be less than the best.

Raoul Walsh: Quite a Character

Colorado Territory was really *High Sierra*, which Walsh had made with [Humphrey] Bogart as a gangster, remember? Well, Warner Brothers decided to make a "cheater," make it again, turning it into a Western. People wouldn't know, so it was a good idea. Anthony Veiller was the producer. Well, they started out trying to get John Wayne. But Wayne was busy; he was contracted, very hot at the time, and they couldn't get him. So they tested everybody at Warner Brothers you could think of. Ronald Reagan, they tested him. They tested everybody. So Russ Saunders, who was Walsh's assistant and who had been an all-American football player at USC and an extra with me, said, "What about Joel McCrea?" And Walsh said, "Why not?"

So Walsh got me over there. He said, "Don't get your hair cut." That was his famous line; he would always say, "Don't get your hair cut." In every Western, whether it was *The Big Trail* or *They Died with Their Boots On* or whatever, he always wanted long hair; he didn't want you to have a nice clean haircut. My hair was usually long, not way long, but just kind of careless. So Walsh then went in to Jack Warner and said, "We can make the picture with Joel McCrea." But Warner said, "I'm not going to borrow Joel McCrea when we've got six actors already in here that we've got to pay." He named who they were, I can't remember all of them. And Warner said, "We've got to use somebody that's under contract, that's being paid."

So Walsh—to show you how Walsh's mind works, he's so brilliant—he lets these guys come in, and he says, "Go to the wardrobe
and dress like a cowboy and c'mon in." Well, they came in with
angora coats and fleece-lined chaps and hats—none of these guys
were Western actors, see? If it had been a Coop, or somebody like
that, they'd have known how to dress. These guys were good actors
but they really didn't know about Westerns. So Walsh would make
a test of them riding a horse, and they wouldn't look too good. He
just let them do it, and let them be lousy. Then he ran all these
tests, six of them, Russ Saunders told me later, and Jack Warner said,
"They're none of them any good." And Walsh said, "Well, you've
gotta use McCrea."

So that's the way I got the part. Then we went down to New
Mexico. Walsh said to me, "Pick your own horse, kid." And he'd
give a macho sign, he'd roll those brown-paper cigarettes; he was an
actor, you know, before he was a director. He said, "How does it
make you feel? Does it bother your ego at all to know that they
tested six other guys and that we really tried to get Wayne in the
first place?" I said, "When the picture opens, I'll be the guy that's
riding out there; people won't know how many were up for the part;
they won't know that Gable might have been up and turned it down;
they won't know any of that. They'll say, 'This is Joel McCrea; he's
in *Colorado Territory*; he plays Wes McQueen.' " And Walsh said,
"You're right." He knew it, but he wanted to see if I felt a little bit
like I was the seventh choice, because I really was as far as Jack
Warner was concerned.

He had his wife down there with him, and Virginia Mayo. He
loved Virginia Mayo and got along real well with her. He'd use Mayo
when other directors, like Wyler, didn't think she was any good;
when she was under contract to Goldwyn, Wyler had to use her in
The Best Years of Our Lives. Anyway, Walsh liked her. He would do
things, like he had a silent shot with her looking after me when I
was escaping at the end there, after we had been married in the
church. He'd say, "We'll shoot this silent . . . all right, Virginia, you
see him going, Wes is leaving, you'll never see him again, they may
kill him . . . all right, all right, now take after him, run, get out of
there, run, you hear they're serving free drinks around the corner . . ."
She'd be going great, and hell, when she heard "they're serving free

drinks around the corner" she'd fall apart. She'd say, "Raoul, you break me up, you can't do that. . . ." So that's the kind of a guy he was; he'd do anything.

He did the funniest things with me. I'd do stuff that I wouldn't have done for any other director, because he was a gutty little bastard. He'd do anything. With that one eye, he'd walk along a four-hundred-foot cliff. I couldn't walk that close to the edge with both good eyes. Anyway, I remember one of the last scenes we did in *Colorado Territory*, when I was escaping from the prison. I ran across this swamp, the dogs were after me, the bell was ringing, and they were all after me. I had to run across this location, which Walsh was familiar with, because he'd made *Objective Burma* there with [Errol] Flynn. There were logs and rocks on the bottom. And Walsh yelled, "Keep running, kid, keep running." He yelled and yelled at me and, boy, I made it. I fell down about four times and damn near broke my leg, but I got up and kept going. And as I came out around the other side, still going to beat all hell, muddy, wet and cold, out of breath, I looked for Walsh to say, "How was it?" I thought he'd say, "Great. We'd have had to use a double for anybody else, but you did it." I said, "Where's Walsh?" And Russ Saunders, the assistant, said, "When he saw you in the middle of your run, he said, 'I think it'll be okay,' and he got in the studio car and he's gone back to the studio." He didn't even wait for the damn thing. He didn't even wait to say "Print." He said, "Let it go." And he was gone, he was gone. That's the way he'd do things. What a character!

He was a wonderful director because he never let a thing die. He would have me rolling the brown-paper cigarettes in a scene. I didn't smoke and I wasn't very good at it, but I could roll those brown-paper cigarettes. He had me doing that, because he never let a scene be static. Every minute, I was moving. I was getting on the horse; I was doing something else; Virginia was coming in; some guy was coming up from behind. Everything was always fluid, so there was never a dull moment when you say, "Oh hell, is anything ever going to happen?"

I once had a picture called *Ramrod*, with a good story, and I tried to get Walsh to direct it. We couldn't get him from Warner Brothers; they wouldn't loan him out. So [producer] Harry Sherman came up with André De Toth. Well, De Toth did the picture; there were long, stalling scenes where I'd stand there for a while, and Donald Crisp would say, "Well, what do you think, boy?" And I'd say, "Well, I'm gonna get Frank Ivy if it's the last thing I ever do. . . ." There was nothing I could do; the direction had to be more fluid. Well, Veronica Lake was the girl and she wasn't any good in it, either; they were married and De Toth loved her so. That was another difficult thing; when you work with the director's wife, this is for the birds. Because he's not gonna be tough with her, you know, or she'll kick his ass when he gets home at night. So you suffer through it, with him. What are you gonna say? "Get me a new girl"? "What, my wife . . ." So *Ramrod* turned out to be a lousy picture.

Director Approval

After a certain point, I had director approval. I didn't for the first, say, twenty years. I remember *Four Faces West*, taken from a story by Eugene Manlove Rhodes who was a classic western writer. The story was called "Paso Por Aqui" which means "They Passed This Way." The fellow who directed that was Al Green, Alfred E. Green. His son is now the head of production at Universal, a fellow named Marshall Green. Al Green was at Warner Brothers for thirty years, and then he did *The Jolson Story* for Columbia. When Harry Sherman, who had produced *Buffalo Bill*, said, "When we do *Four Faces West*, who do you think of as a director?" I said, "Well, Walsh would be great." He said, "We can't get Walsh. He's tied up. I've tried." He tried different people and then he said, "What do you think about Al Green? He's never made a Western." Now Al Green had made pictures with Mary Pickford and George Arliss, you know, but he hadn't made a Western. And I said, "Al Green is a sensitive, intelligent fellow. He doesn't need to have made a Western. Let him do it." And he did it. It worked out great.

Ride the High Country

I was kind of retired, because I had been with the Mirisch Company for five years. Walter had left the Allied Artists group with his brother Harold and came over to United Artists and then the Gold-wyn studios. We did a thing called *Gunfight at Dodge City* where I played Bat Masterson, *Fort Massacre*, and a couple of other things. Then television came in, and those $500,000 or $600,000 pictures that Mirisch were making with me were no longer usable. Because here they were making *Gunsmoke* with Jim Arness, at that time for about $35,000 or $40,000 every week, and people weren't going to see the pictures. So I said, "Well, I'll quit." So I kind of quit; I guess it was about 1958 or 1959; and I didn't do anything from then until about 1962, when Randy Scott brought this property to me. It was called *Guns in the Afternoon*.

It was bought by Burt Kennedy, who had been a writer and a director. He sent it to Randy and Randy said, "This will be fine, but I need another male star and I've never done a picture with another male star. The only guy would be Joel McCrea." So Richard Lyons, who was the producer at MGM, said, "Well, let me see if I can get him." Now I didn't know Lyons; but he called me and I came in to see him, and he and I had lunch together. I took the script and read it and said, "I like it." I said, "But I'll only do it if I play Steve Judd." I didn't want to do the other part. Well, that's not what Lyons had in mind for me, because he thought that I was a little subtler than Randy was, and so it would be a little more deceptive that I would turn and be against him and double-cross him. But I said, "No. If I'm gonna do one more picture, I'm not gonna destroy my image for one picture. My image is Steve Judd. That's the guy who, through integrity, through his own honesty, he's gonna do it; the hell with how bad we were treated and how underpaid we were as marshals."

Well, I told that to Dick Lyons and I said, "Don't say anything to Randy. Just tell Randy, because he came up with the property, that I feel it's his choice to play whatever part he likes, and if he happens to choose the part that I want to play, then I just won't do the picture. I don't want to play the other part." So Dick called us in to have lunch again, and to meet Sam Peckinpah, who had only done tele-vision up to that time. We went to the Brown Derby in Beverly Hills and we had lunch. And I said, "Randy, you're the guy who came up with the project. We're all working because you came up with a piece of property; because that's the hard thing to find anymore, for us, the property. So you have the choice." And he said, "Well, I'll play either one, but if I had my choice, I'd rather play the other guy. I've played the straight honest guy so damn long and so much that this would be more interesting." I said, "You've got a deal, because I want to play Steve Judd." And that's the way it worked out.

Peckinpah was a talented director. He rewrote some of the script, as I recall, and he's a very good writer. Every actor that ever worked with Peckinpah likes him, and does better than they would with somebody else. He's great with actors. But he was a little sadistic with some of the crew, and I didn't like that a bit.

Incidentally, after Clint Eastwood went to Universal, the first thing he did over there was produced by the guy who produced *Ride the High Country*, Richard Lyons, who's a helluva nice young fellow. All I'd seen Clint Eastwood in was *Rawhide* and I liked him; anyway, he said, "I'm gonna run *Ride the High Country* for Clint Eastwood. Would you come in, too?" So I came in, saw it and we had lunch together, and Eastwood, when I died at the end of the picture, he cried. He came out and said, "That's the best scene I've ever seen." Here's a guy hotter than a pistol—getting five times what I ever got—and he was so simple and nice; I really liked Eastwood. He plays very much in the same tradition.

A Certain Sort of Humility

In my career, I've tried to keep it so that people will get what they're expecting. It won't be a big shock. It won't be where, all of sudden, I'm playing some wild thing where I have a psychiatric problem and I want to kick my mother or something. My image is like the image of the Virginian or the role I played in *Union Pacific* or Buffalo Bill or something like that. Somewhat heroic, and really truly believable, and historically fairly authentic, as authentic as you can be. That's the type of thing I could do, that I felt I had something to offer in, rather than attempt something that was beyond my scope. If I stayed within that, not through tremendous humility but just through good common sense, I would enjoy doing it and I would last longer, and maybe entertain. I remember Preston Sturges once said to me, "You have no right to bring people into a dark theater and bore them for an hour." So I figured that this would be one way of not boring them.

Also, I had a certain sort of humility, not so much because I felt insecure or inadequate, but I felt, "I'm just another fellow; I'm another man." Will Rogers was that way, didn't you know? He had that modesty. I did two pictures with Will Rogers, and he and I became great close friends. He was really almost like a father to me, I told him he shouldn't go on that trip—with the one-eyed pilot—I never figured the plane would crash or anything. And I said, "You know, you're a great man. People listen to you. Congress listens to you. The Senate. The president has you to lunch and everything." And he said, "No, all men are great men. I'm no greater than anyone else. If something happens to any man, there's a void; there's a tree gone from the forest." He felt that way. I had that same philosophy, and I loved that man. Will Rogers gave me a lot of philosophy, and a lot of other things. For example, he's the one who really instigated my great interest. I wanted a ranch, but I probably would have waited ten years until I had plenty of money to get it if it hadn't been for Will. He said, "Forget that. Go and borrow some money and buy it. Land in California can't go anywhere but up." And when I was working with him in the second picture, which Booth Tarkington wrote—Fox called it *Business and Pleasure* and David Butler directed it—I found this ranch, bought it, and twenty years later, when I sold it, I made more than I made in thirty-five years in motion pictures. So I listened to his advice and followed it. He was a great humanitarian, a great man. He loved the world.

Mustang Country: Coming Back

Well, I tell you, the things that had been submitted to me, after eighty-two pictures and almost forty years in the business, were not very interesting or exciting; most of them were kind of on the degrading level, which I didn't ever want to do, because I had kind of established an image, such as it was.

I used to talk to Gary Cooper about it. We decided that we wouldn't play antiheroes, that we wouldn't play any degrading roles, because we'd established an image. I remember we met for lunch on the Warner Brothers lot—we were both making a picture at Warner Brothers one time, I was making *Colorado Territory*—and we were talking about it. We were, you know, fairly near the same era, although he started about five years before I did. And Harry Warner joined us that day. He was the one who made a lot of money for Warner Brothers. J. L.—[Jack]—ran the studio but H. M.—[Harry]—bought the real estate and he made millions, more than they ever made on pictures. He said to us, "You two guys are like Kellogg's Corn Flakes. When anyone reads your name, they know exactly what they're buying. Don't disappoint them. It's all right for Bogart to do it. It's all right for Bogart to be a nice guy in this picture and be a heel and kick his mother in the stomach in the next one. But you guys can't do it. You've established an image."

Of course, we both had that in mind anyway, but it was interesting coming from H. M. Warner, because he was a very interesting fellow, one of the older Warner Brothers. Anyway, we kind of did establish an image. And the stuff that was sent to me was so nothing, somebody's sick uncle or something, or a crooked rancher, or a take-off on the real western, you know, where you couldn't grab your gun and you couldn't ride the horse, and stuff like that. I'd never do that, because my whole idea was to perfect my riding of the horse, or doing whatever you had to do in the picture, until it was believable. I didn't want to do an antihero. So I didn't do any pictures for almost, well, I guess it was over twelve years.

And then this picture, strangely enough, was sent to me. They said the only trouble was that the man who wrote it wanted to produce and direct it, and would I mind not producing it. And I said, "I've never produced . . . I don't know how to produce a picture! I don't know how to photograph a picture, I don't know how to direct a picture. I only want to do what I can do." "Well," they said, "That's what we want." I liked the story, because it was a decent kind of adventure, outdoor, and they said that they wanted to make it all in Canada; and I wanted to get away from the studio, because I'd been in those for forty years. So everything fitted in.

I met this young John Champion, who wrote it and wanted to produce and direct it, and we talked. I knew we wouldn't have any conflicts because to me there was no use in getting into a thing that would be a problem, because what am I proving, you know? I've been here too long. But it was really a rewarding experience to do *Mustang Country*. I was surprised that I could pick up everything after twelve years. It was a challenge that way. I did it, and I liked it.

I found myself rusty only in one way. All the stuff with the horse and the action—if I'd have been in a silent picture, I was better than I was before. But if they came in and wanted to change a whole scene the day that you were shooting, like I used to do with Preston Sturges and Gregory La Cava—they'd come in in the morning, and hand you a page you'd never seen before and they'd say, "That's what we're shooting today"—I found that that was difficult. It had to be what I had read and rehearsed and okayed in the first place. Otherwise, I wasn't as quick a study as I had been, and I didn't really think it was necessary to be. We had all agreed on what we were going to do beforehand so we didn't have any problems. Occasionally, some physical thing would happen—something we couldn't get, or it snowed when it wasn't supposed to snow, and we had to change something; I did it but that was work. I had to concentrate on it; I had to think about it. But the rest of it was just like before.

Now Champion is a very quiet, reserved fellow, not a pusher, doesn't push himself at all. He has talent, he knows the business, he's produced a lot of television; he's worked in the business and been raised right around the business. And yet, if he was an aggressive fellow—like, you remember, Jerry Wald, who was there every night at Warners—maybe they would push this picture a little harder at Universal. They're pushing the Gable and Lombard and W. C. Fields things, and everybody's saying that those are unqualified disasters.

The Influence of Coop

Well, I wouldn't exactly say Coop was an influence, because he never said much, you know? He would talk about a third as much as me if he had an interview, and yet you would come away knowing what Coop was like. He wasn't as vocal as I am. He wasn't just a "yep" and "nope" type of guy like they picture him in some film magazines. But he was a fellow who didn't overtalk. He never bragged about himself and he never knocked anybody else.

He was a little bit shy. In fact, he was much shyer than I was.

When he started in pictures, there was a big question as to whether he should be in the business, you know, where you're showing off all the time, because he was very shy and reticent. But it was one of the things that gave him tremendous charm and made women of all ages love him. The older women wanted to mother him, the younger women wanted to go out with him. He and I were friends for an awful long time, from when I first started; when he wasn't married and I wasn't married, we used to go out together and double-date. Then when he was going with the Countess DeFrazo, who was living in Mary Pickford's guesthouse, he would get me to take the countess horseback-riding and stuff when he had to work; because he worked more than I and was in much more demand than I was. That's how much he trusted me, how close we were.

We were very, very close, more in that era than later after he married Rocky. She was quite social and I wasn't. I was kind of— not antisocial, but I lived on a ranch and I stayed out there. So the last, I'd say, five years, I didn't see nearly as much of him as I did before. But he had this kind of an influence: he was quiet, he was sincere, he never made any kind of phony impression. I watched him act. I watched him on the screen. I watched him on the set. And I always felt that he stayed within his bounds. He played with sincerity, and he didn't try to show off or show what a colorful actor he was. Whether it was Sergeant York or Lou Gehrig in *The Pride of the Yankees*, I liked to watch him; I believed him.

But I never copied him because the great disaster, I think, is to copy. You know, a poor guy named James Craig copied Gable. Do you remember that? Well, it was at Metro, he was a guy in stock and he looked like Gable. He had the mustache and everything. He even tested for *Gone with the Wind*. But they said, "Oh, he's just like Gable." Well, who the hell wants the copy? You want the real thing. Gable was a great guy, he wasn't putting it on; that was just Gable. But James Craig was putting it on. He was a nice guy and I knew him and liked him. But he was young and I was young and I couldn't say to him, "Look, kid, don't copy. . . ."

So I never copied anybody. I never copied the best. I watched John Barrymore. I used to go on the set and watch him, when he was older, you know, and had to have cue cards. Even then you saw how great he was. I watched Paul Muni, too. But I never tried to ape anybody. Never, not even William S. Hart, who, as a kid, was my Western idol. I liked him better than [Tom] Mix, because Mix was a colorful guy but Hart was sincere. He thought everything he did on the screen was for real. He was great on authenticity and I admired him. But I didn't try to be like anybody. I never even tried a mannerism or even a thing that made them popular, you know? Never copied Coop at all. The only thing I did was to watch how sincere Coop was in his approach to a thing, how honest he was, and then I tried to be honest in my own way and not go beyond my bounds.

A Theory about Life

All of us are important to everybody else; you're important, I'm important, the waiter and the busboy's important; if you do the job well, you're important. And that's my theory about life. Your life is much more important than your job.

Also I believe you have to believe in a Supreme Being. I don't care what your religion is, you must believe that there's a force for good, and you must believe that if you do right, it's gonna win out in the end. You don't give up your ideals just because things get tough; you stick with it. That was the philosophy of Abraham Lincoln, who is one of my greatest idols. And it was the philosophy of the better men that I came in contact with in the motion picture business. King Vidor was that way; they were God-fearing men. Their egos didn't get in the way.

The Future

As far as I'm concerned, I hate to say I wouldn't do another picture, but I don't anticipate doing another one. I have nothing to prove. I don't need the exposure or the money. Motion pictures are not the end-all. If nothing else, I intend to lay out under a tree and the sun and dream about the old days. Time doesn't weigh heavy on me.

"I was lucky with my timing . . ."

6. Interview with Sheridan Gibney

Los Angeles, April 1983

by Patrick McGilligan

SHERIDAN GIBNEY

(1903–1988)

1931	**Tonight or Never.** Uncredited contribution.
1932	**Weekend Marriage.** Adaptation.
	Two Against the World . Script.
	I Am a Fugitive from a Chain Gang. Coscript.
1933	**The World Changes.** Story.
	The House on 56th Street. Coscript.
1934	**Massacre.** Coscript.
1936	**Anthony Adverse.** Script.
	Green Pastures. Coscript.

	The Story of Louis Pasteur. Costory, coscript.
1938	**Letter of Introduction.** Coscript.
1939	**Disputed Passage.** Coscript.
1940	**South of Suez.** Story.
1941	**Cheers for Miss Bishop.** Coscript.
1942	**Once Upon a Honeymoon.** Costory, script.
1944	**Our Hearts Were Young and Gay.** Script, producer.
1947	**The Locket.** Script.
1956	**Everything but the Truth.** Costory.

Sheridan Gibney took his first job in the film industry in 1931, wrote several classic Warner Brothers films (including I Am a Fugitive from a Chain Gang *and* Green Pastures*), shared a Best Original Story and Screenplay Oscar (with Pierre Collings) for* The Story of Louis Pasteur, *and accumulated two dozen credits over the span of twenty years before the blacklist intruded. Yet he was characteristic of some from his generation in that, despite his success as a scenarist, Gibney thought of himself more as a playwright and never felt comfortable calling Hollywood home.*

His career no doubt suffered as a result of his dedication to the Screen Writers Guild. Gibney signed up early in the organizing campaign and became a stalwart member of the board in the 1930s and 1940s. He was thought to be as fair-minded as he was soft-spoken, and had friends among the archconservatives as well as the

Communists in the membership. Acceptable to both warring factions, twice, at critical periods in guild history, from 1939 to 1941 and in 1947–48, he served as president. This put Gibney in a delicate position when the House Committee on Un-American Activities (HUAC) came to Hollywood in 1947, contributing, indirectly, to his own mistaken blacklisting.

For many years Gibney lived in Montana. In 1983, he paid a rare visit to Los Angeles for the guild's Golden Jubilee, and agreed to reminisce about screenwriting and the early history of the guild.

Tell me a little bit about your background.

I was born at the Marie Antoinette Hotel in New York at 66th Street and Broadway, which is now the parking lot for Lincoln Center. I grew up in New York and Long Island, and I went to Mineola High School and Exeter and then to Amherst College, where I graduated. While I was in college, I wrote poetry but I also wrote plays. My natural vein was comedy, and primarily comedy of manners, which is what all my early plays were. I admired Restoration comedy very much, and I had a natural talent for form, which came out in plays. Comedy of manners was very popular at that time.

I wrote thirteen plays in college, the last of which I sold to David Belasco. It was called *The Wiser They Are*. Shortly after he bought it he died, but I had been so excited about selling this play that I had given up my teaching job at Hobart College, where I had just signed a year's contract, and went to New York. After David Belasco died, the play was peddled all over town for a couple of years, but nobody would buy it. I had given up on it when all of a sudden [producer] Jed Harris, out of the blue, got a copy, read it, liked it, and told my agent that he was buying it for immediate production.

It opened in April 1931 with Ruth Gordon and Osgood Perkins, the father of Tony. The play had a fair run, not too great, but when it closed, Leland Hayward—who was my agent—said he had a job for me in Hollywood with Sam Goldwyn. I had just got married, I was about twenty-seven, and I was broke, so I went to Hollywood for a quick four-week job.

Sam Goldwyn was making a film with Gloria Swanson called *Tonight or Never*, which was a Belasco play about an opera singer who has a wonderful voice, but it is a cold voice; she needs more feeling in her voice, and her manager suggests she have an affair to warm up her voice, which she does. But she becomes pregnant. The play had been made into a screenplay by Ernest Vajda, a Hungarian playwright who couldn't speak English. All he had done was to take the play and put in a few camera angles and that was it. Unfortunately, the play had a lot of exposition in the first act that had to be dramatized on the screen, and that was my job. It was particularly important to hurry it up because Gloria Swanson was pregnant by her then-husband, the Marquis de la Falaise. Since in the opening scenes she wasn't supposed to be pregnant, they wanted to shoot those scenes before she got too big.

Who was your supervisor? Who did you work with?

The supervisor on the picture was Arthur Hornblow, Jr., and the director was Mervyn LeRoy. I didn't work with either of them. All I did was to write the first sequence over at Goldwyn Studios. Mr. Goldwyn was very nice to me and invited me out to his house in Santa Monica for dinner and bridge the first night I was in Hollywood. There were two other people at Goldwyn's house for dinner: Louis B. Mayer and Joe Schenck. I was the fourth for bridge. We sat down to play afterwards, and Sam Goldwyn took me for a partner. He said, "We play for twenty cents a point." I don't know if you know anything about bridge, but at twenty cents a point you can lose up to one thousand dollars very easily. I said, "Well, a penny is all I can play for." Goldwyn said, "I'll carry you for the other nineteen cents." We played about three rubbers, it took about an hour, and we won by something like eight hundred points. I would have cleaned up, but Goldwyn won about $14,000 that night.

Was that normal for a young writer just arrived, to be thrown into such august company?

I know it never happened to me again. [laughs] I also know that Arthur Hornblow, Jr., asked me to come to dinner on the following Monday, my first weekend in Hollywood. I got out to Beverly Hills to his house, I rang his doorbell, and this beautiful girl opened the door wearing an apron. She looked really lovely. I thought she was the maid. Arthur came rushing and and said, "Oh, have you met Ina?" It was Ina Claire, who had just been divorced from Jack Gilbert. She said, "For God's sake, don't tell anybody. Jack is in the other room and he doesn't want anybody to know we're seeing each other because we've just been divorced." Up from behind a sofa popped Jack Gilbert. That was my introduction to Hollywood.

How did you learn to write your first film?

It wasn't a matter of writing films, it was a matter of dramatizing the exposition in the first act.

Did Goldwyn himself appear to have any script sense?

All he knew was that you couldn't have people explain things on the screen that happened in the past, as you can on the stage. All I was told was there should be no explanations. You should *see* it. Well, that's what movies are.

What was your initial impression of Hollywood?

It was very hot and very still and it was almost as though it were unreal. I had the feeling that the whole thing—the landscape, the mountains, the palm trees—was a big set. It looked half-baked, like it really wasn't finished. Like in another hundred thousand years it might be livable. It looked like earthquake country. Anyway I was determined to be a playwright and after my four weeks were up I left. I didn't want any part of it.

Were you credited on the screen?

No, this was before any Screen Writers Guild and the producers determined the credits. Ernest Vajda had it in his contract that he was to get sole credit.

What happened next?

I went back to New York, where another play of mine, called Merry Madness, had been sold, to star, of all people, DeWolfe Hopper, who I thought was dead. He almost was—he was ninety. The play was a farce about a neurotic old man, ideally suited for him, but he couldn't learn his lines. We were out on the road for a month, and then he finally died in Detroit, and that was the end of that play.

So Leland Hayward got me another job in Hollywood. Darryl Zanuck had just become head of production at Warner Brothers, and I came out on a six-month contract. Connie Bennett was getting $30,000 a week; this was considered fabulous money, and it was, with no income tax—and Warner Brothers had a five-week contract with Connie and absolutely no script whatsoever. None. They were in a terrible spot, so they asked if I could make a script out of a play called Two Against the World. I read it and said I could try. It so happened I knew Connie because when I was at Exeter she used to come up to the senior prom with a suitcase full of scotch and horse around with all the boys. I knew her from those days—ten years before. So when I got this assignment, I went out to see her. She was now married to the Marquis de la Falaise—who was getting around—and she had just had a tooth extracted. I remember going up to her bedroom to see her; she was in bed with an ice pack. I said, "Oh my God, you can't possibly appear when you are supposed to ..." which was something like the next week. She said, "Oh, I'm all right," but we got her an extra week—at $30,000. Finally we had enough script for her to start—forty or fifty pages. We did the film in five weeks and I was only about ten pages ahead of the camera the whole time.

What was Weekend Marriage?

Zanuck called me into the office and said, "We have had this Faith Baldwin novel knocking around the studio for five years and we don't know what to do with it. We think there's enough for half a picture but maybe not a full picture. What would you think of taking Weekend Marriage and using that for the first half, and taking Saturday's Children, the Maxwell Anderson play, for the second half?" "Well," I said, "I'll have to read Weekend Marriage." I knew Saturday's Children, of course. It turns out that in Weekend Marriage the marriage fails because both parties are working and they never had time for each other; work breaks up the marriage. In Saturday's Children, it was just the opposite—work is what keeps them happy. Zanuck didn't see any contradiction in this. He thought, well, let's just have them change their mind in the middle of the story! So I did the script, although I don't remember how I worked it out. [laughs]

How did you get involved in I Am a Fugitive from a Chain Gang?

Zanuck assigned me to this book, which he had bought, fresh on the market, called I Am a Fugitive from a Georgia Chain Gang! As I recall, the book was written by the brother [Robert E. Burns] of the fugitive, Burns. It was a kind of a plea for tolerance and, I thought, very moving. The brother came out to Hollywood for four or five weeks to be a kind of story consultant. But I always felt the real fugitive was guilty and the book was a cover-up—not the real truth. That's why I never fell for his innocence in adapting the book to the screen. What I was trying to do was indict the chain-gang system of Georgia, but at the same time not make the fugitive out to be some kind of white-horse hero. The final scene, which really made the picture, was a brainstorm, an afterthought really.*

It's a very unusual ending, still shocking, I think, in its fierceness and ambiguity. I'm surprised Warners allowed it.

I must tell you about the ending. Hal Wallis was the supervisor of the film, and when he read the script he called me and said, "It might need a little something, but in general I think it's great. Except for the ending—we can't use that. It's too strong. Audiences wouldn't accept it." That is when I left Hollywood again and went back to New York. But when Zanuck came back from England, where he had been playing polo with Lord Somebody-or-other, he read the script and what he liked most was the ending.

I thought you'd been working primarily under Zanuck.

No, Wallis. Around this time Zanuck was traveling in Europe.

What was Wallis's advice on the script?

Not to offend anybody, primarily. He was so afraid he was going to lose a customer. He was that type of showman. I had somewhat the same problem with him later on *Louis Pasteur*.

---

*As described by Russell Campbell in *The Velvet Light Trap*, No. 1 (June 1971), the fugitive, named James Allen in the Warner Brothers version, "is driven desperately to a total rejection of society's values" by the end of the film. In the final scene, "Meeting Helen [Helen Vinson] for the last time in an alley at night, he hears a noise and is forced to flee. 'Will you write?' Helen calls to him, as he backs off into the darkness. 'Do you need any money? But you must, Jim. How do you live?' Allen disappears into the night as the image fades to black, and his voice is finally heard in reply: 'I steal!' "

Where does his great reputation come from?

I think Wallis got his reputation through longevity. He kept at it. He always made pictures.

Was he too cautious a producer, in your opinion?

There was nothing adventurous about Wallis. He'd never take a chance. He always wanted to cover his bets. He wanted to be certain that everybody would like it. Zanuck had more guts. Zanuck had other problems, but he immediately saw the value of the final scene.

Did you have much contact with Mervyn LeRoy, this time?

Yes, Mervyn was very, very partial to the script. He would not allow anybody to monkey with it once the script was final. He followed it to the letter. Everything was in my scripts—sets and location were described in great detail. In the other films that I did with Mervyn I was always on the set, whenever there had to be any change at all. Mervyn was very competent, and he became a friend, but he didn't have the spark of genius. I'm not much for the auteur theory, where Mervyn is concerned.

There's another name on the script, the man who followed you—Brown Holmes. Did they make substantial changes after you left?

A very peculiar thing happened, speaking about the need for a Writers Guild. I was back in New York, where I had another play in rehearsal, with Ethel Barrymore, called *Encore*. In the middle of a rehearsal, Zanuck called up Leland and said he wanted me to come right out to make some minor changes in the script. I said I couldn't because I was in rehearsal for my play. Zanuck was furious with me and said I'd never work in Hollywood again.

Ethel couldn't learn her lines either, and we had to stay out on the road with that play for several weeks. She was always dropping little pills into her coffee, and as rehearsals wore on she grew more incoherent and inarticulate. Finally, she did not know the part pretty well—I was cutting it and cutting it until it was bare bones. Suddenly, in New Haven the week before we were supposed to open in New York, she came down with a fever. The doctor came and diagnosed it as double pneumonia. She was out—not only out of the play but out completely for about five years. And she could not be replaced. So that play folded.

Chain Gang was about to open. I went to see the picture in New York with my wife and friends and I was absolutely amazed when the credits came on the screen. When the picture was first released, my name was not on it. In between the time when the picture was finished and when Zanuck told my agent I would never work in Hollywood again, he had taken my name off the picture. This was my punishment. I called up Leland and he said there was nothing I could do about it. There was no guild, nothing could be done.

Did you know Brown Holmes?

Oh, sure, I knew him. He was on the lot. But the only changes he made were in the dialogue in the center part of the script. The important elements of the screenplay were all mine, including the ending. Brown was very sheepish when he saw me again. He felt very bad about the whole thing. We never worked together on the script. I had no actual collaborations at all in the time I worked at Warner Brothers. Most of my collaborations occurred after I went back East, one time or another. It was always somebody writing after me or before me.

What was the audience reaction to the picture?

It was a big box-office picture for those days and it was a shocker. People were shocked.

How did you get back to Hollywood?

After the Ethel Barrymore play folded, I needed another job. I had been working on a Depression story that I thought would make a good movie. It was three-generation story of a poor Norwegian farmer who comes to Wisconsin and makes it rich, and his son loses it all in 1929 on Wall Street. I wanted to submit it, but I thought under the circumstances it would be good to submit it anonymously. Also I thought it would intrigue the Hollywood moguls if they thought this story was being written by the scion of a once rich and important family who had suffered collapse in the market crash.

Leland went out to Hollywood to sell the story. Well, the person who liked it most was Darryl Zanuck! He told Leland that he would buy it, but Leland would have to tell him who had written it. Leland told him he couldn't, because he promised the family he wouldn't divulge the name. Leland left and went back to his office and when he got back there was a call from Zanuck, who said he had decided to buy it anyway. Now would Leland tell him who was the author? Leland told him, Zanuck laughed, and said that was fine with him. I was invited out to do the screenplay.

It was called *The World Changes* and again Paul Muni was going to be the star. My original title was "America Kneels"—meaning that the Crash humbled us—but Jack Warner thought that would depress people. *The World Changes* means nothing.

I didn't write the script, as it turns out; it was assigned to someone else. Zanuck intended to assign it to me, but there was some delay, and I didn't get out to Hollywood as fast as I was supposed to. So the first thing I did for the studio was a film for Dick Barthelmess entitled *Massacre*, about an Indian massacre. That took about eight weeks. And then . . .

The House on 56th Street?

Oh, heavens. I don't remember the actual chronology. Kay Francis, of course, but I don't remember much else about that one.

Can you tell me a little bit about what it was like to be a writer at Warner Brothers in those early days?

Jack Warner used to clock the writers in. He insisted on getting his money's worth. We were supposed to be at the studio at 9:30 A.M. and we'd drift in anywhere between 9:30 and 10. He was always standing at the window with a frown, looking at his watch. They had a writers' building—all the writers were in one building, segregated. We weren't supposed to have any contact with actors or directors. Everything had to go through the producer.

Right outside of Warner Brothers was a tennis court. In my youth I was quite a good tennis player. In fact, I used to play in the tournaments in Forest Hills. Errol Flynn liked to play tennis very much. He asked me if I would play with him at noon. We did and became very friendly. Every noon we'd be out there playing tennis from noon to one. Jack Warner would be standing at the window, fuming at all this horrible time being consumed by hitting balls. We should have been working, or at least thinking about working.

The writers were actually treated almost like slaves. The producers had one terrible habit, of snatching things off your desk. My first drafts are horrible. I didn't want anyone to see them, but the producers always wanted to see them right away and they snatched them off our desks.

We had quite a nice group of writers. We had the Epsteins [Philip and Julius], Mary McCall, John Huston, Niven Busch, a lot of others. Some of them, like Laird Doyle, lived for motion pictures; that's all Laird Doyle ever wanted to do. Others were like me. For the next ten years I always kept my apartment in New York and I would only go out to Hollywood long enough to make enough money to last for the year and then I would go back to writing my plays.

Was there already talk of a guild?

Yes. In 1933 when I came out to Warners I was supposed to get $400 a week as my salary. When I arrived here they were in the midst of what they called the "fifty percent cut," so I only got $200 a week. [Screenwriter] Jay Dratler came by my office and said, "We want to form a guild, so we can force the producers to open their books and show us how desperate they are financially." [laughs] I said I'd be delighted to join and that's how I got involved, at the very beginning of the guild.

Were there pressures not to join?

The bosses warned us that this was frowned upon. Jack Warner loved to warn people. He always sat very close to the writers' table in the commissary, and he would talk in very loud tones so we could hear what he was saying. His language was unbelievable. Nobody would think anything of it now, but for those days it was something.

Was there a tremendous atmosphere of secrecy and fear?

No. Nobody really thought that the guild was going to succeed. You must remember there were seven hundred writers fighting for about two hundred jobs out here. In fact we never had any chance of achieving recognition until the Wagner Act [in 1935]. The NLRB came, in 1937 I believe, and even then, while the producers had to recognize us as a bargaining agent, they refused to make a deal.

I really didn't take a very active part in the guild at all at the beginning. I still had the feeling that I was in alien territory, and didn't belong in Hollywood. While I supported the idea of a guild, I was primarily concerned about the "fifty percent cut."

You went back to New York again, at the end of 1933?

Yes, I was writing plays and I was done with my contract in Hollywood. But the following fall, the fall of '34, I took another job at Warner Brothers. Zanuck was over at Fox by that time, and Hal Wallis was vaguely in charge. The first thing they wanted me to do was work with Max Reinhardt, of all people. He had come to Hollywood after a colossal flop on Broadway in New York, and now he intended to do *Danton* at Warner Brothers. It was based on a famous play in Germany [*Dantons Tod* by Georg Büchner], a classic in verse. Wallis and Jack Warner, I was told, asked him, "Who do you want to work on the script?" He said, "I want your top writer," so they put me on it. [laughs]

I worked for seven months with Reinhardt on this script, during which time he had his two sons, Gottfried and Wolfgang, sitting in my office learning how to write scripts. His wife made wonderful dinners for me. It was a marvelous experience, but I knew from the outset that nothing was going to come of it because Reinhardt's ideas about making movies were far beyond anything Warner Brothers would ever contemplate. Too sophisticated for Warner Brothers, too subtle. He was always thinking only of the play, and I kept trying to explain to him that motion pictures were more than just dialogue, that it was primarily a visual medium. I tried to take a "living newspaper" approach. What I wanted to do was tell the story of Danton from the point of view of the common man, a bystander in the streets of Paris, not the poet's point of view of the great man.

I wrote a script, finally, and it was about three hundred and fifty pages long, which was impossible, of course. [Henry] Blanke was the supervisor, and he of course was partial to Reinhardt, trying to encourage him and coax him along, but just about when I'd finished the script Reinhardt staged in the Hollywood Bowl *A Midsummer Night's Dream* with Mickey Rooney. He staged it more like a German Nibelungen with processions of torches and a lot of spectacle. It was a big sensation, and afterwards Reinhardt announced that before he made *Danton* he wanted to do *A Midsummer Night's Dream* as his first film. So they put *Danton* aside, *A Midsummer Night's Dream* on the screen was another colossal flop, and that was the end of Reinhardt at Warner Brothers—and the end of my script.

I would think a failure such as that, spending so much time on an unrealized project, would be a stigma at the studio.

I think it was, frankly. The next screenplay they gave me to do was Marc Connelly's play *Green Pastures*. They had a feeling I was a good adaptor and that I knew how to adapt plays. Marc had taken the play from the book *All God's Children*. Everything of importance in the play was in the book, which was by one of the Southern poets, Roark Bradford. But Marc had staged the play brilliantly in New York, with the March of Jericho on a moving platform and treadmill. It was spectacular as a play. My job was to take the play and put it into continuity and shots.

Again, Marc Connelly was very strong on being the whole show, and I had to convince him that motion pictures was not the stage. It was another project doomed to failure. I told people at Warner Brothers at the time that you can't get the same effects on the screen that you get on stage. Overcoming the limitations of the stage is one thing, but there are no limitations in motion pictures. The March of Jericho on film is just a bunch of people walking up a hill. And the cast didn't photograph well. If it had been in color, it would have been better. In black-and-white it was deadly.

How did Connelly do the codirecting with William Keighley?

Keighley did all the directing, but Connelly insisted upon codirecting credit. Marc and I became very good friends, however, and in the end I told him I didn't want to take credit on the script because I felt it was his project. This caused great consternation between Jack Warner and Hal Wallis, because they knew I'd done all the continuity.

Somewhere in there was Anthony Adverse.

That was 1935 too. I never understood why Warner Brothers bought that book [by Hervey Allen]. The thing about *Anthony Adverse* was that every time you built up his story to an exciting climax he moved to a different continent and you had to start over from scratch with whole new characters. Just the labor of reading the damn book, twelve hundred pages, which is longer than *War and Peace*! I only agreed to do it if I could come out from New York by ship through the canal, so I could have twenty-one days to read the book. I did come out through the canal, although I never did finish the book. I submitted a twenty-one-page treatment, however, and they were so impressed by the fact that twelve hundred pages could be reduced to twenty-one that they let me write the script. The book bored me, frankly. It's a very phony book.

I gather The Story of Louis Pasteur *was another dubious project—dubious at least from Warners' point of view.*

I'm sure they thought *Pasteur* would finish me off at Warners, because nobody else wanted to touch it. The studio didn't believe in it. They didn't believe in it, at all. Pierre Collings had written a very brief treatment on the life of Pasteur, which Muni was dying to do. Wallis read it, Jack Warner, I suppose, also read it. The only reason they went ahead with the project at all is that Muni had story approval. He had gone into Jack Warner's office and said, "I want to do Pasteur." They showed him the outline, he thought it was a good beginning, and asked if I could write the script.

Why was Muni fixated on doing Louis Pasteur?

I don't know. His wife told me that he had always wanted to play someone with a beard and that is what intrigued him. [laughs]

Had you become friends with Muni?

Muni had been about finished when he did *Chain Gang,* and this revived him. He became, overnight, a box-office attraction. Warner Brothers signed him to a five-year contract, and they gave him story approval, which is very important to what happened with *The Story of Louis Pasteur.* I didn't get to know him at all until I came back to Warner Brothers in 1933 with *The World Changes.* After *The World Changes* we started to become friendly because he liked that story very much and the film turned out very good, with Muni getting older and older, which he loved to do. I really had great admiration for him. He thought of himself basically as a character actor, not in any sense a leading man. And his instincts as an actor were almost always right.

Was Wallis the hands-on producer of the picture?

No, it was Henry Blanke, who also supervised *Green Pastures*. Blanke was very good with writers, very good with me certainly, very patient and understanding and supportive. I always liked Henry. He had taste, unlike Wallis.

Anyway, Jack Warner was just doing *Pasteur* to oblige Muni. When Muni talked to me about the script, he said, "Let's make it as true and factual as possible, a kind of documentary film." I said, "Well, then I have to work with some scientists and I have to re-search some experiments to make it believable. I don't know any-thing about science." I talked to Henry Blanke, who arranged for me to go to the [L.A.] County Hospital. There was a pathologist there who made me cultures of anthrax and other things. I spent eight weeks doing nothing but research, not writing a line. I read all the material I could find about Pasteur. I was so full of research that it only took me about four weeks to write the script.

Pierre Collings, meanwhile, was in the County General Hospital himself, having overdosed on some drug. I think he was a heroin addict. I didn't see him during all this time.

When I got through with the screenplay, it came back from the stenographic department, about twenty copies, and Muni happened into the office. He asked, "How's it coming?" I said, "It's finished." He took a copy and said, "I'll read it over the weekend," and went home.

Apparently Jack Warner also read it on Saturday night, and Jack was horrified. He called up Hal Wallis, who was, I believe, at Lake Arrowhead or Tahoe, and sent the script up by special messenger. Monday morning, when I got to the studio, I had a three-page tele-gram from Hal Wallis, saying that I was to be taken off the script immediately and Laird Doyle was to put on the project. And there was to be no mention in the script of any disease that would frighten women, no experimentation with dogs, because of the Cruelty to Animals Society, no mention of Russian scientists, because that would offend Mr. Hearst, who was anti-Russian, and Mr. Muni could not wear a beard, and the whole story should take place while Pasteur is in college. There he falls in love with the daughter of the dean of the medical school, but the problem is that Pasteur is not a medical student, he is a science and chemistry major! The dean of the medical school will not allow his daughter to marry a chemistry student. "Take it from there . . ." said Wallis.

Also I was called to report immediately to Jack Warner.

Just then Muni came by with the script under his arm, slammed it on the desk, and said, "I love it!" I showed him the telegram from Wallis and he was furious—I'd never seen him so mad. He grabbed a pen and wrote on the cover of the script: "I approve this as written."

So then I went up to Jack Warner's office and Jack bawled the hell out of me. Jack said I had committed insubordination, that no actor should ever see a script unless a producer has first examined it; now they were in a terrible state and it was going to cost the studio hundreds of thousands of dollars because they couldn't make this dog of a picture, yet Muni insisted upon it.

Well, Muni did insist and Henry Blanke was the only other one holding out for it. They gave it the lowest possible budget an A star like Muni could work with, which was $330,000, and they cast it all with company people under contract. They gave it to an unknown director brought over by Reinhardt, who could barely speak English at this time—Bill Dieterle. He could read, but his vocabulary was limited, and he had to have the script translated to him by his wife, who spoke excellent English. And Bill Dieterle hated the script. This is the way we went into the picture.

We had to repaint an old Busby Berkeley set for the palace interior. I remember the whole film was done on a shoestring. I was on the set every single day of the filming to make sure the actors spoke the words I wrote, and to explain the English to Dieterle, who was a little afraid of Muni. Of course Henry Blanke, who spoke German, was there to help also. When it was done, my contract was up and Leland was told I'd never be back at Warner Brothers and I left for London to work on a play.

I was gone about six months, and I got a cable from Leland

saying I should come right home. The picture was nominated for an Academy Award! When I got home I was met at the dock, to my amazement, by the top New York executive of Warner Brothers, who had a limousine waiting to take me to my hotel. Sure enough, I won the Academy Award. But winning the Academy Award meant my salary automatically tripled, and even if they had wanted me back now I was beyond the range of Warner Brothers. So I signed with Zanuck, who was over at 20th Century Fox by now and wanted me to come to work for him.

The aftermath of this whole story is, two years later, Jack Warner was invited to Paris by the president of France and given the highest arts decoration and kissed on both cheeks by the president himself for this wonderful monument to French science. And for years afterward, Warner wouldn't let Muni appear in anything without a beard!

That brings us to 20th Century Fox . . . 1937?

Thirty-eight. A disastrous period, because by this time Zanuck was involved with Alice Faye, Don Ameche, and Tyrone Power. Everything had to be written for them. I was assigned to do *Alexander's Ragtime Band*. This is not my field at all. Irving Berlin, for some reason or other, insisted to Zanuck that I be the writer. Whatever gave him that notion I don't know. Irving even came to my house in Hollywood—I had never even met him—to tell me he wanted me on the script. I worked on it for a while, but I couldn't get anywhere on the script, because all I had in the back of my mind was Alice Faye, Don Ameche, and Tyrone Power. I couldn't stand any of them. Finally, I got a rough draft and gave it to Zanuck and he read it and didn't like it. He called me into his office and said, "How right do you think this is?" I said, "About twenty percent." So he put on another writer, who worked a whole year on the script, and finally the film came out. I remember seeing it, and sure enough, it was Alice Faye, Don Ameche, and Tyrone Power. . . .

Was there anything left of your contribution?

No. But I had a two-year contract without any options, and Zanuck couldn't fire me, so instead they loaned me out. I think they were making money on me. They were paying me, the first year, $1,750 a week, and I think they were getting $2,500 when they loaned me out.

It's surprising that they loaned you out so much, considering that Zanuck liked you.

Zanuck was making pictures then that I just wasn't suited for. The types of things that I had done at Warner Brothers he wasn't doing anymore. The only times I ever succeeded doing anything of any value at Warner Brothers anyway was when it was offbeat or quite different from the typical studio product. Zanuck had his stamp on the pictures he made at Fox, and they were mediocre. There was a trademark of cheapness about them. Fox had a huge chain of theaters and they had a tremendous demand for material and the studio just turned out junk.

Had Zanuck changed in the intervening time?

Oh, yes. At Warners, Zanuck had guts. At Fox, he didn't go out of his way to do anything off the beaten track. Actually, he had an impossible job, because he was trying to do everything himself. He had twenty productions going at the same time, and he was trying to put his stamp on each one. Alice Faye, Don Ameche, and Tyrone Power—it was always the same nonsense. Maybe they could have done something better, those people, if they had the chance, but they never did.

Where were you loaned out?

I did a script for Universal called *Letter of Introduction*, a tearjerker. The only notable thing about that is that it was the film debut of

Edgar Bergen and Charlie McCarthy. John Stahl was the director, an extraordinary character. He was trying to imitate David Belasco with his snow-white hair and cape. He thought he was a magician— hypnotizing everybody. I was working with another writer, Leonard Spigelgass, and every time we'd write a few lines that he liked, John would send us a telegram. You were going to see him an hour later, but he sent a telegram. This was one of David Belasco's tricks, sending telegrams. The whole script was just a conspiracy to whip up the emotions of the audience. John would say, "This is how I want the audience to feel at this point. . . . Here they have to be relieved. . . . Here there had to be suspense. . . ." Poor John—he amused people. But he did have a way of getting what he wanted.

At Universal they didn't care how long a script took as long as we got the right words. This was marvelous, because we spent most of our time at the Brown Derby "discussing the film."

What was Disputed Passage?

That was what we used to call a "polish job," at RKO. As I recall, it was developing scenes that had been skimmed over and bringing them more to life. I wasn't on it for more than four weeks. It was a medical story, as I recall, and I know that Tony Veiller, when he discovered that somebody else had been put on the story, was quite incensed. [laughs] Tony was a friend of mine, but I had nothing to do with the credits. The year that I won the Academy Award for *Pasteur*, he thought he was going to win it for his screenplay based on Maxwell Anderson's play about the Sacco-Vanzetti case, *Winterset*. I won instead and Tony was still mad at me for that.

What about South of Suez?

That wasn't the original title. That's what we used to call an "original." *South of Suez* was from a story treatment of about forty pages that I had sold to Warner Brothers back in 1935 for Paul Muni. They shelved it after he did *Pasteur* and became such an important star. Actually, it was a rather tricky idea about a man who is convicted of his own murder. It took place in the diamond mines and in Amsterdam and all over Europe. When they finally made it, it was without Muni, and I was long gone from Warner Brothers and had nothing to do with the script.

And Cheers for Miss Bishop?

Cheers for Miss Bishop was something I worked on for quite a while. There was a script before mine [by Adelaide Heinbron], but it wasn't right and needed a lot of work. It was the simple story of a dedicated woman teacher who falls in love on one of her sabbaticals in Italy, with this romantic Italian. She comes back to this country and her students and goes on with her teaching, but she never forgets this Italian. Years later, they meet again. Now he wants her to give up teaching and marry him. He should have married her thirty years ago, but, he tells her, it's never too late. She decides that what never was can't be, and she returns to her pupils, and that's the end. It was another tearjerker, an old-fashioned romance. Tay Garnett, I believe, directed it.

Then I did a script for Walter Wanger that was never made. It was based on a novel by Taylor Caldwell about the Du Pont family and the evilest of the munitions makers. A merchants-of-death story. It was just at the time that we were flirting with getting into the war, in '41. I got through with the script, about two hundred pages, about two weeks before Pearl Harbor, and that was the end.

During the late 1930s, I know you were getting more heavily involved with the Screen Writers Guild organizing struggle. I know you were one of the leaders of the liberal faction, and were elected president at two critical junctures in guild history. Can you tell me when and why you became passionately involved?

At the point that I got on the board [in 1937] and experienced the contemptuous treatment that we were getting from the producers, who were so adamant and inflexible and outraged, I had been a member of the Dramatists Guild for quite a while by that time, as I'd had several plays produced, and I knew how the Dramatists Guild functioned. I was trying to further the Screen Writers Guild cause of achieving a similar status, especially with regard to reservation of rights, but the factional infighting among the writers was terrible and played right into the hands of the producers, who could immediately say, "Well, the guild is torn between radicals and conservatives. . . ."

Can you tell me something about the factional infighting and where the liberals stood—where you stood, as opposed to the left- and right-wing groups?

You'd be surprised at who some of the liberals were. One of the most outstanding liberals was Charlie Brackett, who came from a Boston Brahmin family, but he was a true liberal. Dudley Nichols was one of our lead negotiators, and other liberals included the Epsteins, [Francis] Goodrich and [Albert] Hackett, Leonard Spigelgass. There were enough of us to hold the middle, but just.

The fight within the guild was really between the people who wanted the guild to be a union and to establish minimum wages and those who wanted it to be more like the Dramatists Guild and protect ownership of material. The Communists were really keen on the union idea; they couldn't care less about reservation of rights. Many of the people on the right were all for the reservation of rights. What the Communists wanted was to use the guild for political purposes, but they never succeeded. They did succeed in almost destroying the guild, but they never succeeded in subverting it, because they were never in the majority.

You feel the Communist faction was basically a pernicious influence?

Very much so, yes. At the time, especially the 1930s, various causes were seeking support from groups of people. They were always coming in and trying to get the guild or the board to vote to support certain causes. The Communists didn't want to control the guild so far as its real function was concerned. They wanted to use it as a weapon in the war. But the guild had people who were against the causes the Communists wanted to support. What about them? If the guild came out and supported one hundred percent the Hitler-Stalin pact, this would immediately destroy the guild, because half the guild, if not two-thirds, were against the Hitler-Stalin pact. There were many such causes allied with the Communist line, and everybody knew it.

Many times these were good causes—the Communists supported many good causes. Personally I liked the Communists. I liked [John Howard] Lawson. I liked Lester [Cole]. We were very good friends, but we never agreed. It was as simple as this: the Communists believed the end justifies the means, and I don't.

Wasn't that also true of the right-wing screenwriters?

Certainly. One of the causes the right wing wanted us to support was condemnation of the Communists. But the whole idea of the guild was to improve the lot of the writers, and this went out with the bathwater. In the Dramatists Guild there were lots of Communist playwrights, but the Dramatists Guild itself was not used for Communist purposes. My whole fight with all these people was to let the guild be about what it was supposed to be about: the welfare of writers.

Do you think it was injurious to your career to be so involved in the guild effort?

I suppose it was. Jack Warner hated my guts, but then he had ever since I had committed insubordination by showing the *Pasteur* script to Paul Muni and then won the Academy Award. At the negotiating meetings there was always the implied threat of, "Don't you realize you're ruining your career?"

You served as president, initially for two terms, 1939–40 and 1940–41. This was at the height of the internecine debates. Why were you acceptable to everybody?

I think both sides recognized that I was neutral. They believed me when I said that I felt the only proper business of this organization was the betterment of writers. When we had meetings, I didn't take sides. I tried to be fair in letting everyone voice what he had to say. I tried every way that I could to keep politics out of the guild.

The guild finally got its first contract with producers in 1941, nine years after the first petitions and meetings. What are your thoughts about that milestone, in retrospect?

It wouldn't have been signed if it wasn't for the coming war—and Pearl Harbor. All of a sudden the producers wanted labor peace for the great war effort, so they gave us a pittance. The only important thing they gave us was the control of credits. Well, we did establish a minimum wage. We established the fact that writers should earn more than their secretaries, which was a victory. But we got nothing with regard to reservation of rights.

When I first got into the picture business, the main idea of the guild was to achieve the same kind of relationship for the independent contractors that the playwrights had in New York with the managers through the Dramatists Guild. Most of the writers in Hollywood were involved in independent contractor deals on their own time. They would write an original movie and sell it. When they sold it, they sold all rights—for one flat sum. This, aside from the fact that you had no control of the material, was a great financial loss, because these rights became invaluable. I believe that if we had stayed with the Authors League,* that by now we would be functioning with two categories of writers: the employees and the inde-

---

*Under heavy pressure from producers, the nascent Screen Writers Guild's attempt to merge with the Authors League of America was defeated in 1936. Many liberals were part of the bloc that voted for complete guild autonomy, appeasing reactionary members who opposed affiliation with the Authors League. This sounded the first retreat on the issue of reservation of rights.

pendent contractors, with many of the writers moving back and forth between both categories, depending on whether they want to gamble or whether they want salaries. After the guild took in the radio and television writers, the Authors League decided it no longer wanted to be affiliated with the guild, because there's no way radio writers and television writers can hope to reserve rights. They don't have any rights to begin with.

Your first credit during the war had a very unusual comedy premise.

Once Upon a Honeymoon came along in 1941, just shortly after Hitler's blitz into Scandinavia, Belgium, and France. The rapid fall of so many countries seemed to me almost hysterical, tragic as it was. I got this notion about a gauleiter and an American girl stranded in Europe—a singer, an entertainer. She meets this very important guy in Czechoslovakia, who is actually one of Hitler's right-hand guys—although she doesn't know it. He's an advance agent helping to bring about the downfall of Czechoslovakia. He thinks it would be a good idea to marry this American girl so that he can get out of the country and hide his real identity under the screen of being the husband of an American citizen. The girl is rather dumb, but she begins to put two and two together, and begins to realize that every time they move to a different country, the country falls.

I told this story to my agent, who was by now Myron Selznick, and he said, "Tell it to Leo McCarey." Myron arranged a meeting and I told it to Leo McCarey. Leo of course loved comedy, and he saw the possibility of this story. Leo said, "Will you tell it to Cary Grant?" I said sure, so we went up to Lake Arrowhead and I told it to Cary Grant. Cary Grant liked it and asked if I would tell it to the head of RKO. So I told it to the head of RKO, and he said, "You have a deal." The only thing left to do was to get Ginger Rogers to play the girl, and not a single word had been put on paper. This had never happened to me before.

Leo was a terrible drunk, as you probably know, and I didn't see much of him while I was writing the script. But when we got on the set, he sobered up—a little. Leo had a genius for casting, and a genius for getting good performances out of actors. You know, this is really the only thing a director can do in pictures of any value. The rest is done for them. Every scene is shot from twenty different angles, and the selections are made in the cutting room. Anyway, Leo was a brilliant caster, and aside from Cary Grant and Ginger Rogers he got Walter Slezak [to play the gauleiter]—who had never appeared before on the screen—who was just marvelous in this picture. Leo got him out of some road company in New Orleans. Walter had quite a career after that.

What was McCarey's method with actors?

He never gave a direction to actors. Never. His whole idea was to get the most talented, the best possible actors for the parts, and then let them do it. He would never correct the actor. He would shoot things over and over and over again, until he got what he wanted, but he was very patient and understanding and sympathetic. Always joking, keeping them in good humor. I was fascinated, watching him, because what he finally got was the best the actor had to give.

He receives a coscript credit for Once upon a Honeymoon, doesn't he?

He insisted upon it. He didn't write one line. What he said was, I could have the original story credit, but he wanted to share the script credit because he had helped develop the script. Well, he did in a way—we talked it out. But there was no writing. Anyway I didn't care. That was typical of Leo. What I did care about was him cheating me out of $12,500. He was a crook.

The agent told me I got $25,000 for the story and script. I gave $12,500 to Leo, and got a ten-week guarantee at $1,250 a week to write the script. But about seven years later, an IRS man came to visit me and wanted to know why I reported only $12,500 for the story. I said, "Because that's all I got." He said, "According to RKO's tax returns, they paid $25,000 for the story and another $25,000 for the script." "That's news to me," I said. I took this up with Noll Gurney [an agent in Myron Selznick's office], and he finally confessed. He said they wanted to help Leo out, who was so much in debt. Between Leo and the agent, they decided that they would tell me they got $25,000 and actually they got $50,000. Leo ended up with $37,500 and I ended up with $12,500.

You told me that McCarey had a gift for improvisation, but also that you felt it hurt the movie.

It did. He would think up little vaudeville routines that he thought were funny, very often at the expense of important aspects of the story. He thought in terms of gags, like silent comedy people did. Some of the gags I thought cheapened the picture and robbed it of any real comic value. He never could improvise dialogue, but he did improvise Mack Sennett–type things on the set. It went on a bit too long in some scenes, and there were other scenes—Leo wasn't exactly pornographic, but for the times he was salacious—and there were lots of things, because of the Breen Office but also because of the general public, you just shouldn't do.

For example, in the opening scene where Ginger Rogers is being fitted, Leo had an idea. He pretended to be the tailor, coming in to fit her. He measured her behind, taking unnecessary measurements as a comic gag. It didn't add anything to my mind. It distracted. It wasn't what the picture was about. But Cary Grant and Ginger Rogers thought he was just marvelous, and they would do anything he told them to.

What I went through during rehearsals and filming was unbelievable. We made the picture at RKO, and when the day's shooting was over Leo'd insist I go over to Lucy's with him. We'd start drinking and be there until two o'clock in the morning. I'd get to the studio the next morning with a hangover, and some days Leo wouldn't show up—he'd found someone else and gone drinking all night. His wife would call and I'd have to go scouting for him, and I'd usually find him holed up somewhere with a couple of whores. And that day, he couldn't do anything at all. That was Leo.

Even so, the picture turned out quite well. My Communist friends hated it. [laughs] They thought the subject was nothing to make fun of.

Let me ask you about Our Hearts Were Young and Gay.

I got a job at Paramount as a writer-producer, and the first property that I came across that I liked was the book *Our Hearts Were Young and Gay* [by Cornelia Otis Skinner and Emily Kimbrough]. I got the studio to buy it for me, wrote the script, and produced it. I thought I would have more control of the material if I became a producer. I didn't have the patience to be a director, in motion pictures. It's a terribly tedious job, sitting around for hours, waiting for the sets and lighting and makeup to be right. It's so time-consuming. Also I don't have any talent for casting. Anyway, I did have more control of the material as producer, and the picture was done exactly as I wanted. It was very successful.

I still had hopes of getting back to the theater, however, and I had a play I wanted to go east for, so I gave up producing at Paramount. I went east for a year. The play was produced in 1944 on Broadway, but it was a flop.

Ironically, you seem to have had more success in the long run writing motion pictures.

No question about that.

Why do you think that is?

Partly it's luck. I was lucky with my timing. I came along just at the time that talkies were coming in and dialogue was very important. Lots of the old-style film writers couldn't write dialogue, and there was continuing opportunity for someone like me, who could.

Anyway, again I came back to Hollywood, and that is when I sold *The Locket*—first as a treatment, about forty pages. My agent at this time was [H. N.] Swanson. He liked it, but everybody in town turned down *The Locket,* all the major studios and all the independent producers, until it got to RKO and [producer] Bill Dozier. Of course, it's not necessary for everybody to like a script; just one person is enough. Bill Dozier liked it and bought it for his wife, Joan Fontaine at the time. I forget who the leading man was supposed to be, but Joan had another commitment and we ended up with Laraine Day and Bob Mitchum. John Brahm directed it.

John Brahm had, up to this time, not directed an A picture. This was his big break. He had been under contract at MGM, making B pictures. He was very faithful to the script and did a very good job directing it. He was very competent, again not a genius like Leo McCarey or John Ford or [Alfred] Hitchcock, he was more in a class with Mervyn LeRoy. But John had a theater background, and so he respected the script.

It was another one of your stories with a very intricate, tricky construction.

It was tricky suspense. A man is about to marry a very glamorous girl, and about an hour before the ceremony a stranger asks to see him and says that he thinks he owes it to him to tell him a story before he marries this girl. He proceeds to tell him a story of what he went through with this girl when he was married to her, and as the story unfolds you come to a climactic point, where another man enters the picture to pick up the thread and tell about what happened to him and her when he was married to her. That story goes way back to her childhood and it is revealed that she had a very traumatic experience, was punished for something she didn't do—the theft of a locket—and as a result of this has become a kleptomaniac. As the story of the childhood is finished, you come back to the situation in which it was told, and as that story is concluded, you come back to the next situation, and finally you come back to the present and to this man who is about to marry this girl who has become, apparently, a paranoid kleptomaniac. The final scene, of course, is the wedding, because the man has decided to go ahead. I ended the story with the bride approaching the altar and the groom waiting—this is where I wanted to fade out—a "lady or the tiger?" ending. The front office, because of cen-sorship, wouldn't let me. They said, "You can't do this. She's obvi-ously guilty at the end. He can't marry her." I said, "Actually, I don't know that at all. . . ." But they forced me to have her collapse during the ceremony, and then the wedding is called off.

The picture would have been better with Joan Fontaine. She had more of a quality. Laraine Day gave a kind of weird performance, which wasn't necessary, and Bob Mitchum is always Bob Mitchum.

You returned as president of the guild in 1947–48, right on the cusp of the blacklist. Why?

I'll tell you. I was up at my ranch in Montana, in the summertime, August. This was before we had a telephone. The only communi-cation facility was a phone about eight miles from us, where messages and telegrams were received from a city about one hundred miles away. These telegrams were received by a woman named May Hop-per, who would write them out in longhand, and then her husband would get in his car and drive to wherever the ranch was, to deliver the telegram. So I got a telegram delivered to me, which read, more or less as follows: "We the undersigned would like you to run for president of the guild next fall. Please reply immediately." At the bottom of the telegram, May Hopper wrote: "Signed by fifty names."

I didn't know who they all were—left, right, what side they were on. I called up the guild secretary the next time I got to town, and I dis-covered that the instigator was [screenwriter] Ernest Pascal. The fifty names were more or less the middle, the liberal group. Ernest Pascal said I had been suggested by Jack Lawson, because he considered that I would be fair in meetings. On this basis I came back. I ran unopposed.

You were president when HUAC came to Hollywood?

Yes. It was the policy of the board not to cooperate with HUAC, while I was president. As a representative of the guild I joined with

John Huston, Humphrey Bogart, and a lot of other people on that famous flight to Washington with the Committee for the First Amendment. I thought HUAC was completely unconstitutional. It was no crime to be a member of the Communist Party. It was a perfectly legal organization.

I met with Jack, Lester, Ring Lardner, Jr., the whole bunch of them, the morning in Washington before they were about to testify, and I suggested one of them, Jack Lawson, take the stand and refuse to answer the questions to make it a test case of the legality of the committee. I saw no reason why the others had to repeat this strategy and go to jail. Why should the other nine have to go to jail? But they would not take my advice, because this wouldn't suit their purpose. They refused to testify, they all refused, and they did it in a way that had a very deleterious effect on the Screen Writers Guild, not answering questions like, "Are you a member or have you ever been a member of the Screen Writers Guild?"

It would have been better for them and the guild if they had followed my strategy. It appeared in the paper that they had refused to say whether they were members of the Screen Writers Guild, which lumped the Screen Writers Guild in with the Communist Party. That again played into the hands of producers. They could say, "You see. We were right. The guild is a bunch of Communists trying to ruin the industry."

Didn't the liberals in the guild desert the Ten after their testimony? Didn't the liberal middle fall apart?

No, it didn't, not at the guild. The standing of the Screen Writers Guild was certainly impaired. But the board [of the guild] behaved marvelously. After the Ten were cited for contempt and were fired by the studios, the guild threatened to sue the producers on their behalf. When the Waldorf Statement* came out, which said no innocent man or woman would be fired if the guild would cooperate

---

*One month after the Ten defied HUAC in Washington, motion picture executives met in secrecy at the Waldorf-Astoria Hotel in New York City. The Waldorf Statement inaugurating an industry-wide blacklist was the product of that November 1947 conclave.

with loyalty statements, saying they had never been members of the Communist Party, the guild refused on behalf of its membership. When the Ten filed a joint suit against the producers for firing them on grounds of their political affiliations, the guild voted to support the suit and hired a lawyer and put in an amicus curiae brief to protect the rest of the membership. I think the liberals of the guild behaved marvelously, at least while I was president.

After HUAC came to Hollywood, your film credits trickle down to nothing and there's almost a ten-year gap before your next credit, Everything but the Truth in 1956. Why?

After *The Locket*, which I believe was 1948, the entire picture industry went through the most traumatic period of its history. Television arrived and overnight the studios went into shock. Immediately after *The Locket*, I worked on a picture about the great clipper ships that went to China for the tea. I worked for about six months on this script and grew fascinated by the subject. It turned out to be quite a marvelous picture, potentially, but when the television threat materialized and the box office began to fall off for pictures, they shelved anything that would have cost any money, and my script would have been very expensive.

Then I did another script for Dozier, this time really for Joan Fontaine, a thriller about a woman who thought her husband was going to murder her. I wrote it first as a play and up until the end of the third act you really didn't know if he was nuts or planning to murder her.

Another "Lady or the Tiger?" cliffhanger ending. It sounds like that story was a big influence on you.

That's right. But Hollywood doesn't like hanging endings, and that, too, was shelved. Then I did a complete screenplay called "Father's Day" which RKO bought for sixty thousand dollars. It was a story about what goes on in the waiting room of a hospital, among men, when the wife is having a child. It was a cute script, and I needed the money because I was getting a divorce. However, the studio management changed hands and everything the previous management had bought was out.

Everything but the Truth was really a little comedy that Stanley Roberts and I sold to Universal as a story. Stanley and I had some arguments, and I decided I didn't want to collaborate with him on the script. That was about '52 or '53. It then took Stanley about two years to write the screenplay, another year for the picture to be made, and it didn't finally come out until 1957. So *Everything but the Truth* is my last screen credit, but by then I was long gone from Hollywood.

By 1952 there were really just no jobs available in motion pictures. The studios thought they were out of business; they didn't realize they had this gold mine in their old movies. In 1952, I was hired to do—guess what?—adapt "The Lady or the Tiger?" for television. I was working on the script when, suddenly, the producer came in and said, "You have to stop work. We've just heard that you're blacklisted." I said, "Well, what do I do?" The producer said, "I don't know but the front office says you have to quit work immediately." I said, "Can I find out what I'm blacklisted for?" The producer, who was a very nice guy, said he would find out for me. He told me it was Jack Warner's testimony before the House Committee on Un-American Activities, in which Jack Warner had named me, along with about thirty other writers who he claimed put subversive material into his motion pictures. At the end of his testimony, he said he wanted to correct the list and remove the names of Sheridan Gibney and the Epstein brothers. Well, the American Legion went all over the HUAC testimony and included my name on their list of subversive writers and did not include the retraction!

So I had to hire [attorney] Martin Gang, as everybody else did, and Martin Gang had to threaten to sue Jack Warner and take his studio away from him. Jack Warner wrote a letter to Martin Gang, saying that he had never, never in his wildest dreams thought I had put anything subversive in his movies. But there was his testimony! [laughs]

I was disgusted. I was disgusted with HUAC and I was also disgusted that the industry had collapsed in the face of television. I was disgusted that I couldn't get a job. I had been through too much. I was tired.

I decided to move up to my ranch and start writing plays full-time. That was in 1952. I had just remarried and I took my new wife up to the wilds of Montana and built additions to the house and remained there for about three years, writing three plays. Then we went to England, where two of the plays were done in the West End; the third was done in Berlin—my wife was German and she translated for the German theater. Then we came back and had plays tried out all over the country. So it went until about 1960.

In 1960 we came down to Los Angeles to see if I could get back into the picture business. But you know the old saying in Hollywood: "You're only as good as your last credit." And I had had no credits for almost ten years. We moved down here anyway, spending half the year here and half the time in Montana. I did a number of television shows—including *Bachelor Father*, *Thriller*, and *Man from U.N.C.L.E.*—because it was easy to write for these formulaic shows. *Bachelor Father*, for example, was in four acts, each act running something like seven and a half minutes. I did television exclusively for about four or five years, and then I got jobs teaching, first at Cal State–Los Angeles and then, after several years, I moved over to USC. In 1976 we sold our house here and moved back to the ranch. I still did the occasional *Police Woman* or *Six Million Dollar Man* but it wasn't fun or challenging anymore, I didn't really need the money, and finally I gave it up for good.

On the campaign bus with the Gipper

7. Interview with Ronald Reagan

New Hampshire primary, 1976

by Patrick McGilligan

RONALD REAGAN

(1911–)

1937	Love Is on the Air.
	Submarine D-1.
	Hollywood Hotel.
1938	Sergeant Murphy.
	Swing Your Lady.
	Accidents Will Happen.
	Cowboy from Brooklyn.
	Boy Meets Girl.
	Girls on Probation.
	Brother Rat.
	Going Places.
1939	Secret Service of the Air.
	Dark Victory.
	Code of the Secret Service.
	Naughty but Nice.
	Hell's Kitchen.
	Angels Wash Their Faces.
	Smashing the Money Ring.
1940	Brother Rat and a Baby.
	An Angel from Texas.
	Murder in the Air.
	Knute Rockne—All-American.
	Tugboat Annie Sails Again.
	Santa Fe Trail.

1941	The Bad Man.
	Million Dollar Baby.
	Nine Lives Are Not Enough.
	International Squadron.
1942	Kings Row.
	Juke Girl.
	Desperate Journey.
1943	This Is the Army.
1947	Stallion Road.
	That Hagen Girl.
	The Voice of the Turtle.
1949	John Loves Mary.
	Night Unto Night.
	The Girl from Jones Beach.
	It's a Great Feeling (cameo).
1950	The Hasty Heart.
	Louisa.
1951	Storm Warning.
	Bedtime for Bonzo.
	The Last Outpost.
1952	Hong Kong.
	The Winning Team.
	She's Working Her Way Through College.
1953	Tropic Zone.
	Law and Order.

Like Henry Kissinger, who has admitted his secret fantasy of being John Wayne, Ronald Reagan is still playing the movie cowboy—running for president like a wary gunslinger. It's impossible to observe the Reagan-for-president road show without thinking reflexively of his years as a Hollywood movie star. Reagan clearly has his act together, the patter talk, the strategic statistic, the hilarious punchline about the welfare mother vacationing in the Bahamas delivered like a sheriff's quick draw. Same grinning speech, every hamlet. To no other presidential candidate—including born-again Jimmy Carter—does the public effusion, the klieg lights, the hand-shaking rituals, and, yes, the autographs, appear so natural. Reagan has been rehearsing for forty years. Oscar has eluded him, B movies have drained his glamour. But now he is a movie star once again, playing all the roles he was never actor enough for in Hollywood: a Gary Cooper in *High Noon*, "eyeballing" the Russians on Angola, shooting it out with "tinhorn dictators" at the Panama corral.

The supporting cast is stellar. James Cagney, James Stewart, and John Wayne are three warhorses who have endorsed their old friend, the governor. Stewart traveled with Reagan during the Indiana, South Carolina, and Texas (appearing together at the Alamo) primaries, warming up the crowds; the Duke has made several radio and television commercials backing Reagan for president. Other Hollywood notables clambering aboard the bandwagon include Merle Oberon, Efrem Zimbalist, Jr., Ken Curtis and Milburne Stone from television's *Gunsmoke*, producer Hal Wallis, Gilbert Roland, Robert Stack, Pat Boone, and former Miss America Mary Ann Mobley. What an irony that Ronald Reagan has top billing among this crew—it was Sam Goldwyn, according to Hollywood legend who reacted with typical astonishment in 1966, when informed that Ronald Reagan was then running for governor of California. "Hell, no!" Goldwyn supposedly exclaimed. "Errol Flynn for governor, Ronald Reagan for lieutenant governor!" Goldwyn points a moral: Reagan was so invariably the true-blue sidekick in undistinguished

B movies that at first it was difficult for anyone in Hollywood to consider him seriously as a competent leading man, much less a president. Nobody, in 1937, when Reagan signed the standard seven-year contract with Warner Brothers, expected a two-bit actor to metamorphose into presidential timber.

February, New Hampshire

Ronald Reagan likes to say that the Federal Communications Commission made a mistake when, citing the need for equal time by his opponents, it banned his old movies from showing on television during the current presidential campaign. "I've made some movies that, if they put them on television," he says, savoring the clincher, "I'd demand equal time!" Reagan rarely—and with great calculation—mentions his Hollywood career, but he never fails to rouse (laughter, applause) a listless crowd when he does.

Lyn Nofziger was telling me this as we bounced along an icy New Hampshire road on the Reagan-for-president campaign bus.

Pudgy and balding, Nofziger does not look like the smooth political functionary he is—one of the ablest men in the Reagan brain trust. Easygoing, genuinely friendly, he organized the prestige states (New Hampshire, California, etc.) for Reagan, making every decision down to the ham and cheese sandwiches for lunch. He is the man who shuttles local press back to sit with the candidate for five-minute briefings—any longer encourages unfriendly questions—between whistlestops. Nofziger himself cannot exactly remember the titles of Reagan's movies, but he does recall admiring the actor, when Reagan was still a star, in the post–World War II euphoria of the 1940s—Reagan's heyday at the box office.

"Does being an ex–movie star affect Reagan's chances?"

"I'll tell you this," Nofziger said, without blinking. "It helps more than it hurts."

Chewing on an unlit cigar, Nofziger tells me the story of a woman in Florida—she swore proudly that Reagan had made one of his movies on location in her hometown. And another voter in Florida—he swore that his wife danced with Reagan when the actor was still an Air Force cadet. Reagan never made a movie in Florida and he was never an Air Force cadet, but honestly, shrugs Nofziger, what is there to do but shake hands warmly and keep smiling?

"Was it Reagan who secretly requested the FCC ruling?"

"No!" he snapped, momentarily angry. "We were upset. It was an insult to the voters of this country. What does the FCC think? That people are going to vote for Ronald Reagan merely because they liked him in the movies?"

Today, it is tough to remember any of the roughly fifty Ronald Reagan movies made between 1937 and 1964, the forgettable Reagan of such pictures as *Going Places, Nine Lives Are Not Enough, She's Working Her Way Through College*, etc. Bogart, Brando, and the Marx Brothers have countless film festivals dedicated to their careers; Reagan has none. Even Alice Faye has a book devoted to her films; Reagan has none.* His movies are so obscure that several books must be consulted simply to figure out how many he actually made. Seeing them—thanks to the FCC—is another problem altogether. But they are his fame, and worth a bit of digging—for the Ronald Reagan movies are the missing link between actor and candidate.

Long before Ronald Reagan became the ascendant right-wing darling of American politics, he was, in Hollywood, something of a cultural reactionary, cultivated as a patriot in image and style.

Nicknamed "Dutch," he was a gangling radio announcer from Illinois, whose sports broadcasts attracted a national reputation, when he made a screen test at Warner Brothers in 1937. Four days after signing a contract, Reagan appeared in his first movie, *Love is on the Air*, directed by Nick Grinde, playing a brash, irrepressible radio announcer who broadcasts "hot news right off the griddle." Low-budget and formulaic, the movie cast Reagan in the Warner Brothers tradition: a crusader who smashes a ring of racketeers by broadcasting their crimes. The movie has all but vanished today. When I visited the Warner Brothers archives at the University of Wisconsin, the reels were still bound in the original tape—no one had watched the picture, incredibly, since its deposit at the UW one decade ago.

The youthful performer (he was only twenty-six) in *Love Is on the Air* bears an uncanny resemblance to the political Reagan today.

---

*There were not any books about Reagan's film career in 1976. Today there are many—including *The Films of Ronald Reagan* by Tony Thomas, and *Ronald Reagan in Hollywood: Movies and Politics* by Stephen Vaughan.

Then as now, Reagan walks with a hunkering, self-conscious stride, swinging his limbs awkwardly. His emotional gamut seems limited to an annoyingly recurrent gosh-and-golly smile, a great big neighborly smile that occasionally flashes at precarious moments (as he is being fired in *Love Is on the Air*). It's a too, too fleshy smile, slightly off-center, that he beams to advantage on the campaign trail, casting his eyes downward with mock-humility, like a perfect 8×10 glossy photograph. The checkered sports coat he often wears today appears preserved from a Warner Brothers musical in those early days.

Reagan was different, all right. Second-generation at Warner Brothers, he was taller, upright, and handsome, an entirely new beast in the stock company. The Hays Office censors and the years of bitter Depression took their toll on the proletarian Warner Brothers. Bogart, Cagney, and Edward G. Robinson were squat, city-smart, pug-ugly, and against the law. Reagan, with his lopsided grin and aw-shucks manner, inaugurated a new wave, a new righteousness, the smug patriotism of the forties. Warner Brothers specialized in gangsters and molls, upstarts and downbeats—the antiheroes of the American screen. But Reagan, more forties loyalist than thirties rebel, unwaveringly impersonated the hero. He played crusading attorneys (*Girls on Probation*), crime-busting government agents (*Smashing the Money Ring, Secret Service of the Air, Murder in the Air*), record-setting athletes (*Knute Rockne, The Winning Team*), freedom-loving soldiers (*Desperate Journey, This Is the Army, John Loves Mary, Prisoner of War*, etc.), and even conscientious scientists (*Night Unto Night*).

It was an all-American, boy-next-door image, expressed largely as a physical ideal. Six-foot-one, 180 pounds, Reagan was broad-shouldered, with a thirty-two-inch waist and a forty-one-inch chest; his chestnut hair was parted originally to the left and then, after a few movies, austerely to the right. Reagan himself, in his autobiography (*Where's the Rest of Me?* ghosted by Richard G. Hubler), says he was "welcomed like a piece of prime beef" at his screen test. He quotes casting director Max Arnow's incredulous words: "Are those your shoulders?" Old *Photoplay* and *Movie Mirror* magazines abound with beefcake Reagan photos; a typical *Motion Picture* profile is headlined "New Answer to Maiden's Prayers." Often, along with the photos, were the stories about Mr. Nice Guy, soft-spoken Ronnie Reagan who never raised his voice except to argue politics, who never caused dissension at Warner Brothers (no small boast, since many Warner Brothers stars, notably Cagney and Bette Davis, were continually bolting over the feudal contractual terms). The fanzines of the forties were crammed with photos—more photos than articles—of the poised Reagan, smiling imperturbably into the hearts and minds of millions of fans.

With *Love Is on the Air*, Reagan began modestly, grinding out pictures so swiftly that today he likes to joke that they began shooting on Wednesday and wrapped on Friday. Unceremoniously, he was assigned to producer Bryan Foy's prolific B unit, there to make short, unambitious programmers suitable as second features on a Warners double bill. Columnists dubbed him "the poor man's Errol Flynn." The movies were anything but distinguished.

Reagan even had his own shoestring series in neighborhood theaters, all but forgotten today. In three different potboilers, he portrayed a U.S. Treasury agent named Brass, whose adventures included smashing a gang of counterfeiters, halting the illegal flow of aliens, and battling a crook in monk's clothing. One of the pictures (*Secret Service of the Air* in 1939)—which was based on the actual memoirs of U.S. Secret Service chief H. W. Moran—is so middling that it is the only one of his movies, Reagan says, that he himself has so far never seen.

Rarely did Reagan work with the best Warners directors, and when he did, it was usually the occasion for something like Michael Curtiz's *Santa Fe Trail*, a hopelessly muddled slice of history. Reagan played an earnest, unflamboyant George Armstrong Custer to Errol Flynn's heroic Jeb Stuart; with Phil Sheridan, James Longstreet, George Pickett, and John B. Hood, all members of the West Point class of 1854, they track down the dastardly abolitionist John Brown—and execute him, albeit with gentlemanly reluctance. Considerably more impressive is Edmund Goulding's *Dark Victory* in which socialite Bette Davis went blind and perished, despite all sorts of noble medical efforts by brain surgeon George Brent. Reagan played only a minor role, a suitor, in this lavish production. But perhaps he was subliminally influenced by the prestige success, so early in his career, of this crocodile-tears melodrama. For, later in his life his most substantial roles were associated with some bizarre physical tragedy. It was the one curious quirk in an otherwise wholesome career—always the cheap flaw, the fate-ordained tragedy with which to cheat audience sympathy.

Consider, for example, the two movies for which Reagan is best remembered—as gridiron star George Gipp in *Knute Rockne—All-American*; and as roustabout Drake McHugh in *Kings Row*, arguably his best performance (he was nominated for a Best Supporting Actor award). Gipp (Reagan) is a callow, smarmy freshman who is chewing dreamily on a blade of grass when he is first spotted by Notre Dame football coach Rockne (Pat O'Brien). "Take the ball and run . . ." barks the coach. And Gipp dances down the field, sidestepping tacklers with ease. "I guess the boys are just tired," Gipp cracks. Sure enough, the Gipper becomes the star player on the team, revealing himself as humble and decent and clean in the process. But he also reveals a congenital cough and dies in the veritable bloom—not before a win-just-once-for-Gipper speech that, repeated in the locker room later by Coach Rockne, has echoed tearfully down movie-memory lane. Directed by Lloyd Bacon, the movie has dated poorly, and is an agony to watch today. But Reagan has a fresh and honest appeal. It was his first major role in a first-unit production—and it nominated Reagan to full stardom.

Kings Row, another tale of woe, cinched it. An old-fashioned, overblown *Peyton Place* sort of a movie, directed by Sam Wood, *Kings Row* was enormously popular in its day. Reagan played Drake Mc-Hugh, a devil-may-care Romeo whose best friends include a Freudian specialist (Robert Cummings) and a sweet, other-side-of-the-tracks adventuress (Ann Sheridan). A horrible train accident occurs, and McHugh (Reagan) awakes to discover his legs amputated by a lunatic surgeon (who does not appreciate philandering). With the bedside melodramatics of *Knute Rockne*, it is the most famous moment in Reagan's unfamous cinema. Still today, he enjoys telling how he motivated himself for the painful scene. Consulting physicians, psychologists, and disabled people did not help. Rehearsing before a mirror did not help. Only after a prop man cut a hole in the mattress to conceal Reagan's legs—and the scene slowly approached, as he lay there—did a "cauldron of emotions" begin "to terrify me." Reagan's stunned line—"Where's the rest of me?"—became not only the title of his autobiography, but also the tacit motif of his career.

Tragedy piled upon misfortune. Playing, of all things, a veterinarian in *Stallion Road*, Reagan contracts anthrax after a frightened but well-meaning horse kicks him. Epilepsy strikes in *Night Unto Night*, a tolerable soap opera directed by Don Siegel, in which Reagan plays a hopelessly ill scientist in the Florida Keys. Epilepsy again (diagnosed vaguely, since Warner Brothers was worried about box-office impact) is the curse in *The Winning Team*, a sweet-natured vehicle with Reagan playing ailing Hall of Fame pitcher Grover Cleveland Alexander, opposite Doris Day. Reagan built an entire livelihood out of dark victories and winning just once for the Gipper. His one severe disappointment in Hollywood, according to a well-worn movie legend, is that he never got to play the part of baseball pitcher Monty Stratton—whom Reagan deeply admired. James Stewart got the part. Monty Stratton had only one leg.

But even calamity can get tiresome—and Reagan marked his most versatile decade in the 1940s, after *Kings Row*. He was re-teamed with Ann Sheridan for *Juke Girl*, a disappointing social-consciousness yarn starring Reagan as the two-fisted spokesman for downtrodden migrant workers (a rare, and unlikely, role). Raoul Walsh directed him, again as Errol Flynn's sidekick, in the WWII-resistance melodrama *Desperate Journey*. He was tapped for the plum comic part of a lovestruck soldier in Irving Rapper's *Voice of the Turtle*, the hit Broadway play by John Van Druten that flopped on the screen. Former Republican senator George Murphy played his father in the Irving Berlin WWII musical of 1943, *This Is the Army* (then *really* in the Army, Reagan was billed as "Lt. Ronald Reagan"). And present ambassador to Ghana Shirley Temple, then a teenager, played a fatherless youth suspected of being Reagan's illegitimate daughter in one of Hollywood's most preposterous comedies, *That Hagen Girl*. (A scene in which Reagan confesses his "love" for the budding Little Miss Marker was cut after disastrous previews—and the ending, with Ronnie and Shirley climbing aboard a train together, therefore made little sense. "You are left to guess," mused Reagan in his autobiography, "as to whether we are married, just traveling together, or did I adopt her?")

Reagan's star dipped as suddenly as it rose. Drab and gawky—only strong when directed well (which wasn't often)—his persona, like his politics, is irremediably rooted to a certain World War II sensibility of the past. Too stiff, too eager to please, he was "a bit on the colorless side," in the words of one Hollywood fan magazine, "lacking fire or whatever you call that 'something' which really big stars have, or appear to have, and others lack." By the end of the decade, his popularity at the box office began to wane—Reagan was already passé.

Workhorse that he was, he threw himself into union activity for the Screen Actors Guild (SAG), being elected to the first of several terms as president after his discharge from the Army. Actress Jane Wyman, Reagan's first wife, filed unexpectedly for divorce in 1947, complaining that Reagan's growing SAG involvement consumed so much time that there was "nothing left to sustain our marriage." Shortly thereafter, Reagan met his second wife, Nancy Davis, a woman with a more compatible political temperament—she was introduced to Reagan by director Mervyn LeRoy, when she complained to LeRoy about pro-Communist literature being shoved under her door. (An actress of minor renown, Nancy Davis appeared in one movie with husband Reagan, a long-lost little trifle called *Hellcats of the Navy*, released in 1957.) It was during these last uncertain years of the 1940s that Reagan began the slow transition to politics—switched his party affiliation, from Democratic to Republican, became obsessed with the "dangers" of Communism.

The House Committee on Un-American Activities (HUAC) invaded Hollywood in the spring of 1947, and Reagan, from his SAG pulpit, provided crucial assistance to the Communist witch-hunt. Reagan was also instrumental in forming the Motion Picture Industry Council, an ostensibly "patriotic" organization that professed to act as a moderating force during the blacklist. The council gave "unwilling dupes," in Reagan's words, and others wrongly accused of Red sympathies, a chance to clear themselves—if they testified and named other people.

Between the two organizations, SAG and the Motion Picture Industry Council, Reagan developed into a "one-man battalion" (in actor Sterling Hayden's words, from his HUAC testimony), waging war against Communist encroachment in the film industry.

Reagan's Warner Brothers contract lapsed in 1949. The movies stretched fewer and farther between. Paunchy, aging, Reagan could no longer play the romantic male ingenue and he had the range for little else. For the dribblings of a career in the 1950s, he graced a strange variety of motion pictures. Whimsical comedies, anti-Commie potboilers, vehicles for newcomer Doris Day, saddle-sore Westerns, and two mildly entertaining features directed by Allan Dwan, *Cattle Queen of Montana* and *Tennessee's Partner*. Before 1949, when he quit Warner Brothers, Reagan had appeared in thirty-six movies in thirteen years; as a freelancer, he would appear in only thirteen movies during the next thirteen years.

Other movie stars held out against the onslaught of television until well into the 1960s, but Reagan caved in early, and he caved in with a vengeance. Unable to get work in the motion picture industry, he signed for regular appearances on television, becoming the first prominent (he was still president of SAG) example of a crossover star. For eight years, he hosted the *General Electric Theater* series, occasionally acting in episodes—crisscrossing the country meanwhile as company spokesman, speaking at GE factories, honing that capitalism-is-great speech still integral to the repertory today. Then he donned a ten-gallon hat and introduced Western folklore on television's *Death Valley Days*. It was a whole other career, a resurrection. To a new generation of television addicts, Reagan became familiar as a spokesman or host, rather than actor, a straight-talking media guru not unlike Monty Hall, Walt Disney, or Walter Cronkite. Politically, it was like a blank check.

Reagan made one final movie, certainly his best—*The Killers*, directed by Don Siegel, and costarring Lee Marvin, John Cassavetes, and Angie Dickinson. Made for television by Universal, it was thought too violent (especially in light of the Kennedy assassination), and instead was released for theatrical consumption. Taut and brutal, it was actually a remake of the 1946 film of the same name, based on Ernest Hemingway's short story. Reagan plays the only villainous role of his career—the criminal mastermind of the story, a corporation executive who is betrayed by his own hired assassins. Playing against type, with his fading glamour-boy looks, Reagan delivers his most chilling performance. There is irony, as well as terror, in the final, climactic moments of the movie, when he is gunned down a-squirming. It was his last screen catastrophe. Hollywood had lost interest in Ronald Reagan, and Ronald Reagan lost interest in Hollywood. Political horizons beckoned.

The Back of the Bus

The back of the bus, chatting with Ronald Reagan. Reagan turns on the charm when reminiscing about his movies—something he obviously relishes doing. Wrinkled, deep-California-tanned, a complexion that looks buttered in greasepaint, Reagan is not the youngster he is advertised as, but neither is he doddering. Silver patches in the hair, a slight wheeze in the throat. Like all actors, he cannot resist telling his favorite anecdotes over and over again—how he psyched himself for *Kings Row*, why he refused to slap Angie Dickinson in the face ("it was too violent") during *The Killers*, etc. Three Secret Service agents listen in with dull smiles.

The actor-cum-candidate lists his favorite pictures: *Knute Rockne, Kings Row, The Winning Team, The Hasty Heart* (a sensitive soldier-in-the-hospital melodrama, released in 1949) and *The Girl from Jones Beach* (an innocuous little film with Reagan as a commercial artist in search of the perfect cover girl—schoolteacher Virginia Mayo). These are movies in which he is a likable fellow, often "a gay blade going with the girl on the other side of the tracks," in his own words. "You'd better say devil-may-care," he added quickly, flashing a smile, " 'Gay' has a different connotation nowadays."

"Many people," I said, drawing a breath, "think your best movie is *The Killers*—in which you play the villain."

"*The Killers!*" Reagan exclaimed, seeming surprised. "Good lord, there are a few more I thought I shouldn't have made, but especially that one! I always thought *Kings Row* was by far the best. For heaven's sakes." He paused and scratched his cheek. "You know, *The Killers* was never a success the first-time it was made, when John Huston directed it.* It's one of those pictures in which you have no one to root for. There is no good guy. Everyone is a villain. My definition has always been: if the theatrical show is satisfactory, the audience must have an emotional experience and be able to identify.

"But there is a kind of a frustration in an audience that sees a movie, and there isn't anybody to root for. I always had a feeling about *The Killers*. I had never played a villain, which is the way he

---

*Actually, the 1946 version of *The Killers* was directed by Robert Siodmak. John Huston was one of the scenarists.

[Don Siegel] conned me into playing it. When they say to an actor, you've never played such and such, the guy says, oh boy, I've got to do that. I did it but I had an awful feeling, when the picture came out, that everybody was so used to the other, that all the way through the movie, they were waiting for me to turn and be the good guy. They thought I was going to turn out to be all right."

"Did you," I asked, "work best in any special genre?"

"For enjoyment," Reagan answered, "I must confess that I liked the outdoor type of picture. I've always been a horseman, and I could be persuaded sometimes, even if the script wasn't really good enough to say yes to, if it was the outdoors or a western or a cavalry-and-Indians type thing, I was all for it. I just enjoyed that kind of shooting, being out on location with horses. At the same time, I had a career interest in it. Finally, when I got free—I was at Warner Brothers thirteen very happy years—I got a chance at some of the outdoor pictures, finally. This is why I laugh a little bit today when I keep reading in the press that I was a former cowboy actor. I made only three or four Westerns. I also laugh when I keep reading that I'm the fella who never got the girl, because in almost every picture I ever made, I got the girl!"

"Did you have any special methods as an actor?"

Trees and more trees rushed by the window; a woodland road.

"Every actor has his method," Reagan replied quickly, "but I never knew anyone who put much faith in the so-called Method school.

"The thing that you can never put into words is that, in acting, playing a role, there's a fine line . . . so much of what you're doing is the role, the character, and there is so much that is you. In other words, how do you feel, what emotions would you have in this particular situation? No one, I don't care who, has ever been able to define just where that line is. Maybe it shifts back and forward."

"Does being an ex-actor help you in politics?"

"There are things," Reagan said, "in my previous profession that are helpful to what we are doing here—meeting the press, the knowing of those problems, and the ability to communicate. That there is one of the greatest assets of my previous profession, probably. The necessity—not only to the public, but within government itself, in dealing with legislators or others—and the ability, to communicate."

"Does your past Hollywood image—as the likable, all-American hero—give you an edge?"

"Well, I don't know," Reagan answered slowly, choosing his words. "I think, yes, this: I think there is an awful lot in politics that is made up of people voting simply on the basis of liking someone. I never analyzed it much, but the fact that I played, in their memory, over a period of years, as a likable person, must have some bearing."

"Do you ever get the urge—the itch—to act again?"

"First of all," he said quickly, "I'm not very happy about the movies they are making nowadays. It isn't just morals with me, I really think they've forgotten one really important ingredient of good theater, that is, the audience's imagination is far superior to anything you can portray. Good theater stimulates their imaginations. Lord, today you show a wedding night by showing two people having a wedding night, with nothing barred. . . .

"I often used to think about getting older when I was a star and I'd see old actors go down the scale of character parts. I dreaded the thought of doing that myself. I never deliberately set out to do what I'm doing now, you know. I had to be dragged kicking and screaming—as I say at these stops—into running. . . .

"No, not really," he continued slowly, gazing out the bus window. "It was a great, satisfying and successful career. You know, actors always keep dreaming of the one big movie, the one still to come. It so happens that *Kings Row* is the best picture I ever made. But that was always part of the fascination. You always kept dreaming that you had another one coming, and that would be the big one."

Cheers and screams. The Reagan-for-president convoy wheels into the lot of a one-room schoolhouse in upstate New Hampshire. School is dismissed for the day in Reagan's honor. It's SRO. Pink-and-ashen elderly mingle with schoolchildren, the old who remember and the youth who will surely forget.

Reagan strolls self-consciously into the room, the Gipper again (somebody to root for), swinging his arms and shoulders in that terribly boyish way. There is instant recognition, a tremble of waving American flags and an astonishing roar. Who can resist the obvious thought as Reagan's face swings toward the lights, smiling? Here is the aging Hollywood movie star on the comeback trail, dreaming the universal dream of his profession—that last big role still to come.

8. Interview with Dore Schary

Madison, Wisconsin, Summer 1977

by Patrick McGilligan and Gerald Peary

DORE SCHARY
(1905–1980)

1934   *Fury of the Jungle.* Coscript.
      He Couldn't Take It. Story, script.
      Young and Beautiful. Story,
      adaptation.
      Fog. Coscript.
      The Most Precious Thing. Coscript.
      He Couldn't Take It/Born Tough.
      Story, script.
      Let's Talk It Over. Costory.

1935   *Murder in the Clouds.* Costory,
      coscript.
      Storm Over the Andes. Uncredited
      contribution.
      Chinatown Squad. Coscript.
      Silk Hat Kid. Coadaptation.
      Mississippi. Uncredited contribution.
      The Raven. Uncredited contribution.
      Your Uncle Dudley. Uncredited
      contribution.
      Red Hot Tires. Uncredited
      contribution.

1936   *Timothy's Quest.* Coscript.
      Her Master's Voice. Adaptation.

1937   *Mind Your Own Business.* Dialogue,
      script.
      The Girl from Scotland Yard.
      Coadaptation.
      The Big City. Coscript.
      Bill Cracks Down/Men of Steel.
      Uncredited contribution.
      Outcast. Coscript.

1938   *Ladies in Distress.* Story.
      Boys Town. Costory, coscript.
      Love Affair. Uncredited contribution.

1940   *Young Tom Edison.* Coscript.
      Edison the Man. Costory.
      Red Hot Tires. Costory.
      Broadway Melody of 1940. Costory.

1945   *I'll Be Seeing You.* Producer.

1946   *The Spiral Staircase.* Producer.
      Till the End of Time. Producer.

1947   *The Farmer's Daughter.* Producer.
      The Bachelor and the Bobby-Soxer.
      Producer.

1948   *The Boy with Green Hair.* Executive
      producer.
      *Mr. Blandings Builds His Dream
      House.* Executive producer.

1949	*Battleground.* Producer.	1956	*The Swan.* Producer.
1950	*The Next Voice You Hear.* Producer.		*The Last Hunt.* Producer.
1951	*Westward the Women.* Producer.		*Battle of Gettysburg.* Script, producer.
	Go for Broke! Producer.		
1952	*It's a Big Country.* Script (one episode).	1957	*Designing Woman.* Producer.
		1959	*Lonelyhearts.* Script, producer.
	Plymouth Adventure. Producer.	1960	*Sunrise at Campobello.* Script, from his play, producer.
	Washington Story. Producer.		
1953	*Take the High Ground.* Producer.	1966	*Act One.* Script, director.
	Dream Wife. Producer.	1969	*Israel: The Right to Be* (documentary). Script, producer.
1955	*Bad Day at Black Rock.* Producer.		

Someone once described Dore Schary as "tall and avuncular, with soft blue eyes and massive horn-rims, a tweedy Walter Pidgeon version of an American highbrow." As far as it goes, this is a good quick sketch, but it ignores the imposing strength, downplays the sharp intelligence, and misses the most striking quality: on the other side of the Eastern Jewish FDR urbanity was the stark moral stance of a rustic Western hero.

When we talked to the seventy-three-year-old Schary in the summer of 1977, he was in Madison, Wisconsin, to put his autobiography in order. Earlier, he had donated his voluminous papers to the Wisconsin Center for Film and Theater Research; now he was spending his days at the Wisconsin State Historical Society, going through the boxes and boxes of letters, scripts, contracts, pressbooks, and newspaper clippings.

His life makes a fine Horatio Alger story, of a poor but industrious boy from the Jewish section of Newark, New Jersey, who made good—first as a minor comedian in the Borscht Belt (recreated in the only Schary-directed movie, Act One); then as a minor Broadway actor, with parts in gangster melodramas starring Spencer Tracy and Paul Muni; then as an equally minor playwright brought to Hollywood as a junior writer in 1932.

After spending nine years writing films, Schary was put in charge of MGM's B unit from 1941 to 1943, and then went to work as a producer for David O. Selznick for three years, from 1943 to 1946. From January 1947 to June 1948 he served as executive vice president of production of RKO, until that studio was bought by Howard Hughes and constant disagreements with Hughes forced him to resign. In 1948 he moved over to the helm of MGM, where his clashes with another legendary mogul, L. B. Mayer, led to Mayer's ouster in 1951. Then Schary himself was deposed in December 1956.

An anomaly as a mogul in several ways, Schary was regarded as a genuine bookish intellectual; an ex-writer who championed writers; a discoverer of unorthodox *talent who gave first directing breaks to such outsiders as Joseph Losey and Nicholas Ray; an FDR Democrat and staunch unionist. Indeed, Schary fought for recognition of the Screen Writers Guild, an organization hysterically opposed by his MGM predecessor, Irving Thalberg.*

From his executive suite, Schary also spearheaded contribution drives to aid Israel, B'nai Brith, and countless other causes. Groucho Marx quipped during Schary's reign at MGM: "In the old days to see the head of MGM [L. B. Mayer] you had to be dressed like a jockey. Today you ought to be carrying a plaque for civil service."

During his years as the head of MGM, Schary gave the green light to many film classics, including Adam's Rib, The Asphalt Jungle, Lili, Father of the Bride, An American in Paris, Blackboard Jungle, and Singin' in the Rain. *If it was a precarious time for the industry as a whole, MGM, under Schary, still maintained high standards.*

These are all the good Schary tales, but inevitably one is confronted by Schary's conduct during the blacklist period. In May 1947, when the House Committee on Un-American Activities (HUAC) came to Hollywood, Schary, then the production chief of RKO, spoke bravely, stating that under California law, he could never refuse to hire someone because of political beliefs. His testimony, in refreshing contrast to the obsequiousness of Jack Warner and Louis B. Mayer, made Schary a temporary hero.

The Hollywood Ten, subpoenaed in Washington, D.C., that fall, appeared as "unfriendly witnesses" before the same HUAC. After the Ten caused a furor by their public stance, the Motion Picture Association of America called a meeting of producers and executives at the Waldorf-Astoria in New York City. Attending this Malta Conference of the film industry were the biggest of the bigwigs: Harry Cohn, Albert Warner, L. B. Mayer, Spyros Skouras, Samuel Goldwyn, and others, including Dore Schary. Their powwow created the blacklist, which Schary opposed within the meeting. Schary was then chosen as a liberal intermediary to bring the Waldorf Statement before the Screen Writers Guild, where he was heckled and booed.

Schary told the packed meeting of the guild that the Ten had to be fired and blackballed; henceforth, the Hollywood studios would discharge or suspend anyone else found to be Communist. "We do not ask you to condone this," Schary said several times. A few days later, Adrian Scott and Edward Dmytryk, both members of the Hollywood Ten and the producer and director respectively of Crossfire, a frontal attack on anti-Semitism made during Schary's tenure, were fired from RKO. Thus began the "scoundrel time," with Schary later upholding the blacklist at MGM.

When we met him, Schary had maintained three decades of silence on this subject; he said he would explain all in his autobiography—but not before. It was the one awkward moment in our discussion, when we pressed him to explain his role in the blacklist, and he cut us off with a sharp refusal, a hint of the iron fist in the velvet glove.

Surprisingly, when Heyday was published two years later, Schary insisted that he had refused to execute the orders to fire Scott and Dmytryk, and that Peter Rathvon, president of RKO at the time, dismissed the two over his objections. "My feelings then and now are that HUAC acted with malice and with no evidence of the American values that they were supposed to protect," wrote Schary in his book, "that the Hollywood Ten were badly advised and provided an impetus for what happened following their appearance; that the producers behaved cowardly and cruelly."

Schary wrote that he himself did not resign in protest, which many felt would have been the honorable course of action, because "my resignation would in no way clarify the issue." Curiously, Schary said very little else about the blacklist, which left a stain on his career, admitting, "There is some doubt that this account will straighten the record."

Hollywood in the 1930s and 1940s was perhaps the happier time, and Schary was happiest during the interview reminiscing about his salad days as a contract writer.

What were your first impressions of Hollywood screenwriting?

I was brought out there as a junior writer in December of 1932. When I first came to Columbia, there were writers like Jimmy [James M.] Cain and Sidney Kingsley, who weren't really devoted to motion pictures. They came to do well and go back and write a great play or something. But the fellows I gravitated to at the studios shared the same point of view. We were movie fans; I'm talking about people like Joe Mankiewicz, George Seaton, Norman Krasna, and Jerry Wald. We felt that movies could be better than they were. We developed a passion about movies and worked very hard at it. We quit jobs we didn't like, and we refused to take jobs we didn't like.

What were your financial arrangements?

Columbia signed me to a so-called seven-picture contract. My first year I was supposed to get $100 weekly for the first three months,

$125 for the next three months, $150 for the next three months, and $200 for the last three months. By the end of the first three months, I had already done two original screenplays and Columbia picked up my option.

Do you remember the names of the pictures?

Fury of the Jungle and *The Most Precious Thing.* They were produced. But I'd written many other things that weren't—original stories which nobody read. Some were hysterical. So, they picked up my option, provided I'd stay at $100 a week. Then they picked it up again because I'd written two more pictures, one of them called *Fog*; and I did a rewrite on a picture called *Men of Steel.* For a third time they picked up my option—and now nine months had passed. So I went and said, "I think I ought to be getting more, you know. I've done four screenplays." They said to me, "What do you think you're worth?" And I said, "I just want what's in the contract, $200." So they said, "Okay, you're fired. And after you can't get a job, you'll come crawling to Columbia trying to get your $100 a week back." So I left. This was in 1933.

Nice People.

Well, it was typical. Writers, if they had no reputation, were chattel.

How had Harry Cohn been involved in your hiring?

It had been a typical Harry Cohn thing. Yet do you want to know something interesting? As I look back on it, I was lucky and three writers I was interviewed with kind of blew it; they really did. I had the advantage. It was probably because—God knows, I'm not a modest man—but I do not normally come on strong. I come on very slow and very soft, probably because of a natural sense that I don't want to intrude. I went in last to meet Cohn, and that was also lucky for me. There was no room for me to sit down except on the arm of a sofa. These men were asked what they thought they could do, and the first one said that he wanted to write tough newspaper stories. He just didn't seem the type. I could see right away that he was in trouble.

The next fellow I really liked very much, a cute dear guy—he was gay—very discreet; those were the days when gay fellows had to be very discreet, but I knew him from New York. He said, "I want to write about molls, gun molls." I said to myself, "Oh, no!" The final fellow said Hollywood was a stupid kind of business. He wanted to write novels and unless they did what he wanted, he wasn't going to stay. He spoke like this all the time [imitates an upper-class stuffed shirt] and he said, "I write like Noël Coward."

Now I watched the reactions of Cohn and Columbia executive Walter Wanger and Frank Capra and Sam Briskin, who were all there to meet this new breed. Then it was my turn. Cohn asked, "What do you want to do?" I said, "Whatever you tell me to do." Cohn said, "Don't you have any ideas?" I said, "No, I haven't got any ideas. Just tell me what you want, I'll write it." I was fortunate. I might have made a horse's ass out of myself. After I finished, Cohn smiled at me, turned to Wanger, and said, "I told you he wasn't a dame." Earlier, when Wanger read my stuff in California, he had contacted Cohn and said, "Get hold of whoever wrote these three plays. It's a dame named Dore Schary, but she writes like a man." When I had gone to see Cohn at Columbia in New York, he started to laugh. So I kept thinking he brought me to Hollywood as a practical joke. In any event, that ended my immediate problems with him.

And later on?

Cohn had a very attractive secretary, and on a couple of occasions I went up to talk to her about a couple of things; but mainly I wanted to see her because she was pretty. And I don't know, I was skinny and tall, and she came to the writers' office one night. She was very dear and very inviting and perhaps something could have happened. Except that somebody called from downstairs, "Mr. Cohn wants to see you." Now the building was in a rectangle, so Cohn, in his office, could just look over—and I think he saw her coming into my office. Later I was told by the man who fired me, "Don't mess around with Cohn's secretaries." That was Columbia.

Where'd you go from Columbia?

At a party I met Herman Mankiewicz, at that time a top writer at Metro. Jesus, I suppose that's like a young kid going to a party today and meeting Coppola. Anyway, they started to play games at this party. It was a period when people were playing mental games. For reasons I don't know, I have always been good at them. I could do those tricks memorizing twenty-six nouns; then somebody would say, "What was the fifth noun, the fourteenth noun?" and I could tell them. Or they could give me a long number and I could recite it backwards and then repeat it forwards. So we were playing these games—it just happens that I'm also competitive—and I was very good. Mankiewicz was impressed by that. He said, "What are you doing?" I said, "I was just fired." He said, "Come over to Metro to-morrow." So he had me meet the head of the writers, Sam Marx, and Marx gave me a job for $200 a week.

I got an assignment to work with a fellow from the Ozarks, Vance Randolph, a very accomplished writer, a nonfiction writer, who had recorded all the balladry and language of the Ozarks, which is much like Shakespearean English. I don't know if you've ever dug into the Ozark culture, but it's just extraordinary, and Randolph had written some very good books. Scholarly, you know; nobody'd ever read them but universities—he had Guggenheim fellowships for years. He was a real character. He'd been in World War I and he still wore his Army shirts.

They had hired him to write a mountaineer story for Marie Dressler and Wallace Beery about the Ozarks. So I was assigned as an "experienced" playwright, you know, to work with him. He was just a fabulous man. They'd given him a dispensation; he wouldn't work unless he had a spitoon, because he always had a chaw, and he'd—dead-eye—just splat. It was a little disconcerting working with him at first, but he was such a mild-mannered and sly fellow, and I admired that. We were working for a notorious man named Harry Rapf. He was a monster to write for, such contempt for writers.

What was Rapf's position at Metro?

He once owned part of MGM. They bought him out as soon as they smelled they had something important. Then he was a producer. He was going to produce the Marie Dressler and Wallace Beery story. So we wrote, having fun, and I learned a great deal about the Ozarks. Then we submitted a treatment before we worked on the screenplay. We waited a few days and were told to go see Rapf. He had a nice-sized office. When we came in, he was sitting with his back turned; but he knew we were there, you know. I looked at Vance and Vance looked at me and finally I just went "Cough, cough." Rapf turned slowly and picked up the treatment. "I read this. It stinks." And he threw it on the desk.

There was a pause. Meanwhile Vance was standing there in the carpet slippers he used to wear, chawing. I was a little nonplussed, so I finally asked, "Well, Mr. Rapf, what's wrong with it?" He said, "It ain't authentic." That was the magic word, see, so Randolph said, "Mr. Rapf, uh, I really don't know nothin' about, uh, movies. I worked here with this young fella, who I think knows a great deal about movies. I kinda liked the story, but maybe it's no good. But I want you to know something, Mr. Rapf. I've written six books about the Ozarks, got three Guggenheim fellowships, and I've recorded all the ballads; it's kind of recognized that I know more about the Ozarks than any man alive. So when you tell me it ain't authentic, you just pick up that script and stick it in a place which the Lord provided for you."

With that, he went "pffft" and he spat. I've never seen such a spat. If you were doing a cartoon it would be a continuous flow, as if it were coming out of nowhere. With horror I saw this thing spread on the green rug. By the time I turned around, Randolph was out of the office. When I looked up at Rapf, he pointed his fingers at me and said, "You're fired." So I backed out of the office and ran down to see Vance. He'd already packed. He had one of those old bags like a doctor's bag, and he'd put his stuff in. He said, "I already called Sam Marx. He's got my money for me and I'm gonna get a bus and go home.

I'm sorry, but good luck to ya. I'll be writing to ya . . . and bye-bye."

Then he left. Then I called up Sam Marx, and he said, "Yeah, I heard the word, I'm sorry." It was the day before the Christmas holiday, and I was fired.

So you never wrote a picture for MGM?

I didn't go back there until 1936 as a writer. I went to Universal and did a couple of pictures there. But before Universal, my agent got me a job with a marvelous character named Nat Levine, who owned a B picture studio called Mascot Pictures. Levine sent for me and told me he wanted to do a war story, a flying story of some kind. I was to get $900 for the story and screenplay. It had to be an original. So I said fine. I had to report on Monday to a little office on Santa Monica Boulevard; they had no studio, nothing. They rented space. When I got there, the contract called for $750. The Mascot lawyer said, "Mr. Levine changed his mind. He thought you should only get $750."

I thought, "That isn't fair and I don't want to do it." So I tore up the contract and left it on the desk and took my briefcase, pencils, and pads, and I left. I was scared, I don't know why. I got in my car and I just drove. Forgetting I should have called my wife, my agent, forgetting everything. And the more I drove, the angrier I got. Finally I called my wife—by then I was in Santa Barbara—and she was in tears. The studio had called my agent and they were going to sue me. I said, "I'll be home in a couple of hours." I drove back and I called my agent. He started screaming and I exchanged some words with him and I said, "Let 'em sue me." That story got into the trade papers, "Schary Walks Out on Mascot Deal," or something like that.

Luckily, Universal got me a job then, and I did *Chinatown Squad*, and *Let's Talk It Over* before that, a sailor picture with Chester Morris. Then, out of the blue, I got a call from Nat Levine. He asked me to come over and see him. He had by now moved over to Republic Studios and was thinking of buying it. He wanted me to do a picture called *Young and Beautiful*.

It was 1934 and in these couple of years I had gained a little reputation for doing the job quickly, without having anybody else clean up for me, I said, "I'll do it on one condition. I want $100 a day for ten days and I want to get paid cash at the end of each day. Because of what you did to me last time, I don't trust you." Levine said, "Why should I trust *you?*" I said "Because I tell you I'll have it all in ten days." So he said, "Okay," and that's what I did for ten days. Then I came in and gave him the script and said I would do some rewrites, which I did during the next couple of days.

Then the producer of *Chinatown Squad* called me to do this other picture. That was announced in the papers, "Schary returns to Universal." When I came to work, this producer said, "Look, I don't want to get you upset and it doesn't make any difference to me, but here's a telegram." It was from Nat Levine, who said, "I can't understand why you hired Schary. He never finishes anything he starts. I gave him a job and he hasn't done the script and he hasn't kept his word and you ought to fire him." My producer said, "Don't get excited." I said, "I'm not excited." I walked out of his office. I got into my car, drove from Universal to Republic, which was about two miles away, and by the time I reached that studio I was seeing red.

I went through Levine's office doors and the secretary there said, "He's busy." With that, I pushed open his private door and he was sitting in front of a stained-glass window, and he said, "Just a minute!" Then he said something I'll never forget; he said, "I'm the president!"

I took the telegram and threw it at him and said, "You dirty no-good son of a bitch. Make one move and I'll throw you through that goddam plate glass window." All of a sudden I felt arms around me, because I was literally berserk; suddenly I felt as though I was being hit by octopi. There were two cops and his lawyer and one of his assistants, and Levine was yelling, "Throw him out! He's no good!" and the next thing I knew I was literally thrown out of the studio. I didn't fall to the ground, but I staggered out. And I said to myself as I got in the car, "What kind of insanity is this?"

What happened after you left Universal?

After Universal, I went to work at Warners. Warners made some good pictures, but they also made some pretty cheap pictures. I was given a real cheesy assignment, a B picture called *Murder in the Clouds*, and I knocked that off in ten days' time, an original screenplay, with a writer working in back of me. I did something called *Red Hot Tires* and I did something called "Oil"* and then I was working on a W. S. Van Dyne project, *The Blue Moon Murder*, and that blew up.

By that time I was shifting anywhere I could get a job and an extra $25 or $50 a week, because I had started at $100 a week and still wasn't earning much. I tell you, those of us who went out in late 1932 and early 1933 learned a very good lesson quickly about a studio having any moral character. When the banks were closed we all had to take a fifty percent pay cut. When you're earning $100 a week and suddenly you're cut to $50 and the studio is making more money than ever before, you don't feel there is much citizenship.

Then I began a series of very fast moves. In one year, Charlie Brackett and I, though we were not partners, each had eleven screen credits. I think that was '35. Eleven credits. Which was, you know, incredible. But it was all crap, all junk.

Did Young and Beautiful *ever get produced?*

Oh, sure. So, anyway suddenly I got a call from Nat Levine. By then I was hustling and doing fine, making up to $450 a week. I was at the Western lot at Fox, where I did *Your Uncle Dudley* and *The Silk Hat Kid*. Anyway, I went out to see Levine. By now he had bought Monogram and he said, "Look, I made a terrible mistake. I haven't handled you properly at all. I want you to read something, because I really bought something important. I want *you* to do it. This street you are standing on"—I was on the lot where I was thrown off— "this street's gonna be known as Levine Boulevard. And I'll name a street here for you if you'll come in as an executive . . . in charge of writers and stories."

---

*"Oil" may have been unproduced.

I said, "I have to think about that, I don't know." He said, "I'm going to give you a very good salary. Read this story and you'll know what I'm talking about." So I took the story and went home and read *The Front Page*! That's what it was. Everything was *The Front Page*. They had changed the names, but the dialogue was the same.

I thought to myself, "What a schmuck!" I called Levine on the phone the next day and I said, "Nat, that's a good story, but it's *The Front Page*." He said, "It's your fault. If you had been here and read it you could have told me that before I bought it. That's why I need you." I said, "That's why I don't want to go!" He got furious with me. I didn't see him until maybe eight, ten years later. By then, things were rough with him; he was a compulsive gambler. Ultimately, he lost everything he had. When I was at Metro in '53 or '54 he called and asked if I could get him a job as a unit manager . . . by then he had taken to booze and he was just a wreck of a man. Sad story.

What was your speciality as a screenwriter? What were you famous for?

I wasn't famous at all. I had a subculture reputation as that fellow who could get the job done. I had a good story mind, could straighten a story out, or else I could finish a script that was sick if a studio had trouble. The reason I got *Boys' Town* ultimately was because the story wasn't working and MGM had it set up for Mickey Rooney, Spencer Tracy, and Freddie Bartholomew. They'd tried many scripts and finally somebody recommended that I go and talk to them. The producer gave me the material and I said, "I know your problem. You've got it all miscast. You ruin the picture by making it a story of two kids and Father Flanagan. Freddie Bartholomew doesn't rate. This story should be a love story between one boy and the priest. That's the story, throw out Bartholomew. Use him on another picture." He said, "I have to think about that." He called me the next morning and said, "You're right. I talked about it with some people, and go ahead. I want you to go to Omaha and meet Father Flanagan."

Was that unusual in the 1930s—to send someone to do firsthand reporting?

Kind of. Yes. It was winter. Cold as a son of a bitch. And coming from a rather orthodox Jewish family, I'd never actually been in the home of a Catholic priest. I didn't know whether I was supposed to bend my knee or what!

I first checked in at the hotel in Omaha. Freezing! I took a cab out to Boys' Town, and a couple of kids escorted me to his house, a tiny little place. His housekeeper greeted me. She was a nice Irish biddy. Then he came down the steps. I expected robes or something, but he came down in a coat and tie and said, "How are you doing?" I said, "Very cold." He said, "A little scotch will take care of that." We had a couple of drinks and I fell in love with him. He was a darling fellow. He said, "I'm going to tell you something. I kept saying to MGM, 'Don't send me any Catholics. Why don't you get hold of a young Jewish kid? He'll know what I'm talking about.' " I said, "Now what would make you say a thing like that?" He said, "How do you think I got into this business? How do you think this place was built? Because a Jewish man understood what I was doing and gave me money."

Did Father Flanagan comment on your story?

Oh, he loved it! He said, "Now, I want you to go around and spend a few days, meet the boys, and get to know the place." I did. The first director assigned was Jack Rubin. I came back a second time because Rubin wanted to find out more about it. Then Rubin suddenly got myelitis and died; then I got kicked out of the studio. Who do you think kicked me out? Harry Rapf.

At the time, I was being used as a troubleshooter. I was sent from one set of rushes to another, looking at half a picture; they'd say, "What do you think?" and I'd say, "Well, I think this and this and this . . ." "Great ideas, Dore, will you write it out for us?" I'd say, "Fine, but the writer who you already have must know I'm doing it." I was the fair-haired boy. But I knew this about film already—your hair changes color very quickly. That's when Harry Rapf called me into his office and gave me a script to read. He said, "I'm having trouble with it. They tell me you're a very good troubleshooter."

So I read it on a Friday, came in on a Monday, and said, "Well, I don't think you should make it. It's false. It doesn't work. And so-and-so isn't right for the part. You've got very little money in it, forget it!" He rose up to his full height of five-foot seven and said, "It's not your business to tell me what I should and shouldn't make. You know how much you've cost this studio already?" "What could I have cost the studio?" "Three days' work." I said, "I don't know what you're talking about." He said, "I'll tell you what I'm talking about. You're fired! Get out of this studio." So I left and went downstairs.

Now just consider what happened over the weekend. MGM general manager Eddie Mannix's wife, who had been ill, died. So he wasn't in the studio. So the head of the writers said, "Dore, I can't do anything about it, because Rapf is a prominent producer here. If he says fire you, I gotta fire you." So I said, "Well, okay." After Mannix's wife died, his father was killed in an accident, his mother died a couple of weeks later of shock, and then he had a heart attack. By this time, something like ten or twelve weeks had gone by and I couldn't get a job. It was the first period since I arrived in Hollywood that I couldn't work.

What had happened to Boys' Town?

Boys' Town was ready. Finally, I read that Boys' Town was going into production. Tracy hadn't wanted to play a priest again. But he had gone on a binge and when he came out of it he decided he would do Boys' Town.

I couldn't get a job. I had been making $750 a week, which was a lot of money for B pictures, but I had not had a big A picture. Meanwhile, I was working with director Leo McCarey, who signed me to think up a story. He had a title called Love Affair, but he had no idea for the script itself. Who are the people? What will separate them? What will bring them together? How do we do that in high-class terms, in McCarey terms? He was thinking of a diplomat like Charles Boyer. Then I got an idea that the woman should be crippled in an accident and would disappear from his life because she wouldn't want to be a burden. He said that was great. So we cooked up a story in a week.

What had Leo McCarey heard about you?

Same as the others, that I was a good story man. After a week, he said, "The story works and you're going to share the credit with me, but I'm going to get Don Stewart to write the screenplay." I said, "Good luck." I got $750 and he owned the story. So now things were getting very rough because our second child was on the way and I was running out of money. I never had any feeling about saving. Money was mine to spend, enjoy, give, and I took care, thank God, of a lot of people. So I was figuring I'd have to give back some of the furniture which we owed money on and go back to New York and start over. Then I got a call—by now it was September—from John Considine at MGM, who said, "We're previewing *Boys' Town* and I want you to come."

So my wife and I went and the picture was an absolute smash. We *knew*. It all worked like a charm. I came out of the preview and John put his arm around me and said to my wife, "Excuse me, Miriam, I've got to take Dore over. Eddie Mannix wants to say hello to him." He took me over to Mannix and Mannix gave me a bear hug and said, "What the hell are you doing now? You got an assignment with a studio?" I replied, "Eddie, I was thrown out!" He said, "By whom?" I said, "Harry Rapf." He said, "When?" I said, "About three months ago." He said, "You be in my office tomorrow. We'll put you to work. You *gotta* get back to work. . . ." The next day, I went in and sat with John Considine because they were running the picture again. They wanted to take out a scene and both John and I felt very strongly about not taking the scene out; it was the fight scene. We won our battle, then we saw Mannix, I got my job and everything was fine.

Boys' Town was a big hit and in time I got the Academy Award. Two days later, I got a call from McCarey and he said, "I'm taking your name off." He had made *Love Affair* by then. Of course, months had gone by from the time *Boys' Town* hit the street until the Academy Awards. When he said, "I'm taking your name off," there was no guilt operating or anything. I said, "Why're you doing that, Leo?" He said, "Why, you got your award, now I want to get mine."

He was serious?

Goddam right he was serious. I said, "Well, good luck." He said, "I think you're putting the witch's curse on me." I said, "I hadn't thought about it but I may be. . . ." He was nominated for *Love Affair*, but he didn't get an award.

That's not a very nice Leo McCarey story.

No, it isn't. He was funny, entertaining, cut your balls off if he had to.

What sort of pictures did you do when you returned to MGM?

Well, when I got back, I did the Edison bio pictures. Then I did *A Broadway Melody*, and then I did a picture called *Married Bachelor*. I also did some fixing up here and there. I was enjoying myself. I was having great fun and the Writers Guild was negotiating contracts and I was on the committee that got the first guild contract. That's a story that will be in my autobiography.

Were there political projects that were unrealized at MGM?

I worked with John Considine on a project about Simón Bolívar, which I absolutely adored. I loved that story, but it was never made. It's crazy. The reason was timidity. They were afraid of the South American market and South American politics.

I read the Paul Gallico story "Joe Smith, American," and went to John Considine after the studio had said it wouldn't do Bolívar. I said, "John, I read a short story which will make a wonderful little movie and I want to direct it. I want to write it, and I think it's important to do"—because this was just at the time of FDR's pre-paredness program in 1940. So he said, "I can't give you permission, Dore—the only guy who'll give permission for new directors is L. B. Mayer." I had never met Mayer. I'd seen him a couple of times. So John took me up to Mayer's office, introduced me, told him what I had in mind. L. B. said, "Let me hear the story." I told it to him, I had come up with an idea for the finish which was very exciting and very different, and stolen twenty times since. Then he said, "A beautiful story, beautiful story. John, you should buy that story." He turned to me. "Now, why do you want to be a director?" I said, "I want to be a director because I've always wanted to be one. . . ."

What did Mayer say?

He asked me, "Why do you want to do a little picture? Why don't you want to do a big picture?" I said, "Because I think there's a mistake being made by assuming that a little cheap picture has to be a bad picture. . . ." He said, "Have you seen our B pictures? What do you think is wrong with them?" I said, "Well, sir, I think they could be better, I think they ought to be used for young directors and young writers and young actors. You can gamble. You don't have to worry about finding a big audience because I understand if you just get the cost of your picture back, you're happy. These pictures are made for $250,000, and if you gross $350,000, you've got your money back. Why can't these pictures go out and do $1 million if they're important?" Mayer said, "You have anything else to say?" I had some other things to say. Then he said, "I'll let you know to-morrow," and he stood up which meant, you know, *out!*

So I went out with Considine and Considine said, "You never learn to keep your fuckin' mouth shut." He was furious at me. He said, "You blew it!" I was sure I had.

So the next morning I got a call from Mayer's office to be in front of the MGM building at two o'clock. I got the odd feeling that it was going to be some sort of ceremony—that the writers would be lined up and I'd be booed or something and they'd break my pencils. When I got there, his car was waiting, he came out promptly at two, we got in, and we went to the Hollywood racetrack. On the way there, he talked about horse racing; he had a horse running. We saw the race. His horse lost. He said, "That's all right, he ran a good race." Then we went back to the studio, taking about horses. I had no idea what the hell I was doing, but I knew I wasn't going to get fired! What I figured was that he was going to let me direct a picture and give me some sort of caveats. So we got to the studio and he told me to come up to his office. He told his secretary he didn't want any calls. We went in, he sat down and said, "Now, did you mean everything you said yesterday about B pictures?" I said, "Yes, sir, every word." He said, "All right, you're in charge of all the B pictures in the studio." Exactly like that. I said, "I don't know if I can do it." He said, "You can do it." Literally, I didn't know what to say. So I was very candid; I said, "I have to talk about this with my wife." So he said, "I like that, go ahead, let me know tomorrow."

Do you think he had all this in mind before you went to the racetrack?

Oh, sure. What he was doing was giving me a sense of, isn't it great to be riding with the head of a studio in his car? What he was saying was, I like to bet on horses I believe in; and even if they don't win, it's worth it if they run a good race.

Very metaphorical.

Sure. So I went home and got hold of Miriam and I sent for a couple of my dear friends and I said, "What should I do?" They all said, "For Chrissake, do it. Jesus, we've all been sittin' on our tails here wondering when will a writer be in charge of production!" One of my other friends said, "Great, we can all go to work!"

The next day, I called in. We went over it again and I said, "Mr. Mayer, I just want to know how this would work." He said, "You select the stories, you pick the cast, the director, you can pick anybody you want at the studio except the big star, and you run it. I want to find out whether you know what you're talking about. Why don't you buy 'Joe Smith' and do it? Pick whoever you want from the lot—do you know some of the young people?" I said, "You got a lot of wonderful young people who aren't working." They had Fred Zinnemann doing shorts, Jules Dassin doing shorts, and so on. He said, "I just want to put one man with you who'll be in charge of the money, merely to check the budget; but he will have nothing to say, you are the final word." I said, "Who is it?" He said, "Harry Rapf." I said, "Oh, no! I don't believe it!"

Did he respect Harry Rapf?

No. He said, "Dore, he's sitting in his office, he hasn't done anything there for two years, poor man, but he knows cost. He'll be a value to you, and you'll be doing a 'mitzvah,' a good deed." He added, "I'll send for him." I said, "No, I'll go and see him. He's an older man, and I should go." He said, "Well, he'll be very grateful." So I went out into this guy's office; here's this former monster sitting there and as soon as I come in he gets up. He says, "Hello, Dore," and I start to tell him, and he starts to cry. I said, "Harry, please don't do that." He said, "Oh, Dore, whatever you want, I'll do, you just give me the orders, I'm just going to be the office boy." I said, "All right."

What was your new job like?

I went to work, that's all—word spread and writers were crowding my office. I told them, "I can't pay you guys what you're used to getting. My writer's budget for a picture can be at most maybe five percent of my total budget, so you guys gotta turn it out quick. But bring me stories that you like." So they brought me *Lassie Come Home* and one guy brought me *Journey for Margaret*; we went to work and we made pictures. *Lassie*, we made for $400,000, we went way over budget, I had to get approval for that—and we grossed over $4 million.

How did you get the first Lassie?

We went to [Paul] Weatherwax, the guy who trains dogs, said we needed a collie, and he said, "I got a lot of collies." He picked the one he thought would be best, trained it, and then got doubles for it. We had one Lassie that could "grrr . . . growl" and one Lassie that could jump, one Lassie that could do other tricks and then one Lassie who had the soulful face. Then there was *the* Lassie, the quiet, well-trained Lassie, the beautiful Lassie.

You have to remember that when we announced *Lassie*, it wasn't considered much, a B picture; and it was a new director who hadn't done anything before, Fred Wilcox. It was just such a big surprise when we went out to preview it and when the New York people saw it, the New York office, they said *wow! Joe Smith*, by the way, was made for $230,000, and it grossed about a million-eight. And it had a good point of view, very pro-FDR-administration.

But MGM was a Republican studio. . . .

Well, the picture was pro-American and the villains were villains . . . Then we made *Pilot Number Five* in 1943 which dealt with American native fascism. Beautiful, wonderful picture. James Agee gave that one its start with his review in *The Nation*. That was one of the first pictures made by George Sidney. Then we made *The War Against Mrs. Hadley*, *Bataan*; all these pictures had content.

Could you tell us about your collaboration on Storm in the West with Sinclair Lewis?

I had a notion for a film which I sort of visualized as taking place in the area known as the old Middle West, what later became the states of Wisconsin and Montana, etc. I was trying to think of a writer and I said to myself, "Well, I don't want to get a western writer." I wanted someone of real distinction. Inevitably, it occurred to me that Sinclair Lewis might be a marvelous choice.

So I called him up. We had never met, but he knew of me and he was very nice; we talked about some mutual friends. I told him about the idea and he said, "Well, that's very interesting and I haven't done picture work. They once talked to me about my doing *It Could Happen Here*, but that was a disaster." I said, "I would be very happy to offer you a trip to the coast. I'll put you up at the best hotel and send you out here first class." He said, "Well, that's fun. I enjoy getting out there, I have a lot of friends on the coast. When do you want me to come?" I said, "As soon as you can."

So he came out in a hurry. We sat, we talked, and he read an eight-page outline that I'd written. He said, "I love it." So I said, "Why don't you have your representative talk to our people and make a deal?" Which we did. We made arrangements that the story would be predicated on my original notion and the screenplay done by both of us.

What was your notion?

The notion was to do the story of the war (this was 1943) and do it as an allegory and make it a Western. The characters would literally be Hitler and Mussolini and Churchill, but the names would be changed. Sinclair Lewis made up all the names, because he was a bug about names. Hitler became Hyatt, Goering became Garrett, Mussolini became Mollison. Churchill became Sheriff Church. United States became Ulysses Saunders, France was Frenson, Czechoslovakia was Charlie Sloane. We did the entire story like this. We had a wonderful time, and he worked at my home. He was on the wagon then and he was addicted—this was hot weather, summertime—to iced coffee, with a lot of sugar and a lot of cream. He had oceans of this stuff during the period we worked.

He was wonderful company. He kept having to go to the can to pee and then he would come out and come up with statements like, "While standing in front of the bowl, admiring the yellow flow, I had an idea." We had great fun writing the screenplay.

Did MGM like it?

When it was submitted, there was quite a furor in the studio and opposition from Jim McGuinness, who was—I won't say an enemy— an adversary of mine; he was a member of the Committee for the Preservation of American Ideals. He thought I was the moving force for the whole Communist conspiracy. I had a couple of very sharp run-ins with him. So he went to Mayer. McGuinness, at that time, was sort of an executive in charge of story material for one of the units. [Mayer had divided the studio into units to prevent any one person ever assuming the power that Thalberg once had.] So McGuinness reported to Mayer that he'd read the script and he thought it was Communist propaganda. Here's one of the things he said to prove it: when Slavin first appeared in town, in order to quickly identify him, I first focused on the rear of his wagon and you saw a hammer and a sickle. Well, McGuinness said that was Communist propaganda. So I said to Mayer, "Yes, it's Communist propaganda in that it's the Communist symbol, but I don't know what he means by Communist propaganda. It could also be that Slavin is going to be a heavy. He doesn't know." Other people immediately joined in. Then Mayer finally said to me, "I don't think an antifascist picture is important anymore, because after all we're fighting a war." I said, "This isn't just an antifascist picture. It tells about how an entire world community can be taken over by a ruthless man and how you have to be alert to what's going on." Then he said, "No, I don't want to do it." I thought about it a day or so and then I went in and said, "I don't want to be here anymore. I want to quit."

So you left MGM and eventually ended up at RKO, where you became head of production in 1948. Did RKO give you a great deal of leeway to bring in a new stable of directors?

I could do anything I wanted.

How did Jean Renoir get hired?

Jean, as I remember, was under contract to them when I got there, but he hadn't been doing much. Val Lewton was there; Nick Ray.

Why didn't Renoir make a great film at RKO?

That's a tough question. Nothing was in the way to prevent him from making that picture if he had come in with something to do. He had difficulty finding the material that he wanted to do. It was the same way years later with Stanley Kubrick. I had Kubrick under contract at Metro and said, "Search, anything you want to do, let me know." He spent a year looking at three or four pictures a day, reading everything, and—well, a few years later he made *Clockwork Orange*. He gave an interview in which he said, "I'm always grateful to Dore Schary because he let me learn about movies by just watching them. Kept me on assignment."

This was after The Killing?

Yes. I saw that picture and I said, "This guy is something."

So you ended up paying him for a year and he didn't do anything. How did he leave Metro?

His year was up and he came to me and he said, "I'd like to do *Paths of Glory*, a Universal movie." He said, "I've spoken to them." I said, "Go ahead." So he went there, or to whoever owned it.

Joseph Losey—he was one of your discoveries.

Yeah. I gave him his first movie [*The Boy with Green Hair*], and it was Losey who told me that Stephen Vincent Benet's *The Sabine Women* would make a hell of a musical. Tried to buy it then, couldn't get it. Joshua Logan had it under option.

Seven Brides for Seven Brothers?

Yeah.

William Wellman's Westward the Women, *which you produced, is a great, little-known movie and it's from an original story by Frank Capra.*

I loved that picture. Frank Capra wanted to do it at Columbia and he never put it together. Billy Wellman talked to Capra and said, "For Chrissake I can just hear Wellman saying this—you silly Italian schmuck! Why don't you produce that fucking picture and I'll direct it?" And Capra said he didn't want to produce it. Wellman said, "Schary will produce it." So then Capra called me and said, "Is Bill Wellman full of shit or are you really willing to buy the story?" I said, "Yes, I want to buy it. Billy wants to do it and I think he'll make a hell of a movie of it." So he said, "Okay." Then Wellman asked me if Capra could come on the set. But Capra told Billy, "Get lost! You bought the story—make it!"

Was Wellman the sort of director who would fuss over themes and ideas in the script?

No, he would have no feeling about such things; but he would say, "It'll make a pisscutter of a picture. Goddammit, they'll shit in their seats with this fuckin' picture!" This is the way he talked, his language was—oh, some of the things he did in *Battleground*—incredible! You know, there was an old Army expression, when a guy would wake up: "Let go your cocks and grab your socks, we're movin' out." So he told the guys in the tent scene at the beginning of *Battleground*, "You say it." They printed one take of it, and he told the cutters, "Don't tell Schary about it, just run it for him." So they ran it for me and I said, "Tell Bill I thought it was just wonderful and that we're gonna use the first take." So then I went on the set and Bill said, "You son of a bitch, you won't *really* use that first take, will you?"

Did he ever do any writing on his scripts?

No, he improvised, that's what Bill did. Bill to me was the ideal director, for that *Battleground* kind of picture—well, for almost any kind. He was an earthy, gutsy guy. You wouldn't give him *Love Story*. But he would take your script and interpret it and give it all the panache, ambiance, and style that you really wanted; that's what was wonderful about him. He didn't give you all this crap; he didn't change your lines; but he would give you the business; he knew a lot of little mannerisms, and what he did with actors was marvelous.

I thought he gave actors free rein.

Oh, no! He'd say, "Come on, you're actin' like a fag, for God's sake! You don't look like a soldier, you son of a bitch!" He was always yelling and screaming at them. He was incredible! You handed it over to him and you knew it was going to be what you wanted.

What happened when you took over at MGM? The general image of a studio mogul is a sort of bizarre, very eccentric character. Were you scared that you were going to turn into someone like that?

I tell you, I'd been exposed to all of them before in meetings, in labor negotiations and quarrels, and I really didn't have much fear of that happening. If you demand absolute loyalty and you fire anybody who is disloyal, that's a terrible weakness. It's a weakness, for instance, that FDR did not have. He *tolerated* a lot of people who were disloyal to him. He said, "It's their job, as long as they do their job."

Bosley Crowther said in The Lion's Share that the surprise when you took over at MGM was that so few heads rolled— all the Mayer people continued on.

Well, Lew Wasserman [then head of MCA] told me, "Dore, take my advice, when you go in, throw 'em all out. That's the only way it's going to work for you, get rid of 'em. Because they're out to kill you."

Should you have kicked more people out?

Uh-uh. It wasn't worth that much to me. Listen, there are all sorts of benefits that come with power. I knew that if you have power, you must exercise it, otherwise you become nothing. So I had no hesitancy in using whatever authority I had. I would fight for it, I would insist on it, I would risk my job. I did it many times. However, you have to be careful that you don't misuse the power to the point where you become this monster you were talking about. I remember one time when a director and a producer came to see me about a picture. They disagreed with a note I sent them about their script. They began to argue their point. They were both rather discursive men, they could go on for hours. Normally, I endured that, because God knows, I could be very wrong. In this particular instance, I had thought it out very carefully and I had made up my mind that they were following a blind alley. I said that to begin with, and I added, "Look, I'm gonna let you have your turn at bat, but I'm telling you, I think you're wrong." So they went on. I said, "I've listened, and fellas, you're wrong. I'll tell you why." I made what I honestly believed was a compelling kind of an argument to them. They said, "Well, you may be right." I said, "Then I don't want to listen anymore. As long as you admit I may be right." They started in again and I lost my patience and raised my voice and I said, "Now look, I've had enough!" I remember that was the tone I used and there was an instant change. "Well, chief, look, uh, okay. We don't want to press it, we appreciate very much . . ." They began to brown-nose. Then they left. I remember very clearly thinking, "Oh Jesus! Be careful." When I raised my voice and said "That's it!" they immediately changed. And the reason they changed is that the next step is "You're fired." Or "I'm taking you off the picture!" They didn't want to get it to that point. That's dangerous. I've never forgotten that incident. I said, "My God, that's a terrible way to treat writers," and I knew because I'd been through that as a writer.

Are you encountering any special problems with your autobiography?

You're constantly riding between Scylla and Charybdis. You have to be sure that what you're really saying is absolutely true: you also have to be very, very careful that it doesn't get to be simply a story of "I, I, I." You have to try to illuminate the other people that you come in contact with, get a slant on them that they haven't had before.

Did you read Garson Kanin's memoir?

It's really not a memoir. It's an anecdotal book. Gar directed my first play in 1937. I've known him long enough, so that when he asked me about his book, and when he said, "I never heard from you when the publisher sent you a copy, for Chrissake," I told him the truth. "I thought you could have done better." He said, "What do you mean?" I said, "Well, you've got a whole thing in there about the executive dining room and how every executive had a tray with medicines on it. Now what kind of nonsense is that? Did you ever see me there with a tray of pills and things?" So he said, "Well, wait'll you write your book."

Summing up your own career, what did you try to accomplish?

What I tried to do was give opportunity to new filmmakers and I think that I probably gave more young people opportunity than anyone else who acted as an executive for such a comparatively short time. I believe that if someone one day examines the full record they'll find that what I tried to do as an executive I did pretty well. I had respect for the writer, I brought some air into the subject material in films, and I conducted myself with I think mostly good taste and with a deep sense of responsibility to my industry and to my art. That's what I *think* I accomplished.

9. Interview with Robert Stevenson

Walt Disney Studio, Winter 1978

by Patrick McGilligan

ROBERT STEVENSON

(1905–1986)

IN THE U.K:

1932　*Happily Ever After* (U.K./Ger.). Codirector (with Paul Martin).

1933　*Falling for You.* Codirector (with Jack Hulbert).

1934　*The Battle.* Coscript.
　　　Jack of All Trades/The Two of Us. Codirector (with Jack Hulbert).
　　　The Camels Are Coming. Uncredited contribution.

1936　*Tudor Rose/Nine Days a Queen.* Coscript, director.
　　　The Man Who Changed His Mind/ The Man Who Lived Again. Script, director.

1937　*King Solomon's Mines.* Director.
　　　Non-Stop New York. Director.

1938　*Owd Bob/ To the Victor.* Director.

1939　*The Ware Case.* Director, producer.
　　　A Young Man's Fancy. Story, director.
　　　Return to Yesterday. Director.

IN THE U.S.:

1940　*Tom Brown's School Days.* Director.

1941　*Back Street.* Director.

1942　*Joan of Paris.* Director.

1943　*Forever and a Day.* Codirector, coproducer.

1944　*Jane Eyre.* Coscript, director.

1947　*Dishonored Lady.* Director.

1948　*To the Ends of the Earth.* Director.

1949　*The Woman on Pier 13/I Married a Communist.* Director.

1950　*Walk Softly Stranger.* Director.

1951　*My Forbidden Past.* Director.

1952　*The Las Vegas Story.* Director.

1957　*Johnny Tremain.* Director.
　　　Old Yeller. Director.

1959　*Darby O'Gill and the Little People.* Director.

1960　*Kidnapped.* Director.

1961　*The Absent-Minded Professor.* Director.

1962　*In Search of the Castaways.* Director.

1963　*Son of Flubber.* Director.

1964	*The Misadventures of Merlin Jones.* Director.	1971	*Bedknobs and Broomsticks.* Director.
	Mary Poppins. Director.	1974	*Herbie Rides Again.* Director.
1965	*The Monkey's Uncle.* Director.		*The Island at the Top of the World.* Director.
	That Darn Cat. Director.	1975	*One of Our Dinosaurs Is Missing.* Director.
1967	*The Gnome-Mobile.* Director.		
1968	*Blackbeard's Ghost.* Director.	1976	*The Shaggy D.A.* Director.
1969	*The Love Bug.* Director.		

 His name is Robert Stevenson, a solid and unremarkable name, rather like the man himself at first glance. Throughout his career he has remained stubbornly obscure, though he worked under the watchful eyes of such eminences as David O. Selznick, Frank Capra, Howard Hughes, and Michael Balcon, and though now he is a director for Walt Disney Productions. His name does not even appear in Andrew Sarris's authoritative *The American Cinema*, nor—what is more surprising— in Richard Schickel's *The Disney Version*. Yet Robert Stevenson, British-born, has perhaps exerted a more profound cultural influence on his adopted country than any other director. After forty years in the movies, Stevenson, in the words of *Variety*, is "the most commercially successful director in the history of films."

His movies for Disney studios are the movies a generation has grown up with: *Old Yeller, Johnny Tremain, Darby O'Gill and the Little People, Kidnapped, The Absent-Minded Professor, In Search of the Castaways, Son of Flubber, The Misadventures of Merlin Jones, Mary Poppins, The Monkey's Uncle, That Darn Cat, The Gnome-Mobile, Blackbeard's Ghost, The Love Bug, Bedknobs and Broomsticks, Herbie Rides Again, The Island at the Top of the World,* and *One of Our Dinosaurs Is Missing.* His latest film is *The Shaggy D.A.*

Nobody else is within shouting distance of Stevenson's success; Cecil B. De Mille is a piker in comparison. *Variety* estimates Stevenson's total U.S. and Canadian rentals to be a "staggering $178 million, an average of $11 million per film." That translates to roughly $250 million in world rentals, or an estimated gross of $750 million. *Mary Poppins* alone, the 1964 release directed by Stevenson, and the studio's box-office champion, has earned $42 million in rentals to date. Of the nineteen movies Stevenson has directed for Walt Disney Productions since 1957, sixteen have been enshrined on *Variety's* all-time list of top rental films, more than any other director's. The next closest competitor is director George Sidney, the musical maestro with twelve pictures. Then comes Alfred Hitchcock, the master of suspense, with eleven.*

"Undoubtedly, one of the major reasons for Stevenson's success is, as he readily acknowledges, the machine-tooled perfection of the Disney factory," conceded *Variety*, in a recent and flattering profile of the director. "The Disney name on a film is a virtual guarantee of profit in the family market, yet it is also a fact that no other Disney director comes remotely close to equaling Stevenson's record ... Stevenson's films, like the other Disney classics, seldom become dated, and they have a continuing commercial vitality through reissues."

Flubber, leprechauns, levitating nannies, flying Volkswagens, adorable pets, and precocious children are not exactly subjects that endear Stevenson to intellectual critics. Nor does he enjoy fame in Hollywood, where many film people confess to never having heard of him. One reason is that the Disney studio is a hermetically sealed world of trimmed shrubbery and Mousketeer values in faraway Burbank, from which insiders tell no tales. The studio has always been considered a thing apart from the other major studios. Stevenson himself has not ventured outside this world since 1957, when he signed an exclusive contract with Walt Disney Productions; and, in fact, he lives within walking distance of the studio. The other reason is that Stevenson is doggedly modest and protects his privacy with a passion; one's movies, he likes to say, really ought to speak for themselves.

"When I'm directing a picture, what I have in mind is a happy audience, enjoying it in a moviehouse," he explains in *Hollywood Dream-Maker*, a loving and respectful documentary on his career

---

*Variety's all-time listing has changed radically since 1978, when this piece was published, with George Lucas and Steven Spielberg among contemporary filmmakers whose high grosses and rental income have crowded out Robert Stevenson.

produced last year by the BBC. "My friends sometimes criticize me for this attitude, but it isn't mercenary, because every dollar a picture takes in represents somebody's enjoyment and pleasure."

I met Stevenson at lunch one day. He turns out to be a genial, reticent, and witty man with a scholarly intelligence. He wore a sporty polka-dot shirt and spoke in a lilting British accent, although he has been an American citizen since World War II. "Maybe I'm stubborn," he joked. The lunch was arranged at the studio commissary, which Stevenson had not visited since he had suffered a mild stroke. When he entered, uncertainly, scores of well-wishers hurried over to say hello. Clearly, he is a popular man in this, his own little world. Then, speaking in a soft voice, Stevenson reminisced over his long—almost forty features, plus television—and fruitful career.

Like so many important figures of the motion picture industry, Robert Stevenson came to his profession through happenstance and engineering. He was born in 1905 in Buxton, England, one of twelve children. His father, Hugh Stevenson, was a prominent businessman. As a youth, Stevenson attended Shrewsbury and Cambridge, where he was editor of *The Granta* and president of the Cambridge Union. In his spare time, he specialized in aerodynamics. He never watched movies. That is, until he decided to write a thesis on the psychology of the "ki-ne-ma," and one day went to see Joan Crawford in *Sally, Irene, and Mary*. He promptly fell in love with both Joan Crawford and the "ki-ne-ma." As he tells it, he still possesses seventy-five pages of the unfinished thesis.

Shortly thereafter, he went to work for an English newsreel agency, and from there he graduated to writing story synopses of Elinor Glyn and Ethel M. Dell novels for Gaumont-British. He supplemented his meager income by drafting film criticism nightly. Sent to Germany as a representative of Gaumont-British to supervise films in cooperation with the German production company UFA, he found himself dispatched all over the continent. First, he was loaned to a studio in France as dialogue director of *The Battle*, a Charles Boyer picture, and then he was sent to the Libyan desert to supervise *The Camels Are Coming*. In the cast was actress Anna Lee, who was to become his first wife and frequent star. Upon returning to England, he wrote his first screenplay, *Tudor Rose*, and became a director. He was barely thirty.

Tudor Rose, or *Nine Days a Queen* as it was called in this country, was an artistic triumph and a box-office smash. "The new film, being painstakingly accurate, bitterly dramatic, and movingly performed, must be set down as the finest historical picture we have seen this season," wrote Frank Nugent in the *New York Times*, reviewing a season that included John Ford's *Mary of Scotland*. *Tudor Rose* indulged Stevenson's penchant for historical detail—in this case, plot and counterplot for the throne of deceased King Henry VIII—and also featured a young child actor, Desmond Tester, as Edward VI. History and children, interestingly, were to become the director's Disney signature.

The credits followed fast and furiously, movies that are largely unavailable in this country today, because of the Gaumont-British trademark: *The Man Who Lived Again* with Boris Karloff; *King Solomon's Mines*; *Non-Stop New York* with Anna Lee. The first telegram from David O. Selznick arrived after *Tudor Rose*, and the volume mounted until Stevenson succumbed. After taking a year off to write a novel, *Darkness in the Land*, he arrived in America in 1939.

As it developed, Stevenson spent more time on loan than actually under Selznick's commanding gaze. First he went to RKO for a lighthearted version of *Tom Brown's School Days* and then to Universal for a tear-jerking remake of *Back Street*, starring Charles Boyer and Margaret Sullavan. (Stevenson laughingly recalls that a nervous Hays Office censor lurked around the set, anxious about the moral tone, which he resolved by moving a sewing machine into the "other woman's" apartment, hoping the younger members of the audience would assume she was a dressmaker.) Then came *Joan of Paris* at RKO and *Forever and a Day*, a World War II alliance movie that consumed the talents of twenty-one writers and seven directors and producers. The highlight of his early American films was *Jane Eyre* starring Orson Welles and Joan Fontaine. Stevenson shared credit for the script with John Houseman and Aldous Huxley. "I was a little self-conscious," said Stevenson, with a smile, "it being a great classic novel."

"The picture that still bothers me is *Joan of Paris*," Stevenson offered. "That was a stinker. They were trying to make a picture about occupied France, when nobody at the studio had ever been to France. It felt so false. The most interesting thing about that picture was how to show Michele Morgan in a confessional. It had never been done, because the Catholic Church was so strong in America. I had to go see a priest who was the unofficial censor of the Catholic Church, and he showed us a way to do it. As it turned out, it was only a question of [Thomas] Mitchell's attitude. As long as he wasn't going to break the secret of the confessional, they allowed it."

When World War II worsened, Stevenson followed the patriotic course: he enlisted and, wearing a captain's uniform, became an American citizen. He enrolled in Frank Capra's Signal Corps for three years, including overseas duty on the Italian front. Originally, he was supposed to direct a short subject entitled "Know Your Ally: Britain." Director Ernst Lubitsch had agreed to direct "Know Your Enemy: Germany," and Anatole Litvak was set for "Know Your Ally: Russia." "But mine was the only one that ever got finished," said Stevenson. In charge of all camera units during the liberation of Rome, Stevenson took a local pastor aside and persuaded him to ring his steeple bells. As if on cue, the church bells all over Rome began to chime in celebration, too. That was a nice touch, a Stevenson touch, very Capraesque.

"I'm a great admirer of Capra," confided Stevenson, whose own pictures aspire to the dignity and optimism that characterize Frank Capra's cinema. "It's very hard to find fault with some of those pictures, like *Mr. Deeds Goes to Town*. They say something, and yet they're very warm and entertaining. It's a rare gift, a very rare gift."

After his discharge, Stevenson returned to Hollywood, and—after swiftly completing *Dishonored Lady* with Hedy Lamarr and *To the Ends of the Earth* with Dick Powell—he found his contract in the possession of RKO's new chieftain, Howard Hughes. He belonged to Hughes for the next four years—years of political turmoil in Hollywood, and the beginning of the collapse of the studio system; years that he recalled with loyalty to Hughes. "I enjoyed working with him," he said. "He was not the monster people make him out to be. I learned a tremendous amount from him, particularly from a technical point of view. I thought he knew more technically than anybody, except for Walt. Walt knew more. Both of them hated not to know. I remember, once, we were cutting *The Las Vegas Story* and Howard wanted to make a certain cut. The editor made the mistake of saying it couldn't be done, for technical reasons. Well, Howard took it and cut it, and, of course, it worked." Stevenson chuckled.

The Hughes years were a mixed bag, starting with the anti-Communist thriller *I Married a Communist*, or *The Woman on Pier 13*, as it was politely retitled. Nearly every reputable director on the RKO lot, from Joseph Losey to Nicholas Ray, had turned down the right-wing screenplay about waterfront-thugs-cum-Communists. "It was a mistaken concept from the start," Stevenson ruefully remembered. Then followed *Walk Softly Stranger*, a minor yet neglected gem of film noir with Joseph Cotten as a reformed crook on the lam in a small town; *My Forbidden Past*, with Ava Gardner and Robert Mitchum; and *The Las Vegas Story*, with Jane Russell and Victor Mature. "Being Hughes's," said Stevenson of the latter film, "all the girls had to be beautiful, but in those days you couldn't find any beautiful girls in the extras' guild. They immediately went into the Actors' Guild. Therefore, we had to write an entirely imaginary scene with full dialogue, which we had no intention of using, so we could use the girls from the Actors' Guild."

Because he had handled a fair number of retakes for the hard-to-please Hughes, "which wasn't very good for my reputation in the industry," in Stevenson's words, he switched to television in 1952. Over the next five years, he directed more than a hundred television episodes and wrote fifteen television shows. The shows he worked on include *Gunsmoke* (which climbed to number one in the ratings during his association with the program), *General Electric Theater*, *Alfred Hitchcock Presents*, *Fireside Theatre*, *Cavalcade of America*, and *The 20th Century Fox Hour*. Through his television work, he came to the attention of Walt Disney, who was searching for a literate and history-minded director to put together *Johnny Tremain*. "I was hired for six weeks," Stevenson likes to say, "and I stayed for twenty years."

"Walt was the best executive I ever met in my life," said Stevenson. "With all those things he was running, Disneyland and so forth, he never had 'no time' for things. Great ease. He was never flustered. From my point of view, he was a very easy person to work for. If you were working on a story, he would listen to every argument you gave, even if it went against what he said. Then he would only get angry if he had to go over the same ground twice.

"He would be tremendously involved in the script. He would get you started on a subject with a writer and then disappear, and we'd all be working like hell, and, just when we needed him, he'd miraculously turn up. And he would very often lay down the whole skeleton of the story. You see, he had this very interesting gift. When the story was beginning to jell, it was almost as if he went into a trance and spoke in tongues. He began to actually do the dialogue. That was the secret of good writing around here: never interrupt Walt when he was in full cry.

"During the shooting, he wouldn't interfere at all, because he didn't want to make a director nervous. But he followed the dailies closely, and he was involved in every aspect of the production. He was not, as so many people have written about him, dictatorial."

As never before, Stevenson prospered at the Disney studio, helping to create a cinema of magic and virtue that has become classic Americana. It is a cinema of unforgettable moments—the heartrending death of Old Yeller; the spectacular lair of the leprechauns in *Darby O'Gill and the Little People*; the zany airborne basketball tournament of *The Absent-Minded Professor*; the rapturous dance of the chimney sweeps in *Mary Poppins*; the kooky teenagers on the trail of *That Darn Cat*. This latter film happens to be Stevenson's personal favorite. ("It had all those kids in it," he explained matter-of-factly. "I said, 'Let's make it so that the parents are away for the summer.' I'm not very keen on parents. They complicate a story.") They may be children's movies but it is *family* cinema, as Stevenson likes to put it, quoting Walt Disney to the effect that any fool who makes children's movies exclusively will speedily go broke.

Of course, Stevenson's work is tremendously indebted to the anonymous Disney factory. Among the illustrious people he has worked with at Disney are animator Ub Iwerks, art director Carroll Clark, cinematographer Winton Hoch, and matte artist Peter Ellenshaw. Stevenson continuously and generously credits "the team" for his success. The ambitious special effects of the Walt Disney features demand first-rate filmmakers; and the Disney technicians and artists perform feat after mysterious feat for

Stevenson's benefit. For example, the director storyboarded the epic-style *Island at the Top of the World* shot by shot. "The art department took those scenes," said Stevenson, "and analyzed them and discovered that the entire set was basically four very large rocks." Thus the entire picture was shot, at low cost, on the Disney backlot, with only one small side excursion to Norway.

Stevenson's reputation on the set is as the apotheosis of gentility and calm. He tends to discourage significant improvisation, but he is also considerate and open-minded about acting suggestions. "Otherwise," he said, "it tends to throttle the expression of personality. My feeling has always been to start with the way an actor rehearses himself, and, if he's out of key, I make as many tactful suggestions as I can."

There's a story about Stevenson's generosity toward actors. Comic Ed Wynn appeared in several Disney movies, including *Mary Poppins* and *The Absent-Minded Professor,* during the latter part of his career. Wynn's memory was failing, and he had difficulty memorizing dialogue. But his wit was sharp, and so he improvised his lines to wonderful effect as the camera rolled. Stevenson, a stickler for the script, said nothing, merely smiled encouragingly from the sidelines. "I wouldn't let anyone interrupt him," Stevenson remembered. "I just let him go on and on. You see, he had the most wonderful imagination."

As for his fabled touch with small children, the director believes that it is important "to give them the situation and then let them act it out for themselves. I avoid telling them what to do. Instead, I tell them a little story about what's going on, and they will react to that story and express emotions naturally."

He has his "method" of directing animals, too, dogs specifically. "Most of the emotion is read by the audience," he said. "After all, a dog can only do three things: turn his head in the right direction, cock his head, and bark. The dog in *Old Yeller* had the remarkable gift of putting his head to one side and looking quizzical. He was trained according to a particular note on a whistle. Whenever we wanted a quizzical close-up, we simply found that note on the whistle and played it."

Once he was the youngest film director in England. Today at seventy-two, he is one of the oldest active film directors in America.

Since 1963 he has been happily married to the former Ursula Henderson, an associate professor at UCLA, and is a seemingly contented man in every sense of the word. Nor is Robert Stevenson calling it quits. He intends, he promised during our conversation, to work as long as the Disney studio will keep him. Since the attitude toward him at that studio is one of near reverence, he would appear to have little difficulty with further employment. It may even happen one day that scholars will unravel his work and discover hidden significance in those tales of flying Volkswagens (prescience about the energy crisis) and leprechauns (close encounters of the fourth kind).

"I liked the strong characters . . ."

10. Interview with Ida Lupino

Los Angeles, September 1974

by Patrick McGilligan and Debra Weiner

IDA LUPINO

(1918–1995)

1932	Her First Affair (U.K.).
1933	Money for Speed (U.K.).
	High Finance (U.K.).
	Prince of Arcadia (U.K.).
	The Ghost Camera (U.K.).
	I Lived With You (U.K.).
1934	Search for Beauty.
	Come On, Marines!
	Ready for Love.
1935	Paris in Spring.
	Smart Girl.
	Peter Ibbetson.
1936	Anything Goes.
	One Rainy Afternoon.
	Yours for the Asking.
	The Gay Desperado.
1937	Sea Devils.
	Let's Get Married.
	Artists and Models.
	Fight for Your Lady.
1939	The Lone Wolf Spy Hunt.
	The Lady and the Mob.
	The Adventures of Sherlock Holmes.
	The Light That Failed.

1940	They Drive by Night.
1941	High Sierra.
	The Sea Wolf.
	Out of the Fog.
	Ladies in Retirement.
1942	Moontide.
	Life Begins at Eight-Thirty.
	The Hard Way.
1943	Forever and a Day.
	Thank Your Lucky Stars.
1944	In Our Time.
	Hollywood Canteen.
1945	Pillow to Post.
1946	Devotion.
	The Man I Love.
1947	Deep Valley.
	Escape Me Never.
1948	Road House.
1949	Lust for Gold.
	Woman in Hiding.
	Not Wanted. Coscript (uncredited), codirector (uncredited), producer.
1950	Never Fear/The Young Lovers. Coscript, director, coproducer.
	Outrage. Coscript, director, coproducer.

1951	*Hard, Fast and Beautiful.* Director, coproducer.	1969	*Backtrack.*
	On Dangerous Ground.	1972	*Junior Bonner.*
1952	*Beware My Lovely.*		*Deadhead Miles.*
1953	*Jennifer.*		*Women in Chains* (made for television).
	The Hitch-Hiker. Coscript, director, coproducer.		*The Strangers in 7A* (made for television).
	The Bigamist (also acts). Director, coproducer.	1973	*Female Artillery* (made for television).
1954	*Private Hell 36* (also acts). Coscript.		*I Love a Mystery* (made for television).
1955	*Women's Prison.*		*The Letters* (made for television).
	The Big Knife.	1975	*The Devil's Rain.*
1956	*While the City Sleeps.*	1976	*The Food of the Gods.*
	Strange Intruder.	1978	*My Boys Are Good Boys.*
1966	*The Trouble with Angels.* Director, coproducer.		

Nobody played it hardboiled and sympathetic better than Ida Lupino, who hit her stride as an actress under contract to Warner Brothers in the 1940s, in such quintessential studio fare as They Drive by Night, High Sierra, The Sea Wolf, The Hard Way *(for which she was named Best Actress by the New York Film Critics), and* The Man I Love.

But she wasn't satisfied with acting. In the late 1940s, Lupino made the decision to branch out into writing, directing, and producing films. With her then husband, onetime story editor Collier Young, she formed an independent company, which they named The Filmmakers. Their first production, in 1949, was Not Wanted, *cowritten by Lupino. Its director was supposed to be Elmer Clifton; when, early in the shooting, Clifton suffered a heart attack, Lupino took over, the first of her seven films as director. At the time, and for many years after, she was the only woman director in Hollywood.*

The Filmmakers operated on a modest budget. Lupino prided herself on casting unknowns and up-and-comers alongside available stars. The material was earnest and unusual, the scripts were part autobiographical, and the style was often quasi-documentary. Not Wanted *was about unwed mothers.* Never Fear *was about overcoming polio.* Outrage *focused on a rape.* The Bigamist *told of a dual marriage. Ironically, Lupino's most commercially successful film as director,* The Hitch-Hiker, *about a psychopathic killer stalking vacationing businessmen, was her least personal.*

In 1953, on the heels of her divorce from Collier Young, The Filmmakers dissolved. Although Lupino continued to act in occasional feature films, she moved into television with her directing. At first closely associated with the Four Star company (where ex-husband Collier Young was a partner), she developed a particular reputation for handling suspense programs, to the point where she was dubbed "the female Hitch" (as in Hitchcock). In the 1950s and 1960s, Lupino was behind the camera for episodes of many diverse series—including Alfred Hitchcock Presents, Have Gun Will Travel, 77 Sunset Strip, The Donna Reed Show, The Untouchables, The Twilight Zone, Thriller, Dr. Kildare, The Fugitive, Gilligan's Island, Bewitched, The Big Valley, *and* The Bill Cosby Show. *Sometimes she contributed to the teleplays. But Lupino directed only one more film, the cute convent comedy* The Trouble with Angels, *in 1966.*

When she agreed to this rare interview in 1974, Lupino had just returned from location and an acting stint for television's The Manhunter. *A copy of Marjorie Rosen's book* Popcorn Venus, *a pioneering feminist study of films, rested conspicuously on a coffee table in her house. Today Lupino's reputation as a director, especially during the brief, fertile period of 1949–53, continues to grow among feminists and film historians.*

Why did you start your own independent film company, The Filmmakers?

I'd known Collier Young, a literary agent who had been an assistant to Jack Warner and also to Harry Cohn at Columbia. He and I wrote a story, and he said, "What the hell, why don't we get together and form our own company and discover new people and new kids?" I agreed—"Absolutely, that is what I would love." We did it.

What prompted The Filmmakers to make Not Wanted?

It was a darned good idea—the story of the unwed mother—that we thought should be presented. The girl should be able to get sympathy from the family. Without being too messagey we were trying to say, "Don't treat her like she has some terrible disease. So she made a mistake."

Was the story your idea?

No. Another writer thought of it, but we only used about four of his pages. I did most of the screenplay.

How did you break into directing?

I did not set out to be a director. I was only supposed to coproduce *Not Wanted* since we had this wonderful old-time director, Elmer Clifton, to make the picture. About three days into the shooting, he got heart trouble. Since we were using my version of the script, I had to take over. My name was not on the directorial credits, however, and rightly so. This gentleman, as sick as he was, sat throughout the making of the film. I'd say, "Elmer, is it all right with you if I move the camera, if I do this, and so forth and so on?"

Our editor on this picture happened to be Alfred Hitchcock's editor for *Rope*, William Ziegler. I would run to the phone every five minutes and say, "Bill, listen, I want to dolly in and I think I'm reversing myself." On the first picture he helped me out. He would come down to the set.

On the second film we got Bill again. The picture, *The Young Lovers*, was based on my original story about a young woman dancer who contracts polio, and I cowrote the screenplay. I'd run to the phone again, but this time he'd say, "Uh-uh, you're on your own. I'm cutting right behind you. You can't afford for me to come down on the set." So that is how I became a director.

You acted with many fine directors. Did any of them influence your directing?

Not in style. I had to find my own style, my own way of doing things. I wasn't going to try to copy anybody. But certain directors, like Wellman, Charles Vidor, Walsh, or Michael Curtiz, couldn't help but rub off. And Robert Aldrich, God knows it was a delight to work for him in *The Big Knife*. He's not only a fine technician, but he certainly knows the actor. He digs down into your role and pulls things out you weren't aware were there.

Did Raoul Walsh ever instruct you in editing?

He used to let me watch him in the cutting room. I wouldn't bother him, but I'd ask him certain things, you know, about "lefts-to-rights" and "rights-to-lefts" and "over-the-shoulders." As for splicing the thing, I didn't go into that.

Most of The Filmmakers' pictures were made for under $160,000. How did you manage?

Our scripts couldn't call for floods, tremendous fire scenes. We never compromised, but we also always made sure that we were going to bring the picture in for our budgeted price.

As a matter of fact, we used to sell our pictures personally whenever possible—going out on the road, hitting towns and cities, getting magazine coverage while we were shooting. Still, we were lucky that we got backed for our first and second pictures. And when Howard Hughes, then head of RKO, became interested in the company, we received RKO financing, production facilities, and distribution in exchange for half of our profits. It was rather rough on independents that way. We did not become millionaires. We were lucky to get out.

Why did you decide to make Outrage, the story of a rape victim?

Actually, I just felt it was a good thing to do at that time, without being too preachy. After all, it was not the girl's fault. I just thought that so many times the effect rape can have on a girl isn't easily brought out. The girl won't talk about it or tell the police. She is afraid she won't be believed.

I didn't think it was one of my better directorial efforts. There were certain things in it that I thought were rather touching and really true to life, but we tried to get artsy in places.

The subject material in many of your films was fairly unconventional for the time.

Yes, I suppose we were the New Wave at that time. We went along the line of doing films that had social significance and yet were entertainment. The pictures were based on true stories, things the public could understand because they had happened or had been of news value. Our little company became known for that type of production, and for using unknown talent. Filmmakers was an outlet specially for new people—actors, writers, young directors.

I thought Mala Powers's performance in *Outrage* was exceedingly good, considering this was her first film and she was only seventeen. She still had to have a schoolteacher on the set. We discovered Sally Forrest and Hugh O'Brian in the second one, Keefe Brasselle in the first. We never had the opportunity to screen-test them because we were too poor.

Who else directed for Filmmakers?

A lovely man, Harry Horner, who was one of the industry's finest set designers, was made the director for "Day Without End."* Although we were practically autonomous from RKO, when it came to introducing new directors Mr. Hughes was a little leery. Don Weis, for instance, was our script consultant, and we had a script all prepared for him to direct. But it took weeks trying to find Howard Hughes. We had put out quite a bit of publicity about Don, and there was a short at Metro he had a chance to direct, and so we lost him.

---

*Filmed as *Beware, My Lovely* in 1952.

Why did you decide to make Hard, Fast and Beautiful, *about a tennis-player daughter pushed into competition by her aspiring mother?*

These things happen—the ambitious mother and her daughter and the not sticking to the rules of the game as far as playing it straight is concerned. Again, this picture was based on a true case slightly altered—to this day I will not say which case. Actually, no good came of it for the mother. The gal bowed out of the tennis business.

You are known for playing spirited, tough, offbeat roles. Is this the kind of woman character you like to work with as a director, or write about?

I never wrote just straight women's roles. I liked the strong characters. I don't mean women who have masculine qualities about them, but something that has some intestinal fortitude, some guts to it. Just a straight role drives me up the wall. Playing a nice woman who just sits there, that's my greatest limitation.

Many of Filmmakers' pictures focused on women's issues.

Not all of them. I directed *The Hitch-Hiker*, which was a true story, the William Cook story about a hitchhiker murder, and that certainly was not a woman's story at all. And I made *The Bigamist*, and this definitely was the man's story.

*Did you write the screenplay for **The Bigamist?***

No, I believe it was Malvin Wald, but it struck me as very well written. The challenge to make Lucille, the first wife, completely understanding towards her husband, interested me very much.

Why did you act in as well as direct **The Bigamist?**

I was forced to do that. Joan Fontaine wanted me as the director but said I must also play the other woman because having another name added value.

Was it difficult both to direct and to act?

I'm not mad about combining the two. It takes me morning, noon, and night to pull the thing through just as a director, and then to get in front of a camera and not be able to watch myself . . . Unfortunately, I was in all the scenes with the people who could watch me. Joan couldn't watch me because we had to hurry her back to Paramount. And Eddie O'Brien couldn't because I was in every scene with him. I had to have my cameraman tell me when I was overdoing it. When I was acting, I still had to say, "Cut, print, cut, print." I think I needed a separate director.

When you both directed and produced a picture, was that difficult?

No, it was an ideal way, but that was because it was all done together. Filmmakers was a family group. We all contributed ideas, we threw them into the pot. Four years, and I never had a happier period in my entire life. I'm very sorry that my partners chose to go into film distribution. If they hadn't, I think we still would be going today. We should have stayed an independent company, with distribution coming from whichever high-level outfit gave us the best break. I thought it was very wrong, but I was outvoted. And sure enough Filmmakers didn't make it distributing their own pictures. We didn't get the right playing dates in the right houses. We weren't very wise to step into a field which we didn't know too much about.

How did you become a director for television after Filmmakers went out of business?

I was asked to direct Joseph Cotten in *On Trial*, a series presentation on the trial of Mary Seurat, who was hanged as a suspect in the Lincoln trial. It was shot in three days, with three or four days to prepare. I sat up day and night doing all the research I could on the assassination of Lincoln. Television—there's nothing rougher, nothing rougher. And from then on it became like a snowball. They'd book me in advance because they had to have answers in advance and I couldn't direct movies again until 1966, with *The Trouble with Angels*.

What are your favorite directorial efforts?

Well, I don't think I did a bad job on *The Bigamist*. I like *The Hitch-Hiker*. I think they were really good. There's been some television shows I've done that I like.

Which television shows?

There's been so many, it's a little difficult at the moment to pick out which, but there have been one or two from *Mr. Novak* that I like my work on. There is one *Hong Kong* I like very much. A few on *Thriller* I think are pretty good.

What makes a picture you direct turn out well?

It's a matter of chemistry. A combination of a good script that is possible to shoot in the time allotted, a producer I am completely simpatico with, good actors, and my cameraman. The night before shooting and during that very first shot I always have butterflies in my stomach. But once I get the first few shots in the camera, well then, the stomach starts to settle down.

Communication with my actors is also very important. Being

close to them. I understand their problems. I'm not saying I do awfully good work, but I've done some pretty good stuff.

What genres have you been channeled into in television?

The producer who started me began me in westerns. He had seen *The Hitch-Hiker* and the next thing I knew, I was directing *Have Gun Will Travel* with Richard Boone, *Hong Kong* with Bob Taylor, *The Fugitive* with David Janssen, *Manhunt*, *The Untouchables*. Who, me? I thought. Here I'd always done women's stories and now I couldn't get a woman's story to direct.

In what type of picture do you think you do your best work?

I would not be good at *Doctor Zhivago*, *The Longest Day*, the tremendous plains of war. I don't believe that is my channel. I mean if I were going to decide whom we should have as a director, I would not choose me. Suspense pictures, yes. Robert Aldrich things, yes. *Whatever Happened to Baby Jane*, yes. That I would say is my slot. Suspense.

Not women's pictures?

I think I fit into the women's pictures category, too, but I don't consider myself only a women's director.

You were among the few woman directors in Hollywood. Were there any problems?

I guess I was a novelty at the time and it would have been difficult to become a director then if we hadn't had our own company. But as a matter of fact, most everyone went out of their way to treat me like a buddy. After all, I'd worked with practically every crew in town since 1934. And because, well, I don't act like a man. My way of asking a man to do something on a set is not to boss him around. That isn't in me to do that. I say, "I've got an idea, and why don't you see if it feels comfortable because I think it would be effective."

Listen, if a woman came to you and said, "Honey, gee, I don't know what to do. We've finished this and I'm not quite sure whether we should send it down or what grain I should use. I'd like to do this, but, well, what do you think?" You'd want to help me, wouldn't you? Well, all right.

What would you like to be doing nowadays?

Really, my dream is that some dear old man would see my old movies on television and leave me an oil well in his will. Then I could do good things for the people I like. And I'd want to live on a ranch. I'm definitely small-town, the country type.

Would you want to direct more films?

It would be lovely as a hobby, wouldn't it? Like Liz Taylor and Richard Burton. They can act whenever they want to because they are so damn rich.

I will have to get going again myself. I've been in front of the camera for so long. I've had offers to direct but they would have taken me out of the country, which would have meant leaving my home, my daughter, being away from here months and months on end. It's a rough setup.

That's where being a man makes a great deal of difference. I don't suppose the men particularly care about leaving their wives and children. During the vacation period the wife can always fly over and be with him. It's difficult for a wife to say to her husband, "Come sit on the set and watch."

"You're talking to a screwball . . ."

11. Interview with William Wellman

Cape Cod, July 1974

by Patrick McGilligan and Debra Weiner

WILLIAM WELLMAN

(1896–1975)

1935	*Call of the Wild.* Director.		*The Story of G.I. Joe.* Director.
1936	*The Robin Hood of El Dorado.* Coadaptation, director.	1956	*Gallant Journey.* Coscript, director, producer.
	Small Town Girl. Director.	1947	*Magic Town.* Director.
1937	*A Star Is Born.* Costory, director.	1948	*The Iron Curtain.* Director.
	Nothing Sacred. Director.		*Yellow Sky.* Director.
	The Last Gangster. Costory.	1949	*Battleground.* Director.
1938	*Men with Wings.* Director, producer.	1950	*The Happy Years.* Director.
1939	*Beau Geste.* Director.		*The Next Voice You Hear.* Director.
	The Light That Failed. Director, producer	1951	*Across the Wide Missouri.* Director.
1941	*Reaching for the Sun.* Director, producer.	1952	*It's a Big Country.* Codirector.
			Westward the Women. Director.
			My Man and I. Director.
1942	*Roxie Hart.* Director.	1953	*Island in the Sky.* Director.
	The Great Man's Lady. Director, producer.	1954	*The High and the Mighty.* Director.
			Track of the Cat. Director.
	Thunder Birds. Director.	1955	*Blood Alley.* Director.
1943	*The Ox-Bow Incident.* Director.	1956	*Goodbye, My Lady.* Director.
	Lady of Burlesque. Director.	1958	*Darby's Rangers.* Director.
1944	*Buffalo Bill.* Director.		*Lafayette Escadrille.* Story, director, producer.
1945	*This Man's Navy.* Director.		

 William "Wild Bill" Wellman was nearing the end of a publicity tour for his book A Short Time for Insanity when we tracked him down at the Cape Cod residence of his brother. The director's decidedly free-form remembrance of things past had been written ten years earlier during a hospital stay for back surgery, while Wellman was under the influence of heavy painkillers. Agreeing to an interview, Wellman interrupted work on his next book, Growing Old Disgracefully* for which, he said, he had already written the ending, modeled after the ending of his friend Ben Hecht's novel Gaily, Gaily. A copy of Hecht's book rested on a coffee table.

We were invited to stay for lunch. James Cagney, the reclusive star whom the director had launched in The Public Enemy, interrupted by phone from Martha's Vineyard to arrange a boating trip with Wellman for the coming weekend. Serving the food, and occasionally chipping in comments, was Wellman's wife since 1933, the

---

* *Growing Old Disgracefully* was never published.

former Dorothy Coonan, once a Busby Berkeley dancer and one of the leads in another of the director's Depression-era dramas, Wild Boys of the Road.

Wellman, born in a Boston suburb in 1896, was an admitted hell-raiser as a youth who escaped hometown shackles by joining the Lafayette Flying Corps in France, just in time for World War I. This background indelibly marked him and inspired one of his specialties as a director. Wings, *the first Oscar-winning Best Picture in 1927, was followed by other air adventure films, including* Legion of the Condemned, Young Eagles, Central Airport, Men with Wings, *and* The High and the Mighty. *Wellman's first book,* Go, Get Em!, *published just after the war, chronicled his experience in the Flying Corps, and then served as a bookend to his career by inspiring the storyline for* Lafayette Escadrille, *made in 1958, his last film as director.*

Among Wellman's hundred-odd films, a list which begins in the silent era with Dustin Farnum and Buck Jones two-reelers, are many other types and styles. The best-known titles, which include Call of the Wild, A Star Is Born *(for which he wrote the original story),* Nothing Sacred, Beau Geste, The Ox-Bow Incident, *and* The Next Voice You Hear, *suggest a director who could be as tender as he was tough, whose swagger disguised his sensitivity to people and ideas and pictorial beauty. The least-known William Wellman films include neglected works as well as more than a handful that are "just plain lousy," as the director himself was always the first to cheerily confess.*

At seventy-eight, lean, tan, and rock-jawed, "Wild Bill" relished his sobriquet and seemed little tamed. For several hours Wellman reminisced about his long, colorful career: five marriages, fistfights and drinking sprees, bitter feuds with top stars and producers.

What do you remember about your youth?

I was born in Lyndon Place in Brookline [Massachusetts] in a big, huge house on February 29, 1896, leap year. And I did something I think no one has ever done. I dropped a stink bomb from two stories up on the principal's bald head. Of course, that was the end of my scholastic career.

I'm the only uneducated Wellman—except for my voice. I have a very resonant voice. It's the only thing I have ever been educated in. I was trained at the Boston Conservatory. I love voices. Directing Ronald Colman is like directing the greatest voice in the world.

I had a very dear friend then. We used to take cars at night and "exercise" them. We always brought them back, but one time we got caught. So we were both put on probation by the city of Newton for six months. I had to report to the probation officer of the city of Newton, who just happened to be my mother. So I thought that maybe it would be a good time for me to get out of the house.

I went to work at a candy company called Fish's Green Seal Chocolates. Well, I ate so much candy that I never ate candy again for two years, and I never sold a pound. Then I went into the cotton business, and I didn't sell much of that. I tried to learn the wool business but I used to watch movies when I went out on the road. So I never sold a pound, or whatever the hell you have to sell when you sell wool. Then I went to work in a lumberyard, and there I was a success.

What movies did you use to watch?

Earl Cummings, Bill Russell, and Lotte Pickford—now what does that mean? They were three in some sort of big serial that I watched all the time. I can even remember the names.

When, and why, did you join the Lafayette Flying Corps?

I wanted to fly, and the only way to fly was to join the Lafayette Flying Corps. Finally, through one of my uncles Francis L. Wellman, who wrote *The Art of Cross-Examination*, I got into the Flying Corps at age nineteen or twenty.

I'm very proud of it. I think we were the first group of Americans who volunteered before America was in the war. We volunteered and made history, and I'm proud of it. I really am. The French and the United States governments wanted to get together a flying unit. The French hoped that it would bring the Americans in, and the Americans wanted to do something to help. So William K. Vanderbilt formed the Lafayette Flying Corps, and out of it came a certain group of young guys like myself, Tom Hitchcock, David Putnam, Frank Baylies, George Mosely, the ex-All-American Yale end, and Blumenthal, the ex-Princeton center.

They were a wonderful group of boys. I think the average age among us was nineteen or twenty. The youngest of us all was Tom Hitchcock; he was seventeen. He was the only one that I remember who really and truly thought that America should be in the war, and that was his reason for joining. My reason was because it was the farthest place from Newton, and because I wanted to learn how to fly. Tom was killed during World War II. He had his own group, and he was just about to take them to the front. They were doing one last maneuver, a power dive, and he never came out of it. He was too old. He never should have done that dive. He went right into the ground.

How did you meet Douglas Fairbanks?

I was a very fine hockey player as a youth, and he was playing in a thing called *Hawthorne of the USA* at the Colonial Theater, with Phoebe Foster and Fred Stone. He used to come down and watch us play at the Boston Arena. The hockey team was different then. It had seven players, instead of six as it does now. There was the goalie, the point, the cover point, two wings, the center, and a rover. The rover was the fastest skater and the dirtiest player. I was the rover.

So Fairbanks was intrigued by me, and he invited me over to meet him and his group at their box. He asked me to go backstage, which I did, though I didn't even know what backstage meant. And we became very dear friends.

Then, when I got into the Lafayette Flying Corps—you know how, pardon me for saying this, newspapers tend to exaggerate things—you would have thought I won the war. He sent me a cablegram which I still have in my safety deposit box, saying that, "When it's all over, you'll always have a job."

At that time, the government wanted two veterans to get out of the French corps—the French let them do it—and join the American Air Corps. I was one of them; Doug Campbell was the other. Campbell chose Mineola, and I chose North Island [in San Diego] to teach pursuit, and all kinds of fighting maneuvers. So from North Island I used to fly up on weekends and land on Doug Fairbanks's polo field. It was there that I met everybody. I met Charlie Chaplin and, of course, his wife; Mary Pickford, Pola Negri, Wallace Reid—you can name them all, everybody. And that was the start of it.

Then, after the war, he made me an actor, so called, in *The Knickerbocker Buckaroo*. I saw myself and it made me sick. I went to him and I said, "Look, I don't want to speak disrespectfully of acting, but I'm a lousy actor." He said, "What do you want to be?" I said, "I want to be a director."

So he got me a job as a messenger boy at the old Goldwyn Studios, and I worked my way up from that to everything. I was an assistant cutter—thank God, for that's where you really learn—an assistant property man, assistant director, and eventually a director. I made one picture called *The Boob* which I'm very proud of. In it was a girl who was the star called Lucille Le Sueur. When Mr. Goldwyn and all of the other Napoleons of the studio—of course, I hate producers; they didn't like me but I made money for them so I still worked for them—when they saw the picture, they fired me because it was so bad. They changed her name from Lucille Le Sueur to Joan Crawford. So I enjoy the distinction, which I'm very proud of, of having made the lousiest picture Joan Crawford ever made.

Incidentally, wherever I've been, I always start by telling the audience that I've made lousy pictures, and I'm the only director that does that. [William] Wyler and [Frank] Capra and all the others—even Jack Ford—they all talk about their successes. The only other one that does what I do is Raoul Walsh, whom I'm crazy about. He's my favorite because he's the same kind of a guy. They asked him once, when we did *The Men Who Made the Movies*, how do you make a picture? He said, "I get a story that I like and I make a picture." That's the way he makes a picture. People ask me how to direct. I can't tell anyone how to direct. You can ask [George] Cukor and he'll tell you from now to doomsday. Or Frank Capra can tell you, or a lot of other guys can tell you. Howard Hawks can tell you. I can't. I don't know how.

What films influenced you when you first began directing?

I must have seen *The Big Parade*—and I was broke—some twenty-odd times. Not to copy King Vidor, just to learn. Then I'd go home and try to be a better director than Vidor, though I never succeeded.

That one I loved, and I like to see good pictures nowadays, but they've got to be good. What's the one I just saw? It's an odd name. The star played in *Midnight Cowboy*. *Conrack*. Did you see it? Did you love it? I did, and I loved the other one: *Sounder*. That's one of my favorite pictures. Jesus, I would have loved to hear someone say, "Do you know who directed that? Wellman did." That scene where she ran and ran to meet that poor guy on those crutches . . . goddam, boy, I tell you, I cried all the way down.

Naturally, I loved *The Sound of Music*. I loved *Patton*. I loved *Love Story*. I loved *The Sting* because George Roy Hill is a very dear friend of mine. And I loved his first one much more than I did *The Sting: Butch Cassidy and the Sundance Kid*. I think *Butch Cassidy* is a much better picture than *The Sting* and I told him that.

But I don't go and see these other kinds of pictures, these *Deep Throat* things or any of that sort . . . I'm not interested in them. I tell you, frankly, it's going to end, whatever it is, and I'll tell you why. It's going to end because I think that the gals are going to suddenly realize that they are being made suckers out of, which they are. When they get angry, which they're going to, the whole thing is going to change.

When anyone asks me what's wrong with the business today, I say where are the [Gary] Coopers, where are all the wonderful stars that we had? There are none of them, and that's what's wrong with the business.

You know where they found Cooper? He was driving a bus in Yellowstone Park, and one of these wonderful guys spotted him. He had funny little mannerisms, and they hired him. His first picture was a western with Ronald Colman. [*The Winning of Barbara Worth*, 1926]. Then he did *Wings* and I gave him his first starring role there. He was nineteen. I kept him down in San Antonio on location for nine months because I was very fond of him. He was a wonderful guy.

His big scene [in *Wings*] was where he said goodbye to Buddy Rogers and Richard Arlen, who were a couple of kids. He forgot his talisman, which he always carried, and it was on the bed. No one knew about it except the audience. He used that wonderful smile that he had, that wonderful—it was just—well, stardom just stuck out of his face. It hit you. It's indescribable. And then he also did something with his nose.

He came to my suite that night, and all the other actors were gone. I had nothing left but the dogfight and I was waiting for clouds. And he came up to my suite and he said—he called me Mr. Wellman—"Mr. Wellman, couldn't I please do that all over again? You're not paying me anything. I'm getting very little." I said, "Look, Coop, you're the only one that could get away with this. Anyone else would try it, I would throw them right out of my suite. Just for fun, tell me what is it you didn't like."

Now—you can't use lousy language in your interview but I'll tell it the way I said it—I said, "Now, what did you do that was wrong?" He said, "Well, I picked my nose in the middle of the scene." I said, "You just keep right on picking your nose, and you'll pick your nose into a fortune. Always back away." Which is what he did. Jimmy Stewart became the second nose-picker—not quite as good as Cooper but an awful good one. Now that means nothing other than that was just his odd way. Very natural, and he became one of our biggest stars.

Frankly—this is a silly thing—the thing that makes stars is something they're born with. No one ever acquired it. For instance, who's our big stars today? Bogie, he's dead and he's one of our biggest stars. [John] Wayne, of course, but he's so old that he's beginning to have trouble. Where are the Coopers, where are the Colmans, where are the [James] Cagneys, where are all those women?

Have you ever tried to think of all the women that we had at one time—the Norma Shearers, the Greta Garbos—oh God, all right—the Marilyn Monroes? Who do we got now? Barbra Streisand, the girl that sings so beautifully, but she is hardly in their class as far as I am concerned, though I'm not speaking disrespectfully of her. She has a magnificent voice and I love to hear her sing.

But those women had something about them that was natural. A guy in the audience looks up and says, "Oh, Jesus, I'd love to have that." That's what it is. A certain appeal, certain sex about them without throwing it at you. It was just there.

We haven't been able to see Beggars of Life, *your first talking picture. Did you have difficulty adapting to sound?*

Beggars of Life is the best silent picture I made in my life, and we can't find it anywhere. It was written by Jim Tully, and it was a beautiful picture. Silent. It had the first sound in it because Wallace Beery sang a song. That's all.

There wasn't any difference between silents and sound. Some directors couldn't do sound, and I could do anything. What the hell! Look, all I wanted to do was to cut down the dialogue so that I wouldn't be making a stage play. So I cut down dialogue and rewrote it as a motion picture so that you could see something that was beautiful.

The producers called us in and said that there are three stage directors who are going to take part in all of your pictures, sharing the whole thing, moneywise and everything else. George Cukor, John Cromwell, and George Abbott. Abbott was the best of them all, stagewise, and he never could make a picture. Cukor has been very successful with gals, with ladies' pictures, nothing else. And Cromwell was all right until he became political.

Anyway, all of the directors [at Paramount] sort of sunk down in their chairs but I got up and I said to the guy that was running the studio, "There's something that you have forgotten. I have a seven-year contract, and there isn't one thing in it that says I have to use a stage director. And I won't use one. If one comes on my set, I'll kick the hell out of him." I got away with it. Later on, they said, "Do you mind if they come to sit on your set?" I said, "Not if I can see them, and I have twenty-twenty eyesight." So I stayed away from them, but some of these poor guys had to suffer with them.

So that was my experience. If anyone else could make a picture, I could make it, and I didn't need some goddam stage director telling me how to talk. Of course, talking on the stage is entirely different. In pictures, you talk the way you and I talk. That's the way I always talked.

How did you get involved with **The Public Enemy?**

You know the story of Jimmy Cagney, don't you? In *The Public Enemy*, Eddie Woods was playing the featured role. Jimmy was the second man. Oh, it's a terribly long story to tell.

A couple of druggists [Kubec Glasmon and John Bright] met me on the lot when I was going to lunch. They had a book called *Beer and Blood*, and they asked me if I would read it. Well, I asked them to lunch. They seemed like very nice guys. They came to lunch and, boy, I'll tell you, they stayed to lunch for a very long time. I liked *Beer and Blood* because it was an odd couple of things. I read it and loved it, and I took it to Darryl Zanuck immediately and he read it that night. That's when he was really working—when he was working, he was great. The next day he called me up and I went over to his office and he said, "Tell me why I should make it." He had just made *Little Caesar* and *Doorway to Hell*. But this mixture of *Beer and Blood* intrigued me. It was fantastic, so I told him that I could make it the toughest picture of its kind. He said okay, go ahead. So we did. We got it all ready.

He went to New York. I worked Thursday, Friday, and Saturday. Those days, we worked Monday, Tuesday, Wednesday, Thursday, Friday, and Saturday, *plus* Saturday night. It was wonderful—no one interfered, no unions, no nothing. It was great; you were used to it. Then when you got through with a picture you took it easy for a few weeks, and then you went to work again.

Anyway, I shot for three days, and then on Sunday, with my head cutter, I saw all the stuff that I had taken those three days. Something was wrong, and I realized it. I asked him to get another reel that Eddie Woods and Cagney were together in, and I realized that I had the wrong man in the wrong part. So I called up Zanuck, who was in New York, and told him, and he said, "Make the switch." So I put Cagney in the main part and Eddie Woods played his pal. Cagney became a great star, and I'm a lousy motion picture director—but that's between the two of us.

Who thought of Cagney's famous grapefruit sequence? We have read that it was inspired by your anger at your wife at the time.

That's right. I almost did it to her but I didn't, and the next day the scene came up, so I did it in the scene. I changed it. The scene read that he threw half a grapefruit at her, and instead of doing that, I had him squash it in her face. Not a very exquisite thing to do. And it became legendary. I don't know why, I guess it is. Zanuck claimed that he thought of it, but I answer him in my next book. He's a goddamn liar. I print the page from the script the way it was written. I have forgotten who it was who wrote that he threw the grapefruit at her—I imagine it was either one of the two guys that wrote the story or the guy [Harvey Thew] who wrote the script. I've forgotten which, but I know it wasn't Zanuck. And it wasn't me. But I did do the other thing.

Did you supervise your own editing in those days?

I made a picture so that you didn't have to worry about how to cut it, because you could only cut it one way. Cagney said to me, when we had our fortieth wedding anniversary back in Southern California—Jim and his wife, Bill, came to the party—he said, "Bill, do you remember how long it took you to make *Public Enemy?*" I said, "No, I don't." He said, "Seventeen days." I guess I said, "Are you sure?" He said, "Yes, sir." So I guess Jim must have kept track of it. It took us seventeen days and nights.

I had one trick. I always rehearsed. I had a rehearsal, a real rehearsal—positions, dialogue, and everything else. Then I had a camera rehearsal so that the actors would know. Then when the camera rehearsal was all over, I said, "Okay now, that's fine, now what was wrong, what you do think, what do you think, what do you think? All right, let's do it again. Once more." So we did it once more. And I threw that take away, and I used the camera rehearsal, because the camera rehearsal had a spontaneity about it that you couldn't get if you did it a million times. I couldn't.

And the actors never knew. If you made mistakes, you could go in and take another angle. It's very easy if you knew what you were doing.

Did you have a lot of leeway choosing scripts at Warners?

To a certain extent. They had a great story department, and Zanuck always knew what the best story would be for me or Lloyd Bacon, or for whoever his directors were. They bought all the best things and they would say, "Jesus, that's good for Wellman," and they'd give it to me and it really was good for Wellman. Zanuck was the guy who did all of the choosing, but if you got ideas, such as I did with *Beer and Blood*, well, he let me do it. He was a very fair and a very bright guy. For instance, Ruth Chatterton could never get along with any director, and I had had trouble getting along with any star. So he put the two of us together and we made a couple of very successful pictures. One of them was called *Frisco Jenny*; it's about a very famous San Francisco madam. You never had to reject scripts. Warners had such a beautiful story department.

What kind of stories appealed to you the most?

I don't think the kind of stories mattered, but who was in it and how it finished. For instance, *A Star Is Born*, which I wrote, I loved it. I wrote it from memory; it is about John Bowers mainly, because he had a voice which was not good when pictures started to talk.* The same thing happened to Jack Gilbert—they both killed themselves because of it. There are so many tragedies in the picture business.

---

*After talking pictures came in and his career faded, handsome silent-screen star John Bowers became an alcoholic, and in 1936 he committed suicide by drowning. His life and death were part of the inspiration for the original *A Star Is Born* and subsequent remakes.

Did you always work closely with your scriptwriters?

I worked with a writer, and when the script was all finished, I had an agreement with the studio that I could take an extra week and get all these wonderful writers to cut dialogue. We'd make a game out of it. It was wonderful. Seven or eight-line speeches would come down to one or two lines. So it gave me a chance to still make a motion picture. They didn't mind—all of them, Ben Hecht or any of them. They understood perfectly because I said we've still got to make a motion picture.

Usually, I changed nothing. I didn't have to; it was all so well written. I had beautiful writers. How can you write better than Ben Hecht? Producers thought they could write better than God. I hate them. I remember I had one story that I was crazy about. Ernie Gann wrote it. He is one of the finest writers that I've ever met. We did *The High and the Mighty* together. It was his story and he wanted to change it. He thought he could improve it. We almost had fistfights because I said, "Look, I won't let you change one bloody thing. It's what I want, it's the way you wrote it." He's thankful right now. We did it the way the story was. The only addition that I put in was a young kid character, who happened to be played by my youngest son [Michael Wellman]. I wanted a young kid to come out with that Mae West jacket on him. He had a wonderful time and a great experience that he'll remember the rest of his life, and it gave me something to play against, because it was pretty rugged doing all that in that enclosure of the airplane with those different groups.

What was your relationship with Jack Warner? We understand he changed the ending of Wild Boys of the Road. We love that film, but the ending seems so different from the rest of the film.

The ending of *Wild Boys*! Actually, it never did end. Jack Warner is one of the most despicable men I've ever known in my life. You can print that anytime you want to. I hate him. He changed it. It was sickening. The poor judge looking at his son and . . . it was supposed to be a sad ending, really. They all were supposed to go to the place where they were keeping all the kids, and all that sort of stuff. It was a sad ending.

He changed that just as he changed *Lafayette Escadrille*, and I got out of the business. Because it was never called *Lafayette Escadrille*. "C'est la Guerre," that was the story, and it was a beautiful story. He changed that and made that into a happy ending and I said, "Oh, the hell with it." I got out and I've never made a picture since.

Did he interfere with any of your other pictures?

No, those were the only two. Jack Warner interfered only on a few occasions, and unfortunately, there were a couple of them that were mine. He didn't like me. He's supposed to say very funny things and he asked me once, "Why don't you laugh at some of my jokes?" I said, "Because I haven't heard one that was funny yet." Which was true, I hadn't. He had a whole bunch of laughers with him, guys that would follow him and they'd roar. They didn't even hear what the hell his *bon mots* were anyway, and they would laugh. I didn't like him, but he had sense enough to have Zanuck and [Hal] Wallis. Those two gentlemen produced all of his pictures. I was a Zanuck director, and there were others who were Wallis directors.

Your wife, Dorothy Coonan, plays one of the lead roles in Wild Boys of the Road, doesn't she?

You remember the little girl in *Wild Boys of the Road?* Well, that's Dottie, of course. She's great but she hated it. She was a beautiful dancer, one of the leading dancers in the Busby Berkeley group, and I had had the toughest time in the world to get her to marry me.

Then, when she finally did—she was nineteen and I was in my late thirties—I realized I had something that was all mine. There was a great mystery about her and there still is. We've been married for forty-one years, and I'm scared to death of her. She's the only woman I've ever been afraid of—I say this nicely but I am—and I idolize her.

We had tough times, too, of course, because I was drinking then. I went on the wagon once for ten years, but then I came home drunk. We were living in Berklee Heights in a house that sort of went down. The bedrooms were on the second floor, the playroom was on the third. I came home and she said, "How are you, darling?" and I rolled all the way down the stairs. I went off the wagon, but not for too long. But it's pretty bad when I do.

Dottie housebroke me and saved my life. She gave me seven kids. Not only that, but she gave me girl, boy, girl, boy, girl, boy, girl. She called her shots. They all idolize her, too. We have twelve grandchildren, and another one coming.

How did you become involved with The President Vanishes?

[Producer] Walter Wanger was a very dear friend of mine. He said, "I have a story that is very unusual and would you read it?" I read it, I liked it, and I did it. Well, it was political, true, but I didn't do many political pictures. I loved all the old guys that were in it; I had no star. It was wonderful. It was also Rosalind Russell's first film. Jesus, she was beautiful then. I saw it at this retrospective my son organized in Los Angeles. It's all cut up now; you can hardly recognize it. They've taken bits and pieces out of it, it's just unbelievable.

You directed two films for David O. Selznick, A Star Is Born and Nothing Sacred. What was your relationship with him?

I answer *Memo from David O. Selznick* in my next book. David Selznick's memos were completely different than the relationship we had together. I never found out about his point of view until he died and I read his memos. He said a lot of things and I answer every single one. He didn't like directors, so I was probably the only director who made a couple of pictures for him without having some other director come in. I made *A Star Is Born*, which I also wrote, and *Nothing Sacred* with [Carole] Lombard. He used to have all these memos coming down every morning, none of which I ever read. I threw them in the trash can, but it gradually gets on your nerves, you know. I said, "Oh God, one of these days I'm going to go out of my head."

Myron Selznick, his brother, was my agent, you know. He was the king of them all and he had it in my contract that David could only come down on my set a certain number of times. I don't know how many they were but, of course, he didn't live up to it. He would never interfere; he would just sit there and look. But I had odd ways of spoiling his time when he was there. Any producer coming down and watching a director work I think is crazy.

You began to produce your own pictures, beginning with Men with Wings?

Yes. I was producing and directing then. I produced and directed *Beau Geste*. I produced and directed eight pictures, including *The High and the Mighty* and *Island in the Sky*. Then, suddenly, I realized that producing's not for me. I didn't ever want to do it again. It's too much work. It's not fun; all of the fun went out of the bloody thing because I was the producer. I hate producing. Being honest, producing is taking care of the financial end, nothing else, and I suddenly realized that making deals with actors and then trying to direct them was an impossibility. So I went to the studio then and I said, "Cut the producing clause out of my contract, I'm going to be a director from now on." But I wanted to be sure that I worked for the producers I liked, which I did. I just didn't have brains enough to do both things.

Who were your favorite actresses to work with?

To tell the truth, none of the girls wanted to work with me. None of them, because I wouldn't let them wear makeup. They'd say to me, "Well, what do you want me to do?" I'd say, "Make up the way you would if you were going to go out and have lunch." They'd say,

"What about the lines in my face?" I'd say, "That's what I want. I don't want to photograph a statue. I want to photograph something with some character."

[Barbara] Stanwyck and Loretta [Young] and [Carole] Lombard were great. But, of course, you could photograph Lombard or Loretta with nothing, for God's sakes, nothing—they were so beautiful. Especially Lombard. Lombard had had an automobile accident and one of the sides of her face was hurt, but I could still photograph it. And Stanwyck, of course, was a brilliant actress. She could do anything. I did five pictures with her.

What about Ida Lupino?

Oh, I loved her. Well, I brought her into the business. Actually, she found me. She broke into my office, I didn't even know who the hell she was, and she said, "I want to play [the part of] Bessie and will you play Colman?" "No," I said, "I can't play Colman but I'll do the best I can." We played that big scene [from *The Light That Failed*], and she played a scene in my office like I had never seen in my whole life. So I took her to the head of the studio, to [B. P.] Schulberg, and said, "She's Bessie."

Mr. Colman had different ideas. He wanted someone else. So he brought his gal in to Mr. Schulberg. I said, "Look, I don't give a damn." I didn't; Colman didn't like me. I said, "If you use Colman's girl, then you can get yourself another director." I was under contract to them, and Mr. Schulberg told Mr. Colman, "Mr. Colman, Mr. Wellman has done some very fine pictures for us, and he's going to do this picture. If you don't want to do it, I'll sue you." So that quieted him down, but he never forgave me for it. It was always "Mr. Wellman," "Mr. Colman." So Schulberg straightened it all out, Lupino played the part, and it made her a star. She is a magnificent actress.

Since I'm talking about this, I was telling you about this retrospective in Los Angeles recently that my oldest boy arranged. One of the pictures he showed was the Colman picture, *The Light That Failed*. Tom Laughlin of *Billy Jack* helped finance it; he's a very dear friend of mine. So, anyway, I hadn't seen this picture for thirty-five years. I couldn't look at it because Colman was in it. Finally, I looked at it again, and, I'm being very egotistical, I'm not ashamed of it at all. It's a helluva picture; it really is. He's great and [Walter] Huston's great and Dudley Digges is great and Ida Lupino is fantastic, and I did a helluva job.

Who were your favorite actors to work with?

You must remember, I'm not a very lovable sort of guy, I'm not. But I did love Bob Taylor. He only did two pictures with me—*Small Town Girl* in 1936 and then twenty-five years later we did *Westward the Women*. Bob was wonderful, though I missed on the picture. And I'm crazy about Joel McCrea, one of the nicest guys I've ever known. Bob Taylor, Joel McCrea, Cagney—though I only made one picture with him, and that was his starring picture.* But that's Hollywood. Hollywood isn't as big as a picture as you think it is. Strangely enough, you can know people in Hollywood and never see them.

[Clark] Gable and I did three pictures together. We had a row, though; I think it was in the middle of *Call of the Wild*. For reasons I don't care to mention. I called him for it, which I shouldn't have done, in front of my company. But, you see, I was always at an advantage with an actor because an actor makes his living with his face. I don't; I'm behind the camera. He was a bigger man than I am, but I'd had a pretty rugged boyhood. Gable's face might have turned out a little different. I might have ended up in the hospital, though I doubt it. He would end like a character man. So it was one of those things. I was going to hit him if it got to that point. I had a frightful temper, and if it got to a point like that, yes.

I hated [Spencer] Tracy. We just didn't like each other, that's all. He was the kind of a guy who, when he got loaded, he didn't get high, he got terribly low. Well, you know his whole history. He and I just didn't like each other. We had a lot of fistfights and I always beat him because he'd start talking and I didn't talk, I hit. The one thing you learn when you fight, you better do your hitting right off the bat. We just didn't like each other. I did one picture

---

*Actually, Cagney also had a small part in Wellman's *Other Men's Women/The Steel Highway*, made in 1931, before *The Public Enemy*.

with him, long ago. I can't even remember the name of it [*Looking for Trouble*, 1934].

Didn't you work frequently with Richard Arlen, when you were at Paramount?

I only made a few pictures with Arlen. I was too tough with Arlen. He went to the big producer and said, "I won't work with Wellman anymore." They called me in and told me that and I said, "Well, that's an easy answer, I won't work with him anymore." Which I didn't. I could have used him in a lot of other pictures too. He faded pretty quickly.

I was a rough guy to deal with, and the actors and actresses knew what they were up against when they took the job. They knew, with me, they were going to be directed by me.

Who is George Chandler, who is in so many of your pictures?

George is my friend, the only real friend I have. I've got some few nice acquaintances, some medium acquaintances, some acquaintances that don't like me, but I'm talking about friends. Sometimes at night, especially at night, when you can't sleep and everyone else is asleep and it's quiet, just try to figure out how many friends you have. Now by friends I mean someone who would do anything in the world to help you, give you anything, do anything. I bet you can't think of more than one. If you can, you're a superman. I got one. I had two. Of course, I had a group of friends, all fliers in the Lafayette Flying Corps, but they're all dead. George Chandler is the only friend that is alive.

He played in thirty-six of my pictures. If I got a little screwed up—I had a reputation of always knowing what I was going to do, which is not true—if I got a little screwed up every once and a while, I signaled him. He'd do something to upset everything. Then I'd ball the hell out of him and call a ten-minute coffee break. I'd go into my little office and work it out. I'd come out and it would be all done. He was that kind of a friend, a wonderful guy.

How would you describe your visual style?

Composition was my great faith. Composition. Jack Ford and I started dilly-dallying about, moving cameras all around. Then we got loaded together one night and he said, "Do you know? We're a couple of goddam fools." I said, "Why?" He said, "Because we're moving these cameras around. My wife heard someone in an audience saying, 'Why did Ford move the camera . . . ?' " And he was right. The camera movements started to get so tricky and everything else that the audience was looking at the wonderful camera movement. They forget that there was a story or what it is about. So we never did it again. We went right back to just lovely composition. Wonderful composition, that's all.

Of all the cameramen you worked with, which was the best?

My son Bill and I once tried to figure out how many cameramen I had in close to a hundred pictures. A lot of them are lost, you know. Most of the pictures I made with Dustin Farnum are gone, and all but twelve of the pictures with Buck Jones are gone, so it's pretty hard to tell just how many I did. But it's close to a hundred, one way or another. We tried to figure out how many cameramen I had in all those pictures, and we figured twelve. I can't tell you who was the best, it's awfully hard to say. I wouldn't want you to print it because they were all so great. In *Wings*, Burton Steene was the big man. He died in my arms later on when we were doing a dolly shot back at the studio with Clara Bow. He fell back into my arms, dead. He was the greatest aerial photographer then. Bill Clothier was the next best. I took Bill out of the air, made him my cameraman, and made him sign a paper that I drew up legally which said he would never fly in the air again—because those guys were apt to kill themselves. They were all wonderful but they were just goofy.

Did you ever do any of your own aerial photography?

No. The last time I flew a plane was in *Wings*. I had a trick flier who couldn't turn a Fokker over. Well, that's the simplest thing in the world, because in the first place, you get rid of all the gas. You just have enough gas so you can circle and get your height and come down and then turn it over. So there's no danger of fire or anything of that sort. You're strapped in and if you know how to do it, you can loop it a couple of times. He couldn't do it. So I went up and did that, and that was the last time I've ever flown.

Wild Boys of the Road *seems to be very left-wing, while a film like* **The Iron Curtain** *seems almost right-wing in comparison. What are your politics?*

I can answer that by a little quip. I did a picture called *The Ox-Bow Incident* and another picture called *The Iron Curtain*. In *The Ox-Bow Incident*, I was accused of being on the left. In *The Iron Curtain*, I was accused of being on the right. I don't care what it is, my politics are the screwed-up politics of the world. I vote for the guy I think is the right man, I don't care what he is. I loved Eisenhower. I did the last twenty-two minutes of the incandescent lamp show with him.* I played golf with the man, and I was crazy about him. He may not have been a great president but he was a great leader. I've forgotten now whether he was Republican or Democrat, and I don't give a damn. He was a great leader, and I wish to God we had one right now that was not a politician. I hate politicians.

---

* Wellman is referring to *Light's Diamond Jubilee*, an all-star variety program on the seventy-fifth anniversary of the invention of the lightbulb broadcast on television in 1954. Wellman directed the sequence featuring President Eisenhower. The show was produced by David O. Selznick.

Isn't The Iron Curtain *what might be called a "political message" picture?*

Oh, *The Iron Curtain* wasn't a message picture. I had nothing to do with it politically. I just felt that it was a lovely story, and since it was a beautiful story I agreed to do it. Really, I'm being very honest. I'm not trying to avoid anything.

I'm very proud of what happened to *The Iron Curtain*. It's the greatest thing that's ever happened to me in my whole lifetime. They won't allow a Wellman picture in Russia. There's not a Wellman picture in Russia, nor will there ever be one, because of *The Iron Curtain*. Yes, I'm very proud of it because I don't like the Russians.

The picture was considered very important at the time, wasn't it? It was one of Hollywood's first Cold War pictures?

I don't know. All I know is that we had a helluva tough time doing it. I did it in Canada somewhere, and they ran a car into one of my assistant cameramen. He broke his leg. They didn't get me, but they damn near did. It was exciting, because I was young then.

Who are "they"?

The Communists.

Soviet agents in Canada? The KGB?

I don't know who the hell they were. I only know they didn't like me because I represented something else. I know we're having trouble here [in the U.S.], but, God almighty, if you think it's tough here, we're sitting easy compared to what it is in other countries.

Were you involved at all with the House Committee on Un-American Activities during the 1950s?

No, because they knew very well what a screwball I was. Look, I'll be very honest with you. I cry when I see the American flag. I still do. I love this country.

Were you influenced by any particular authors? Ernest Hemingway? Jack London?

No. I never read anything but [sports columnist] Jim Murray—do you know he is?—of the *Los Angeles Times*. I read him all the time. And I read [political columnist] Joseph Alsop, who just died recently. That's all I ever read. I never read—they accused me on *Yellow Sky* of doing what?—something by Shakespeare. One of my friends in England wrote and told me that the criticisms said it resembled something of Shakespeare's. *The Tempest!* Hell, I've never read *The Tempest!* I have never read Shakespeare. I never read fiction. I just read the things that I was going to make pictures out of, or the stories that I wanted to do. You're talking to a screwball.

You wrote your book, A Short Time for Insanity, while you were in the hospital for back surgery over ten years ago?

I wrote it all when I was under sedation. Green Hornets—a combination of various dopes. I was really having a rugged time. Under those conditions, I would think of things that I never would think of under ordinary conditions. My thoughts were never finished, and they were never in continuity. I decided that I would write everything down, not to publish, but just to have eight books made, seven for my kids and one for my lovely wife. Then Ernie Gann—he was a great flier and a great friend of mine—we did *Island in the Sky* besides *The High and the Mighty*—well, Ernie Gann read it and he said, "You're crazy, put it out." So I put it out.

A lot of critics have said that they liked it but that I should write an autobiography. I can't write an autobiography. I think autobiographies are the most boring things in the world. They want me to start telling all about the pictures I made with Dustin Farnum. Who the hell gives a damn about Dustin Farnum or Buck Jones or any of that sort of stuff? I just wouldn't know how to write an autobiography. The book that I am doing and finishing now is really and truly much worse than the first one. It's screwy completely.

This new one will be called *Growing Old Disgracefully*. I'm retired, you know, and I made so many pictures that I sometimes think maybe I might have made a very bad mistake in not doing more writing and reading. But then I think, if I had done more reading, I wouldn't have made as many pictures as I did. I wanted to make every kind of picture that was ever made. And I have. So I have decided, to hell with it. I'm glad I didn't do any more reading.

I have just finished the finish of my second book. I tried to get a finish something like Ben Hecht's in *Gaily, Gaily*, but it's not as good as Ben's.

[reading]

"Do I remember all the past as it really was? No. I remember it as one remembers seeing from the air a packed stadium without seeing its faces, as one remembers snatches of love, not sure of the names of whom they were with. To the memory of those I loved and flew with. Some of the words were theirs, most were mine, but they were still a part of those ghostly figures of my past that I can never forget. I've made my living by making motion pictures, by reading the stories written by fine authors, and eventually, I was to transpose them into a movie of success, to be seen and enjoyed by millions. Despite the beauty of the words, there was a very necessary ingredient to be added: imagination. Especially in the manner of the action those words suggested. To one director his way, to me my way. It was the foundation of a style formed by the repetition of a hundred pictures, all completely different in content and spoken and acted by hundreds of actors and actresses, and written by at least a few hundred authors and scriptwriters. I digested many of their styles, their humor, their tragedy, their actor-like utterances, but not necessarily their ideas. As a matter of fact, I always looked on many of my writer friends, such as Gene Fowler and Ben Hecht and the delightfully quiet Lamar Trotti, as superb actors. They performed in their writing. They gave me a style all my own, good or bad, usual or unusual, and they are a part of it."

I'm a screwball, you know. I always write the front first, and then the end of it.

Do you have a favorite film?

The Story of G.I. Joe. Ernie Pyle's *G.I. Joe.* I think it was the best picture I ever made. I loved Ernie. One hundred and fifty of those kids worked for me and they all—this is a sad story—they all went to the South Pacific. Ernie went to the South Pacific too, and none of them ever came back. It's kind of terrifying, because all of these kids I grew to know and like. I got them extra money and everything else, then suddenly it was all over. Even Ernie didn't see his picture. I didn't want to do the picture, you know; I myself hate the infantry.

How did you get involved with Robert Riskin and Magic Town?

Robert Riskin was Frank Capra's partner. When they were together, Bob wrote and Frank directed, and their pictures were the best pictures either of them ever made. They had an argument of some sort and they split up. That was a shame, because neither one of them ever became as good, really, as they were when they were working together. So Bob Riskin came to me and said, "I want you to do *Magic Town.*" I said, "Well, let me read it." I read it and I said, "Look, Bob, this is Capra's story, not mine. I don't know how to do this thing. I'm not interested in it." Well, he talked to me and begged me and said, "I'll help you." I said, "Oh, I don't want any help. It's just not the type of story that I would do." You know that because I've never made anything like it but that one. Well, anyway, he talked me into it. I did it because I was very fond of Bob Riskin, and I did the best job I could. I don't think it was a very good picture.

It was like this. [so-so gesture] Well, I don't like pictures like that. Either they should be that way or this way, one or the other. I did the best I could but it wasn't my type of picture. Frank would have pinned my ear down if he had done it. But I did much better than he could have with some of the pictures that I made. He couldn't do all the type that I did. For instance, I don't think he could make *The Ox-Bow Incident* as well as I could. I really don't.

How did you end up directing The Next Voice You Hear? *It's such an unusual story.*

I was under contract to Dore Schary, who ran the studio [MGM]. We did *Battleground,* and then he wanted me to do this one. I said, "I don't want to do it because it's got a message; I don't like those goddamn things." But [Eddie] Mannix, who was the production manager, said, "I'll bet you ten thousand dollars that you can't make a picture in two weeks at MGM." I said, "Okay, you've got yourself a deal." I made that goddamn picture, and one day I got $10,000 under the table. It was worthwhile, one of the reasons why I made it.

Why did you team up with John Wayne's production company in the 1950s?

He wanted me and he paid for me. I made six pictures, three with him, one with [Robert] Mitchum and two others. I also made one of the best pictures that I've ever made in my whole life in 1956, though the public didn't agree with me. But to hell with them. *Goodbye, My Lady.* You've got to see it. Warner tried to change the title to "The Boy and the Talking Dog" or some silly thing. It was called *Goodbye, My Lady* and it was a beautiful picture. One of the best pictures I ever made, I loved it. It was the story of a kid [Brandon de Wilde] who had to give away his dog. That's all; it was that simple. It was also one of [Sidney] Poitier's first pictures. He had a good part in it, a wonderful guy.

What is the common element in every William Wellman picture, whether it is a comedy or drama or western?

Jesus, that's a tough question to answer for a dummy. Tempo.

Rhythm?

Well, that's one word. I call it tempo. Tempo is the word, tempo. My pictures didn't lag very much. If they were bad, they got over very quickly, I'll tell you that. Tempo. Because sometimes, with some directors, well, people talk and they talk and they talk so slowly. They say things over and over again, they are so repetitive. It's awfully hard to listen to. Just tempo. I think that's what it would be, I really do.

How do you rate yourself as a director? Were you influenced by other directors?

No. Jack Ford maybe, because Jack and I were very dear friends. Someone once asked Jack who's the best director. This was just before he died—I was with him when he died—and he said, "Bill Wellman's the best—but next to me!" Which I'm not. Jack Ford was the best, with no exception. He was the best because when you suddenly realize it, Wyler was a great director but he did all women's pictures. Frank Capra is a great director but he did all the political sort of pictures. Goddam Ford could do anything, and I could do anything. I've done kid pictures, musicals, mysteries—the whole bloody mess. It's wonderful. Now some of them were pretty bad . . . but, anyway, when I did quit, at least I could sit back and say that I had accomplished what I wanted. I had made every type of picture. And I'm very proud of that. That's what I wanted to do.

On the set of Family Plot

12. Interview with Alfred Hitchcock

Universal Studios, June 1976

by Patrick McGilligan

ALFRED HITCHCOCK

(1899–1980)

1922   *Number Thirteen/Mrs. Peabody.*
        (unfinished, two-reeler). Director,
        Producer.

1923   *Always Tell Your Wife.* Codirector
        (with Seymour Hicks).
        Woman to Woman. Art director,
        coscript, assistant director.
        The White Shadow. Art director,
        coscript, assistant director.

1924   *The Passionate Adventure.* Art
        director, coscript, assistant director.

1925   *The Blackguard.* Art director, script,
        assistant director.
        The Prude's Fall. Art director, script,
        assistant director.
        The Pleasure Garden (U.K./Ger.).
        Director.

1926   *The Mountain Eagle/Fear o' God*
        (U.K./Ger.). Director.
        *The Lodger/The Case of Jonathan
        Drew.* Director.

1927   *Downhill/When Boys Leave Home.*
        Director.

Easy Virtue. Director.
The Ring. Story, script, director.

1928   *The Farmer's Wife.* Coscript, director.
        Champagne. Coscript, director.

1929   *The Manxman.* Director.
        Blackmail. Adaptation, director.

1930   *Elstree Calling.* Codirector (with
        Andre Charlot, Jack Hulbert, and
        Paul Murray).
        Juno and the Paycock. Coscript,
        director.
        Murder. Coscript, director.
        Mary/Sir John greift ein! (German-
        language version). Coscript, director.
        An Elastic Affair (short). Director.

1931   *The Skin Game.* Coscript, director.

1932   *Rich and Strange/East of Shanghai.*
        Adaptation, director.
        Number Seventeen. Coscript,
        director.

1933   *Waltzes from Vienna/Strauss's Great
        Waltz.* Director.

1934   *The Man Who Knew Too Much.*
        Director.

1935   *The 39 Steps.* Director.

1936	*The Secret Agent.* Director.		1949	*Under Capricorn.* Director, coproducer.
1937	*Sabotage/The Woman Alone.* Director.		1950	*Stage Fright.* Director, producer.
	Young and Innocent/The Girl Was Young. Director.		1951	*Strangers on a Train.* Director, producer.
1938	*The Lady Vanishes.* Director.		1953	*I Confess.* Director, producer.
1939	*Jamaica Inn.* Director.		1954	*Dial M for Murder.* Director, producer.
1940	*Rebecca.* Director.			*Rear Window.* Director, producer.
	Foreign Correspondent. Director.		1955	*To Catch a Thief.* Director, producer.
1941	*Mr. and Mrs. Smith.* Director.			*The Trouble with Harry.* Director, producer.
	Suspicion. Director.		1956	*The Man Who Knew Too Much* (remake). Director, producer.
1942	*Saboteur.* Story, director.		1957	*The Wrong Man.* Director, producer.
1943	*Shadow of a Doubt.* Director.		1958	*Vertigo.* Director, producer.
	Watchtower Over Tomorrow (Office of War Information documentary). Codirector.		1959	*North by Northwest.* Director, producer.
1944	*Lifeboat.* Story (uncredited), director.		1960	*Psycho.* Director, producer.
	Bon Voyage (four-reeler for British Ministry of Information). Director.		1963	*The Birds.* Director, producer.
	Aventure Malgache (for British Ministry of Information, never released). Director.		1964	*Marnie.* Director, producer.
			1966	*Torn Curtain.* Director, producer.
1945	*Spellbound.* Director.		1969	*Topaz.* Director, producer.
1946	*Notorious.* Story, director, producer.		1972	*Frenzy.* Director, producer.
1948	*The Paradine Case.* Director.		1976	*Family Plot.* Director, producer.
	Rope. Director, coproducer.			

 Hitch, as he likes to be called, always dresses in a navy blue or black suit, decorated by the thin red Legion of Honor ribbon. His assistants also dress severely, in respect, a strange formality in the Hollywood of today. His set evokes an Old World, not merely closed to visitors (as it is) but hermetically sealed, a throwback or capsule of time. Hitch dominates it by sheer presence, and by a mystique that visibly awes his crew. They eye him distantly, turn quiet when he approaches, call him "sir." Short, plump, his is the most famous profile in film. He bobs when he walks, like a sea-tossed buoy, and his bowling ball figure is, like his movies, at once scary and comic.

On a June day, between takes, a chauffeur waits to drive Alfred Hitchcock back to his bungalow, also on the Universal City lot. He will await the next call there. Or, if things are moving swiftly, he will sit inside his mobile van, just sit there, clasping fat, pink hands thoughtfully, his face impassive. The small room has a writing desk, pencils, a full-length mirror, three leather chairs, and a rolled copy of the Sunday *Times* and *Telegraph*. It is here, in this silence, that Alfred Hitchcock will endure the ordeal of filmmaking, which can last so very, very long in its delays.

His assistant director, young and harried, in suit and tie, appears to present a lineup of children for a Sunday school sequence the following day. Hitchcock himself looms in the doorway, solemnly and wordlessly inspecting the scrub-brushed kids whose mothers wait expectantly nearby. A few murmured words to his assistant, and two lucky girls and a boy are chosen. The director returns to his lair. His assistants are legion, devoted, constantly astir. They make many of the minor decisions during shooting, while the director sits like a grim, inscrutable buddha, the ruler of all he surveys.

Three or four women, especially, long-time personal assistants, supervise the progress of the production. Once the key subordinate was secretary Joan Harrison, rumored to be the minister of casting; she went on to become the trusted producer of television's *Alfred Hitchcock Presents*. Today, as ever, the central figure is "Madame" (Mrs. Hitchcock), Alma Reville, once a script girl and editor and assistant director in England, later a coscenarist on many Hitchcock features. He is utterly attached to her. Her exact contribution is a mystery, but she appears on the set with regularity, whisking Hitch away to privacy.

The master of suspense is seventy-five, encumbered with a pacemaker and shooting his fifty-third movie, one half century after he began his celebrated directorial career with *The Pleasure Garden* in Munich, Germany. He is the last, with George Cukor, of the active early-film veterans. The new movie, which he wrote in collaboration with Ernest Lehman over a two-year span, is called *Family Plot*, based on a novel by Victor Canning that involves two intertwined stories, a kidnapping, and a fake psychic. It will be familiar Hitchcock terrain: innocent persons drawn into a web of sex, fear, and crime. It stars Karen Black, Bruce Dern, William

Devane, and Barbara Harris—although the real star, of course, is Hitch.

Born on August 13, 1899, in London, Alfred Hitchcock, as a lad, studied mechanics, navigation, and art, among other things, before signing on to pen titles for British Famous Players–Lasky at age twenty-three. He shortly became immersed in all aspects of film production (he is credited, for example, with the adaptation, dialogue, assistant direction, and art direction for *Woman to Woman* in 1923), and, ultimately, he became a director. In his native England, he directed the first "talkie," *Blackmail*, in 1929, and such classics as *Murder*, *The Man Who Knew Too Much*, *The 39 Steps*, and *The Lady Vanishes*, before moving to Hollywood, under contract to David O. Selznick, in 1939. In America, Hitchcock flourished, creating such masterworks as *Rebecca*, *Suspicion*, *Shadow of a Doubt*, *Notorious*, *Strangers on a Train*, *Rear Window*, a second version of *The Man Who Knew Too Much*, *Vertigo*, *North by Northwest*, *Psycho*, *The Birds*, and *Frenzy*—to name a certain few.

Perhaps no other film director has achieved his international stature (François Truffaut compared him to Kafka, Dostoevsky, and Poe) and, what's more, his common-day box-office recognition. Even the average moviegoer is versed in the Hitchcockian credo: the essential but trivial plot gimmick or what Hitchcock calls the "MacGuffin" (the uranium samples in *Notorious*); the stress on pure, visual cinema and montage (over seventy shots in forty-five seconds in the *Psycho* shower scene); and his expected cameo appearance in nearly every Hitchcock picture (in a newspaper's weight-loss advertisement in *Lifeboat*). The signatorial walk-on was "strictly utilitarian" at the beginning, Hitchcock has said, later a superstition and gag, and finally a "rather troublesome gag" that distracted the audience. Still, the cameo is part of Hitchcock's carefully cultivated public image, and he takes it seriously. He banned all visitors and nonessential crew from the set on the day he shot his own appearance in *Family Plot*—fittingly, as a shadow behind the door of the Registrar of Births and Deaths.

The heat was oppressive, even inside the drafty Universal sound stages, as *Family Plot* was being shot in the summer of 1975. The unit publicist was besieged by buffs and scribes, everybody convinced that Hitchcock was directing his last picture. The director himself only chuckled at this thought, and then pointed to his Universal contract (he is actually believed to own a small percentage of the studio), which calls for two more. Yet, he often seemed subdued, languid, almost bored. I found him, one afternoon, resting in his mobile van, and I asked him whether moviemaking was still as much fun as it once was—fifty years ago.

"There are so many imponderables today," he said, in his sticky, macabre drawl. He raised an eyebrow. "Costs are so much higher, and therefore the watching of costs becomes half the operation. One time, when costs were low, we didn't care. We just shot and shot. In the days of the silent pictures, we always shot out of continuity because we didn't have the quality of character in those days. But now people say to me, 'Well, can you do this particular scene, because, costwise, it makes it easy for us to do the picture.' I say, 'Yes, but wait a minute, you're choosing a scene at the end of the picture, and I don't know my character until I've shot the first scene.'

"I'm giving you an example of how the economics are liable to sometimes interfere with the flow of the character and narrative which you have in your mind, and that is one of the problems you have to face today. It takes a lot of the fun out of it because there isn't that freedom that you like to have, ideally. The way one would like to shoot a film would be in its continuity of narrative.

"I will say this," he continued. "In my personal experiences, I am not pressed at all. They ask my personal production unit, 'Is it possible to do this?' I have to say, 'Well, it can be done, but it's going to be difficult.' In a sense, freedom of activity, which I have, becomes an embarrassment, because I have a duty not to spend money all over the place. Although they like to talk about film art, there is an element of industry in it.

"We know that film is an art form of the twentieth century, but it carries with it many liabilities. What would a painter think if I handed him a canvas and said that it cost $750,000; here's an easel which costs $500,000; here's a box of paints which costs $250,000; here's a palette which costs $800,000; and a set of brushes that costs $500,000. Now paint me a picture, and at least get me my money back. The artist would say, 'You're crazy.' "

Hitchcock directs from his chair, seated, virtually immobile, but for an occasional tilt of the head, a nod, a grunt of approval or humorous quip. He studies each scene with apparent disinterest, puffing his Dunhill cigar leisurely, and giving directions, when necessary, in a ponderous voice. Mainly, he converses with his director of photography (Leonard J. South, who operated the camera for the late Robert Burks on many Hitchcock films), his assistant director, and the script girl. Scenes are normally accomplished in one or two takes. I asked him whether he is ever surprised by what ends up on the screen.

"No-o-o," he replies, a slight smile playing on his lips, as he elongated the word. "I know the film by heart, cut by cut. Don't forget, I've been an art director, I've been a scriptwriter, I've been an assistant director. I've done all the jobs in this business. A lot of directors haven't. They've come from writing or the theater. Not to say that they aren't good but they are, to some extent, in the hands of the technicians.

"As you noticed, you've never seen me look through the camera. The reason is because there is a rectangular screen. That's what we're aiming at and, in my mind, I can see a screen. I can talk to the cameraman in his own language. 'Where are you cutting, give her a haircut, do this, do that.' So all the technical side is very second-nature to me."

Of the acting side, the stories about Hitch are rife. It is said that he once compared all actors to cattle; he himself cannot remember ever having precisely said such a thing, although he has been questioned about it ever since his arrival from England. More likely, he says with a patented leer, he said all actors *behave* like cattle. Acting is the least important element of his cinema; because he is, in some ways, a disciple of Kuleshov's theories, his actors are frequently called upon to emote less rather than more. Only Hitchcock knows that they may end up as little more than the closeup of an eyeball in a particular scene. He talks little with them, as a rule. Casting is the last step, rendered almost as an afterthought.

Through the years, there have been notorious battles. And, indeed, a close reading of *Hitchcock*, François Truffaut's conversations with the master, reveals that Hitch was never really satisfied with anybody, save the reliables Cary Grant and James Stewart. To Ingrid Bergman, during the making of *Under Capricorn*, he offered the consolation "Ingrid, it's only a movie!"; he clashed repeatedly with Kim Novak during the shooting of *Vertigo*. Often repeated is his advice to Paul Newman, when the "Method" star approached him during *Torn Curtain* to inquire about his motivation. "Learn your lines," Hitchcock supposedly informed him, "and don't speak to me until after the film." It seems that this unsavory reputation has been with him since as early as 1940, when he directed his only screwball comedy, *Mr. and Mrs. Smith*. Carole Lombard ribbed him one day by building a three-sectioned corral on the set, with a young cow in each, name-tagged for the three principals, Lombard, Robert Montgomery, and Gene Raymond.

There were minor skirmishes, too, during the making of *Family Plot*. Roy Thinnes, originally cast in the movie, was replaced shortly after shooting began on the vague complaint from Hitchcock that he was not "strong enough" (which may mean that he was, in fact, too strong). Hollywood wags point out that Hitchcock at his press conference in the local cemetery earlier in the month kept referring to Thinnes as Roy Scheider. The director said it was a slip of the tongue, but more whimsical observers saw malice aforethought.

Karen Black, no small star in 1976, and a free-spirited devotee of Scientology, brushed mildly with Hitchcock over her role, a kidnapper who, in one scene, must disguise herself as an oldish woman. She is required to play the part (over her protestations) with an unnaturally husky voice, lowered on Hitchcock's command to heighten her malevolence. Her efforts to inject some personality into the dialogue were met with typically Hitchcockian reminders to stay low-key. One day, Black made an amusing mistake that tested their goodwill. Generously, she informed Hitch about the "loose thread" on his otherwise immaculate suit, only to realize instantly, by his droll sangfroid, that she was indicating his beloved Legion of Honor ribbon. They nevertheless managed to sustain a friendly rapport; her good humor won him over. Some days, as shooting droned on and tensions rose, she could be observed fondling the back of Hitchcock's head, as he sat mute.

Worrying most, almost complaining, during my visit to the *Family Plot* set, was the man who replaced Roy Thinnes, an actor named William Devane, who was impressive on television as JFK in the much-praised reenactment of the Cuban missile crisis. Devane, a talented actor who in the spring of 1975 also directed an acclaimed Los Angeles production of Eric Bentley's *Are You Now or Have You Ever Been*, met Hitchcock only five minutes before his first scene. Devane was to play the key villain. The director told him, "You're William Powell," and later, only "Be lighter, lighter."

"I can add three colors to his palette if he'll let me know what's going on," Devane explained. He was talking during a break in his dressing room, alternately grimacing and chuckling over the situation. "He's not interested in what makes the people tick. He's interested in what makes the story tick. I've seen this character in every film Hitchcock has ever made.

"One day, I had a line, saying, 'You know how funny well-to-do people are.' He asked me, "Would it be too much trouble to say rich?' I said to him, 'Only a lower-class person would say rich. Someone born to money would say well-to-do.' He thought a minute and then said exactly the same thing back to me. I said, 'Wait a minute. That's exactly what I said to you.' He said, 'Go ahead and fake it.' He doesn't talk at length about anything. He ends up by saying. 'Fake it.' "

The conversation whetted Devane's appetite for a confrontation, and he walked over to Hitchcock's mobile lair and entered determinedly. Moments passed. Not a raised voice could be heard. Finally, Devane emerged, with the same lost, head-shaking expression. "He didn't reveal anything to me," he explained. "He just continued to explain to me how the film was being shot. I said, 'You'll let me know if we're going in opposite directions?' He said, 'Yes.' "

Devane laughed resignedly.

"It's tiring to work with a genius."

But Hitch usually has his favorites, in this case Bruce Dern and Barbara Harris, who play the psychic medium and her cabbie boyfriend. They are the more interesting roles, to his way of thinking, and he lavishes attention on the actors who play them. Dern (once affectionately called a "calf" by Hitchcock) could practically coax laughter at will from the veteran director, whom he so admired that he visited the sets on off days to quietly observe his technique. Dern worked with Hitchcock once before, when, as a sailor, he was fatally bludgeoned in *Marnie*. He even managed to discuss character with the director one day for half an hour, although, admittedly, it was a one-sided talk.

"I did all the talking," Dern explained. "He opened up by saying, 'Bruce, it's been a long time.' I said, 'Yeah, twelve years. The last time you saw me, you had me beaten to death with a fire poker.' He said, 'Yes, who would ever have thought you would end up being my leading man, much less a leading man at all?' I said, 'If you hang in there long enough, it can happen to anybody; if it can happen to Jack Nicholson, it can happen to me.' Then we talked a little bit about the wardrobe; he told me to lighten my hair; and I suggested a few things to him about the character.

"He doesn't get in the actor's way at all. I don't know what everybody's been talking about all these years. Once you're in his form—there's no changing that at all, for anyone—then you have the freedom to do what you want. He doesn't give you things to do, but when he does give you something to do, you do it, because he's absolutely right. You can't fight him, you must accept the fact that he is the best. Once you do that, you're in."

With Barbara Harris, Hitchcock seemed positively polite and gracious, a consideration that shows in her merry performance. Directing a critical psychic seance, he even went so far as to stand and gesture balletically to demonstrate an especially difficult movement in her trance. He thanked her for her perspicacity after the lengthy scene, and when she wondered aloud whether that complicated word had anything to do with sweat, he remarked with dry wit: "Perspicacity has nothing to do with the underarms; it means alertness." Everyone broke into laughter.

"I know what I want, but you don't always get it," he remarked later of his performers, still entrenched in his mobile van. "Some of them are extremely efficient. They can take direction very easily. 'Slow down, speed up, make this point.' " He grinned like a pumpkin. "I have an actor in this picture—Bruce Dern—well, he's absolutely surefire. One sees an actor like Bruce, and you see a tempo. You say, 'Speed it up there, and don't make that pause so long.'

"They're very different," he continued, "from the Method actor who says, 'I don't know what I might do there; I have to feel it.' They're not very helpful in this business. They may be fine in the theater. But they're taught to improvise, which, to me, is a very risky word. They're taught that at schools! I remember an actor saying, 'Well, I went to such and such a school, and I was told to improvise.' I said to him, 'That's not improvising; that's writing.'

"And what for? What for?"

The silence was thunderous. He asked the question as if it answered itself, spreading his palms slightly; for a director who so meticulously plans everything, in his head and on paper, before arriving on the set, it was the utmost heresy. "I improvised in the office a year ago on this," he said, thrusting his fleshy lower lip forward into a pout. "I don't have to improvise." I left him there alone, staring noiselessly into space, as the set whirled in preparedness outside. No doubt he was thinking up something gruesome—for actors and audiences alike—for Hitch's fifty-fourth.*

---

*Alas, there would be no fifty-fourth. Hitchcock died on April 29, 1980, with *Family Plot* his last finished film.

About the Contributors

JOSEPH McBRIDE is the author of thirteen books, including *Frank Capra: The Catastrophe of Success, Steven Spielberg: A Biography, Orson Welles, The Book of Movie Lists,* and the critical study *John Ford* (with Michael Wilmington). His forthcoming biography of Ford is called *Searching for John Ford.* McBride's Howard Hawks interview book *Hawks on Hawks* was chosen by the Book Collectors of Los Angeles as one of the "100 Best Books on Hollywood and the Movies." McBride's scripts include the cult classic film *Rock 'n' Roll High School* and (with George Stevens, Jr.) five of the annual American Film Institute Life Achievement Award tributes to legendary Hollywood figures. He was twice nominated for Emmy Awards for those AFI specials and won the Writers Guild of America award for the tribute to John Huston. He writes a regular column on movies for *Irish America* magazine and is a contributor to *Boxoffice.*

GERALD PEARY is a film critic for the *Boston Phoenix* and a member of the National Society of Film Critics. He teaches film studies at both Suffolk University and Boston University. He edited *Quentin Tarantino: Interviews* and coedited several anthologies, including the pioneering 1977 book *Women and the Cinema: A Critical Anthology.* His "Superstars of Dreamland" appeared in *The Best American Movie Writing 1998.* He was Acting Curator of the Harvard Film Archive, and is editing the first book of interviews with the late filmmaker John Ford.

DEBRA WEINER has lived in New York, Paris, Berlin, Bangkok, Boston, Montreal, and Vermont. She has written for *Playboy, Outside, Travel & Leisure, Glamour,* the *New York Times,* the *International Herald Tribune,* the *Boston Globe,* and the *Wall Street Journal.* Her short fiction has been published in the *Douglas College Review.* Presently she is writing screenplays in Chicago, where she lives with her husband and son, Sam.

PERMISSIONS

All interviews, except those with Sheridan Gibney, Dore Schary, and Robert Stevenson, were originally done on assignment for the *Boston Globe* and appeared first in that newspaper in abbreviated form.

The full Clarence Brown interview was published as "Clarence Brown at 85" in *Focus on Film* (U.K.), No. 23 (Winter 1975-6).

The René Clair interview was published in *Take One* (Canada), Vol. 3, No. 4 (Jan.-Feb. 1973).

The Alfred Hitchcock interview was published as "Hitch" in *The Movie Buff's Book 2*, edited by Ted Sennett (Pyramid Books, 1977).

The Ida Lupino interview was published in *Women and the Cinema: A Critical Anthology*, edited by Karyn Kay and Gerald Peary (E. P. Dutton, 1977).

The Joel McCrea interview was published in *Focus on Film*, No. 30 (June 1978).

The Ronald Reagan interview was published as "Reagan Stalks 'The Big One' " in *Take One*, Vol. 5, No. 3 (Aug. 1976).

The Dore Schary interview was published in *Take One*, Vol. 7, No. 8 (July 1979).

A shorter version of the George Stevens interview was published as "A Piece of the Rock: George Stevens" in *Bright Lights*, No. 8 (1979).

The Robert Stevenson article was published as "Who Is the World's Most Successful Director?" in *American Film*, Vol. 3, No. 5 (March 1978).

A portion of the Raoul Walsh interview was published as "Raoul Walsh Remembers Warners" in *The Velvet Light Trap* (Madison, Wis.), No. 15 (Fall 1973), and in its entirety the piece appeared, in French, in *Positif* (Paris), No. 454 (Dec. 1998).

The William Wellman interview was published in Swedish as "Alla jävla sorters filmer" in *Chaplin* (Stockholm), No. 147 (June 1976), and in French in *Positif*, No. 396 (Feb. 1994).

The Sheridan Gibney interview has not previously been published.

Filmographies are based on *Variety's Film Reviews*, *The Motion Picture Guide*, Ephraim Katz's *The Film Encyclopedia*, the *New York Times Film Reviews*, the *International Dictionary of Films and Filmmakers*, the *Museum of Broadcast Communications Encyclopedia of Television*, *Leonard Maltin's TV Movies and Video Guides*, and information provided by the interview subjects.

Photographs are courtesy of Photofest, Archive Photos, Walt Disney Productions, and the author's private collection.

Index